Harvard's Secret Court

WILLIAM WRIGHT

HARVARD'S
SECRET
COURT

The Savage 1920 Purge of

Campus Homosexuals

St. Martin's Press

NEW YORK

www.stmartins.com

Excerpts from letters of Harvard personnel and other Harvard records are reprinted courtesy of the Harvard University Archives.

Book design by Fritz Metsch

Library of Congress Cataloging-in-Publication Data

Wright, William, 1930–
    Harvard's secret court : the savage 1920 purge of campus homosexuals / by William Wright.— 1st ed.
        p. cm.
    ISBN 0-312-32271-2
    EAN 978-0-312-32271-7
    1. Harvard University—Students—History—20th century. 2. Gay college students—Massachusetts—Cambridge—History—20th century. 3. Discrimination in higher education—Massachusetts—Cambridge—History—20th century. I. Title.

LD2160.W75 2005
378.744'4—dc22

2005047702

First Edition: October 2005

10   9   8   7   6   5   4   3   2   1

This book is dedicated to all the men and women

who have courageously struggled against determined,

sometimes brutal, efforts to keep them

from being who they are.

Contents

Author's Note

MUCH OF THE information in this book is based on copies of records kept originally by Harvard's Secret Court in which student names have been redacted by the office of the Dean of Harvard College. The copied documents can be found in the Records of the Dean of Harvard College, Disciplinary Records 1891–1923, Redacted Copies (call number UA III 5.33, Box 668). Through the research of *The Harvard Crimson* and by other means, the actual names have been determined and used in this book. It is important to emphasize, however, that in the letters and Court notes generously provided by the Harvard Archives, the actual names do *not* appear.

An additional point: With the dialogue in chapters 3 and 7, some liberties have been taken. In all important aspects, however, the information in these scenes is based on known facts.

Prologue
A Dark Place

THE FIRST MOMENTS on wakening were the good ones. Unsure of where he was, even who he was, he luxuriated in the sweet potential of an unfolding day. Then as the stark, drab room came into focus, reality settled on him like a massive weight descending gently, implacably onto his chest, where it would lock in place until he returned to sleep that evening: he was in a hospital and could not leave.

In those first moments of awakening, he could often recall his dreams, but only for a minute or two. Then they too would evaporate, along with the feeling of optimism and freedom. He dreamed of those people who had wronged him and were made to regret it—the Portuguese workers he had caught stealing at the mill, the black kids in Montclair who had tried to extort money from him, his insurance agent who called himself a friend yet tried to defraud him of his due. He had given them all a good thrashing. And then there were his true enemies, the two closest to him, his wife and mother, two wicked women who had been sent to punish him. He had no idea why. He had taught them both a few lessons, but they had won out in the end. They had defeated him and he was here. But he did not dream about them.

If he was born in 1891, he'd only be fifty-six now, but around the hospital he was known as the Old Man. Just one more injustice he had to live with. He knew he didn't look good. He refused to exercise, even to work in the greenhouses, and they'd pulled all his teeth, in some harebrained scheme they thought would cure his illness. That sort of thing makes a man look older. With his thinning hair turned gray, his paunch, his flabby arms, and his collapsed mouth, it was no wonder they saw him as old.

He had refused their offer of dentures. Let the world see what they had done to cure a sane man of mental illness. He knew that a lot of the other patients, most of them, if truth were told, felt they didn't belong here. He knew that. But not only did he know he was as sane as the guy who decided these things, Dr. Eisenstein—probably saner, from the way that Bavarian charlatan played chess—he knew *why* he had been put there. His family wanted to be rid of him—especially Lucy, whom he never should have married. The children were too young for such plotting, but Lucy, she had been born scheming. Too grand to move to North Carolina, too grand to have a business meeting in someone's kitchen, too grand to have a husband out of work.

How had they come to hate each other like two Siamese fighting fish? No one could make him as angry as she could, drive him into such a fury. Of course he had thrown hot water on her. They said it was boiling. True, it was in a pot on the stove. It was very hot, but probably not boiling. Well, boiling water purifies. That's what she needed. Evil woman. Evil, selfish, *cruel* woman.

If the others called him the Old Man, it was only behind his back. He'd heard them often enough. To his face they all called him Mister—inmates and staff. He was the only patient who got a Mister tacked to his name. They respected the fact that he was smarter than all of them, had attended Harvard, spoke four languages, was a chess master, and was working on the second volume of a landmark book on paleontology and evolutionary theory. If that wasn't worth a "Mister," what was?

As a foretaste of hell, the place wasn't so bad. He had his own room—one of the few who did—and he was allowed his books. He also had a second chair for visitors. Sometimes he would permit another patient to come in for a chat. No one else had the privilege of having a visitor in his room. He never had visitors from the outside. Lucy had tried to come see him, drove right up to the building a few times, but he had refused to see her, of course. Well, there was that one time she had gotten in. He had fixed her, all right. Turned his chair around and sat with his back to her until she left.

What did she want? To give him a box of cookies and apologize for destroying his life? For locking him up in this mausoleum for his remaining days? He'd been here for seventeen years. She'd see to it they never let him out. According to actuarial tables, he had a good twenty more years to go.

At least he had managed to use his brains to get out of doing chores. It wasn't like earning a million dollars or winning the Nobel Prize, but it was a sizable achievement in a place where everyone had to do chores. By writing letters for patients, advising them, doing small favors, he could always get others to take over his work schedule. He never had to sweep floors or work in the kitchen. For the most part, the Taunton hospital was well run and clean. Others talked about a smell—not human or animal or medicinal, more of a musty smell—but he'd never noticed it.

He looked out the window. Ornate Victorian flourishes on the eaves, some wrought-iron filigree—more architectural detail than you'd expect to see on a public building that was used to house the discarded. But gloomy, dark, and oppressive. A high-security temple to the fantasy that humans can be protected from other humans. The world was full of scoundrels and villains. Humans were just a subspecies of primates. Their superior intellects may have produced wonders but also enabled ever more ingenious ways to vent their irrelevant and destructive hostilities. How absurd to think society could lock up a token handful and make the world safe. And he was on *their* side, the side of decency and morality. They should thank God a few like him would stand up to the vicious and depraved, the morally bankrupt, the real scoundrels—would show these villains they had tried their evil tricks on the wrong person. For this, he was locked up.

He felt sleepy. It was time for Dennis to show up. Dennis always checked in to make sure he was all right, not up to any mischief. More of a jailor than a nurse. They should know by now that he'd give them no trouble—unless they tried to put him in the showers. They knew damn well he hated showers, refused to take them and would fight anyone who tried to force him. Dennis had to lose a tooth to learn this. Hit it square with his belt buckle. You'd think they'd get tired of the violence they provoked. What did they want to prove? A tub bath was the only civilized way for a gentleman to clean himself. Showers were for livestock—or inmates of an institution.

He stripped down to his BVDs, turned off the overhead light by the wall switch, and got into the narrow bed. The rules said he had to leave his door open at night, so a shaft of hall light fell across his floor. As he wriggled down into the hard cot, he glanced over at the room across the hall. As usual, there was Jimmy lying on his stomach under his bed, watching him. The old man rolled over and went to sleep.

THIRTY MILES DUE north of the well-landscaped Taunton State Hospital is the equally verdant and formerly ivy-swathed Harvard Yard, in one shady corner of which sits the Nathan Marsh Pusey Library. This building, one of twenty-nine Harvard libraries, houses the Harvard Archives, the university's huge collection of every conceivable record of the university's curricula, faculty, employees, buildings, organizations, clubs, and, of course, students.

Anyone seeking information about a former student fills out a slip that will send a researcher into the library's vast stacks. Rows and rows of files and boxes contain the records of everyone who has passed through Harvard, three centuries of the nation's best and brightest. Here one can find the student or faculty files of countless great men—Emerson, Longfellow, Theodore Roosevelt, Thomas Wolfe, W. H. Auden, Leonard Bernstein, and many more figures of major historical or cultural importance. Here also are the records of countless men and women who led inconspicuous lives of great distinction in the arts, science, government, education, and business.

And finally there are the records of those few who ended their days at Harvard in disgrace. Among this sad group were the victims of an extraordinary purge of homosexuals in 1920, a purge that was kept hidden for eighty years and has only recently come to light. It is a sad tale of reckless student indiscretion, to be sure, but far more than that, of a mighty institution run amok and, in the name of morality and righteousness, wielding its immense power in a brutal and destructive way.

It is a story of values skewed by uninformed views of one aspect of human behavior, of judgments based on Old Testament moral injunctions that are now disputed by biblical scholars, all of which resulted in many wrecked lives and a number of tragedies. Most puzzling, the sexual activity that the university saw as a crisis could have been dealt with, even stamped out, in a far less harsh way. The furious excesses of the administrators indicate that they saw the situation not just as a disciplinary issue, but as a deeply moral one. If Harvard as an institution is a triumph of learning and the resulting wisdom, as most people would agree, the purge of homosexuals in 1920 and the Secret Court that carried it out are perhaps the most egregious of its failures.

Part One

THE

STUDENTS

1

A Death on High Street

———✦———

THE INSTANT MARY ANNA WILCOX woke up that morning in May 1920, she knew something was very wrong. It wasn't the smell of gas, which at first she didn't notice. It was Cyril's behavior. He had been quiet at dinner the night before, none of the lively chat he'd kept up since coming home. He had always done this, even when she knew he was feeling sad or out of sorts. Even in the few days since he had been sent down from Harvard—just a temporary suspension after all—he had seemed in good spirits.

Last night was different, and then the quiet from upstairs after he went up for the night. Usually she could hear her son moving around his rooms—the third-floor bedroom, which was directly over hers, or his oh-so-private den, which he forbade her to clean. Every night she would hear him tidying, rearranging furniture, or just pacing. Often she would not sleep till the sounds stopped and she knew he had settled down for the night.

But on the previous evening, from the moment he had gone up for the night, she had heard not a sound. Now as she lay in bed, willing herself awake, the realization of why she sensed trouble hit her like a blow to the back of her head. She smelled gas.

Without waking her husband or putting on her dressing gown, she flew out of bed. "Oh my God, oh my God," she said over and over as she raced up the stairs. Pushing open the bedroom door, she saw her twenty-one-year-old son sprawled fully dressed on his bed, one arm hanging limp, his fingers touching the floor. A terrible smell told her he had vomited, yet his brown hair was neatly combed, his handsome face looked serene. His skin appeared paler and pinker than usual, and his lips were an unnatural red. The open, unblinking eyes told her beyond question her son was dead.

She let out a scream, then groped her way to the hall landing and screamed again. No words or names came from her mouth, just a primal wail of agony. Her older son, Lester, was the first to bound up the stairs, followed by her husband, George Wilcox. Lester ran to his motionless brother and put a hand on his head. Then climbing onto the bed, Lester began giving Cyril artificial respiration, causing the mattress to bounce madly.

"This bed's too soft!" Lester yelled. "Father, help me get him to the floor."

Gently the two men lifted the body and laid it facedown on the rug beside the bed. Lester, still in his pajamas, his eyeglasses slipping from his nose, straddled his brother and began furiously pumping his rib cage. Mary Wilcox put a knot-tight fist in her mouth and moaned while her stunned husband placed an arm around his wife and looked on in shock.

"George, call for an ambulance," Mary half cried, rejecting Cyril's death. "We must save him."

Her husband hurried from the room and down the stairs.

Lester pumped on his brother's back for the forty minutes it took the medics to arrive. Two men in white coats had to pull Lester from the inert body so they could make their examination.

"How long you been working on him?" one said.

Lester shook his head. "I don't know. Ten minutes."

"It has been longer than that," his mother said.

"Okay. A half hour."

With cold authority, Mary Wilcox addressed the two men. "My son's been trying to get his brother to breathe for a good forty-five minutes."

When the family doctor arrived, the medics stepped aside so he could make his examination. After seeking a pulse and applying his stethoscope to Cyril's chest, the doctor looked up and confirmed what Mary had known since she had first entered the room.

"I'm sorry to tell you," he said, "but this boy is dead and has been for several hours."

WHEN A MEMBER of any family takes his or her life, it leaves a wound, permanent and painful, for all the survivors. Gradually, however, it fades into the package of catastrophes and triumphs that inform every family history. Cyril Wilcox's sad end was different. The death of this one insignificant and emotionally troubled Harvard student would have enormous ramifications lasting decades and would impact immeasurably the lives of many people, including a Boston political boss, a federal judge, a Broadway producer, three Harvard deans, and the university's president. A number of those who were deeply affected did not even know Cyril Wilcox.

AMONG THE OLD families of Fall River, Massachusetts, the Wilcoxes were prominent and well liked. Because of the town's burgeoning Portuguese and Italian population—"Catholics" was the pejorative classifier—the Protestant descendants of early settlers had congealed into a self-contained tribe that had grown more insular than is customary for such groups. Although length of residence was less important than wealth and ethnicity, the Wilcox family went back as far as any in the area. One forebear, Thomas Wilcox, had fought in the American Revolution and brought glory to the family as part of the group that, with dazzling boldness, kidnapped the British commander General Richard Prescott from his headquarters near Tiverton, a short distance from Fall River across the Rhode Island border.

Subsequent generations of Wilcoxes had economic ups and downs but always maintained a firm foothold in the town's respectable middle class. The father of the now-dead Cyril was George Thomas Wilcox, a handsome man with a reputation for a good and kindly nature. He was one of seven brothers, three of whom had distinguished careers. One, a colonel in the U.S. Army, had served as an adjutant to General Pershing during the recent war. Another had prospered as an executive of a manufacturing company, while still another had founded his own firm, the R. A. Wilcox Paper Company, and had grown wealthy.

George Thomas had started out inauspiciously, working in a pharmacy, but when his wife, Mary Anna, came into a modest inheritance, he opened his own store. The Wilcox Pharmacy quickly became one of Fall River's three top drugstores, the one favored by the old families. While far less rich than his two businessmen brothers, George Thomas provided his family with a comfortable life: a roomy house on almost-fashionable High Street and good educations for the two sons.

The younger, Cyril, had graduated from a local high school and had done an additional year at Exeter. In spite of lackluster grades there, he entered Harvard in the fall of 1917. Cyril was a good-looking young man, charming and outgoing. He was known to the girls of his Fall River circle as an excellent dancer and was considered a budding ladies' man.

His brother, Lester, on the other hand, was somber, studious, and highly intelligent. He had attended a local high school, then entered Cornell in 1909. Disappointed that Cornell did not offer the courses in advanced mathematics he wanted, he transferred to Harvard. Although he had been at Cornell for a year and a half, Harvard would not give him any academic credits. Still, he earned his degree in three years, graduating with the class of 1914.

Academically, Lester did well enough to have been offered a teaching grant at the University of Chicago so that he could attend graduate school there. His mother, a formidable, strong-willed woman also from an old Fall River family, came down forcefully against this impressive offer. She insisted Lester go to work in one of Fall River's textile mills, the backbone of the local economy, to "pay back all the money I spent on your education." In the worldview of Mary Anna Wilcox, a bachelor's degree from Harvard was not a passport to intellectual pursuits, but rather a badge of social distinction and, even more, a potent business asset.

Yielding to his mother's wishes, Lester took a job with a textile firm, misleadingly named the Granite Mills, where he did well. After two years he left to serve with distinction in the U.S. Navy during World War I, returning to the mill when his tour ended. In his position as a cost accountant, he discovered that the company was suffering substantial loses through systematic employee theft. With the help of the police, he set up a trap one night and caught the perpetrators in the act. He agreed not to press charges if they would leave not only the company, but Fall River as well.

This episode was characteristic of Lester Wilcox. He had a powerful sense of right and wrong, coupled with sharp and fearless responses to perceived injustices or immorality. The mill owners, who already felt Wilcox had a talent for the textile business, were greatly impressed by his daring solution to a serious problem of which they had been unaware. A short time later, when Lester was only thirty-two, they named him plant superintendent.

The Wilcoxes were a tight-knit clan. In spite of the disparity in economic status, the seven Wilcox brothers remained close and had frequent family gatherings. They prided themselves on being fun-loving folk and approached their socializing with zeal and imagination. When it was time for another party, whichever family was in line to host the event would send out invitations in verse. The others were expected to respond in verse; the replies would then be read aloud at the gathering. Many in the family were musical. Mary Anna Wilcox played the piano; her husband, the cello; and Lester, the violin. Others were brought in to form quartets or quintets to perform for the family.

When Lester found a girl he wanted to marry, Mary Anna disapproved, even though his choice was from an equally prominent Fall River family. First arguing that her son could not afford to get married, she then expressed her doubts that the girl would "fit in" with the high-spirited Wilcoxes. She eventually acquiesced to Lester's determination but never warmed to her daughter-in-law, who turned out to be as strong-willed as she was.

If Lester had meekly given in to his mother's career scheme, Cyril threatened to be more of a problem. Her younger boy had shown disturbing artistic leanings, which Mary Anna had been quick to squelch. When he wanted to hang curtains in his third-floor bedroom, she had vetoed the idea as too feminine. The same judgment blocked his desire to wallpaper his adjoining den. She barely tolerated his disagreeable cat.

What most dismayed Mary Anna was Cyril's interest in becoming a professional actor. To her, this was akin to becoming a floorwalker or a beautician and far from what she had in mind. At Exeter, he had done well in only one course, elocution. Whenever a touring acting company played Fall River, Cyril had wangled ticket money from his disapproving mother and joined the handful of solitary, often good-looking youths who, impeccably groomed and dressed, infiltrate the audiences of theatrical productions everywhere and for whom the event means far more than just an evening's entertainment. Mary Anna resolved to put an end to such folly, just as she had ended Lester's academic pipe dreams. Had Cyril aspired to be a writer, a musician, or a painter, her reaction would have been just as strong. In such artistic fields, she saw nothing but risks. Solid careers were supposed to deliver a man from financial worries, not add to them.

At Harvard, Cyril had almost failed his freshman year. In April 1919, Harvard's administrative board placed him on probation for a month, and he did terribly on his final exams, getting one pass, one B, two Cs, and five Es. Harvard suspended him, but after applying himself at summer school, he was readmitted in the fall of 1919.

By the spring of 1920, Wilcox was once again in academic trouble. His adviser wrote to Assistant Dean Edward Gay, "Wilcox seems to me a bright enough chap, but he doesn't study apparently." His midyear grades were dangerously low—three Ds, a C, and an E. On March 17, he received a warning letter from Dean Gay: "This will, I fear, be your last opportunity to make good at Harvard. If your grades in April fail to meet the requirements, the Board could do nothing but request that you withdraw."

Just before the all-important examinations, Cyril arrived at the office of Dr. Roger Lee, the head of Harvard's department of hygiene and a man who would play a prominent role in the events to come.

Cyril had a bad case of hives, which Dr. Lee said afflicted people under severe strain. When the hives were cured, Cyril suffered from what Dr. Lee described as "an hysterical attack." He never took his exams and was allowed to withdraw from Harvard for health reasons. The hope was that, in time, Cyril could straighten himself out physically and emotionally.

LATER ON THE day that Cyril's body was discovered, May 14, 1920, *The Fall River Daily Globe* ran a front-page story with the following headline: SON OF DRUGGIST GEORGE T. WILCOX FOUND DEAD IN BED. The article said the death of "the well-known young resident" resulted from a "partially opened" gas jet, and that he had been dead for five or six hours when he was found at six A.M. In spite of the suggestive circumstances, the paper refrained from calling the death a suicide.

In subsequent days, the family said that Cyril had been in good spirits since returning from Harvard. A cousin remarked that when she had met his train from Boston, she had found Cyril to be remarkably cheerful considering the circumstances of his departure from school. To the rest of the family, Cyril seemed happy to be home. He had been so happy to see his beloved cat, Schmaltz. The only member of the family who had reason to suspect suicide was Lester Wilcox, to whom Cyril, on the night before his death, had confided that until recently he had been involved in a homosexual relationship "with an older man" in Boston.

It is not known whether Lester reacted to Cyril's confidence with anger or pity, but his subsequent behavior leaves no doubt that he deplored homosexuality. It is not known if he chastised Cyril, but it is certain that he placed considerable blame on the older lover, and later on Harvard, for his brother's collapse into this unspeakable depravity. However Lester expressed his dismay at Cyril's announcement, his reaction could not have implied any tolerance of homosexuality, leaving Cyril feeling even worse about himself.

The Wilcox family always talked openly about Cyril's "suicide." This suggests that, when they discovered his body, they found unequivocal evidence, such as towels stuffed in doorjambs and window cracks. He may even have left a note. If such evidence existed, it was destroyed before the arrival of outsiders. This would not have been unusual in a day when suicide, among God-fearing families, was considered a sinful disgrace.

IN THE DAYS following Cyril's death, the Wilcoxes were immobilized by shock and grief—especially Lester, who had greatly loved his brother. He was little prepared, therefore, to handle a fresh blow that arrived in a letter addressed to Cyril dated May 10. It was written by a fellow student, Ernest Roberts, the son of a former Massachusetts congressman who was still a political power in New England. The letter was written on stationery with a simple heading printed at the top: HARVARD UNIVERSITY, CAMBRIDGE. Lester opened the letter and read it through twice. Later events indicate that he did not show the letter to his parents. It began:

> *Dear Cyril,*
> *I am a rag, I hadn't heard from Paul for three weeks (or at least it seemed that long) until last Sat. But then I got a letter explaining all. The dear old thing is the same precious lover as ever. He was laying off and went for a motor trip up thru the Catskills . . . these same people promised to motor him to Boston. Then I get my innings.*

In the ensuing paragraphs of desultory chit-chat, Roberts writes about mutual friends who have landed jobs as "features" in *The Greenwich Follies,* adding, "Aren't my lovers flying high?"

Thus enters a major character in the complex drama that Cyril Wilcox's suicide precipitated. Ernest Weeks Roberts was the son of a wealthy and influential congressman from the Boston area. Like Wilcox, Roberts was a Harvard sophomore who found more amusing ways to spend his time than studying. In spite of his lurid sex life with males, Roberts was unofficially engaged to a young woman, Helen Smith, who lived with her parents in suburban Boston. He often stayed with Helen for days at a time, telling Cyril she was the kind of girl to whom he could "tell everything."

His reference in the letter to his high-flying lovers reminds him of projected conquests, and he adds a startling parenthesis about his fiancée's younger brother, an eighteen-year-old named Bradlee, whom Roberts later describes as "the sweetest thing, and so funny, always saying cute things in such a naïve way."

The aside to Wilcox conjures up a sexual ruthlessness that would surely have alarmed most Harvard deans, not to mention parents of students. Roberts boasts: "I haven't made Bradlee yet, but my dear wait, when I do it will last for 2 days and 2 nights without taking it out."

A giddy, offhand remark about another student, Kenneth Day, would have major ramifications. "Ken is being sucked foolish by anyone and everyone he can lay hold of. I almost regret bringing him out; however he still maintains his same Jane old self. I do him . . . once in a while, for diversion."

Roberts says how relieved he is to be taking a break from his sexual decathlon by visiting his girlfriend in Brookline. It is a pleasant change, he says, being "chaste, not chased." Although their friends are having the same wild parties in his Harvard rooms, he's glad to be absent. Roberts passes along gossip about mutual friends, making snide comments about each. Catching himself, he adds, "I love the way I am panning the crowd, but dearie, aren't you kind of glad to be out of it?"

The letter makes clear that Roberts is in the same academic hot water that had brought about Wilcox's suspension, but he is confidant that he can bamboozle Assistant Dean Murdock into allowing him to remain in school. He must, however, make a visit to his parents, who have summoned him for a conversation about his poor performance at Harvard.

But Roberts doesn't dwell on such unpleasant subjects, and the letter quickly returns to his romantic life—mocking a student who expects to spend the night with him, another friend seen at the theater with a new lover ("Quite young and good looking, but swarthy. Black hair etc."), and the fun he is having in Brookline—playing cards with gossipy old queens from Boston and being tricked out in drag by his two female cousins for photos. ("We can take [the pictures] in their yard and then I can get some good-looking evening wraps etc. More darn fun . . .")

Roberts ends the letter on a note of sober reflection about his wild life that would be more suitable for a burned-out jade of sixty than a twenty-year-old Harvard sophomore: "Between you and me, I think I have had my day, that is so far as getting next to every queer diz that comes along, and these terrible faggoty parties, bore not to say disgust me."

He signs his letter, "Always your kindred soul, Ernest."

Although Lester Wilcox already knew of his brother's homosexuality, he was nonetheless stunned and horrified by the letter. Like many in his day, Lester considered male-male sexuality an offense against the natural order, something that was practiced only by those of the lowest moral character and most wanton depravity. But also like many others, he did not think of an individual as being indelibly, unalterably a "homosexual." This rigid concept of a permanent state of being, a distinct category of human, was a relatively new idea in 1920. Rather, he saw such men as weak individuals who had fallen into practices many might try if they allowed carnal urges to overwhelm their moral boundaries.

In his struggle to mitigate the iniquity of a brother he loved, Lester quickly decided that yielding to circumstances in this way was even more likely for one as young and inexperienced as Cyril. In their conversation, Cyril had told Lester his lover's name, Harry Dreyfus, and that he had just broken off with him. That Dreyfus was older than Cyril reinforced Lester's conviction that Cyril had been an inexperienced and innocent victim of an unscrupulous and predatory pervert.

But the letter undermined this rationalization. Everything about it disgusted Lester: the flippant tone, the women's names for men, the casual boasting about disgusting sexual acts, the ruthless plotting of future conquests, and—hanging over it all like a putrid cloud—the strident lack of shame about the most shameful conduct. While Lester clung to the notion that his brother had been victimized by depraved villains, he could not escape the letter's revelation that Cyril was deeply involved with them. Most difficult for Lester to bear was the letter writer's damning assumption that Cyril was a willing collaborator in this depravity and would be amused to hear about it.

2

Shaken Harvard

———◆———

WHILE LESTER WAS assimilating his shock and working out a course of action, a second letter arrived for Cyril, this one as repugnant and incriminating as the first. It was from Harold Saxton, he would learn, a recent graduate of Harvard who was supporting himself tutoring students. Lester read this letter with more of the cold eye of a detective seeking evidence than the appalled sibling learning more details of his brother's secret life.

> *Salome's Child:*
> *I had hoped that "time" would provide me with much cheering dirt, but, alas! Not a speck have I for the dish-pan.*

The remainder of the short letter is filled with tips on buying wigs and drag, and has one item of significant gossip about a man called "Harry" who would later turn out to have been Cyril Wilcox's lover.

> *"Dot" tells me that Harry is married again—something very "Majory", says she.*

He concludes the letter on the same cheery note: "Are you <u>ever</u> coming back to the 'fold'? Say when!" Then he signs it, "Toujours Moi."

Lester Wilcox's digust quickly turned to rage, but not at Cyril. His anger intensified and focused on two targets: Harry Dreyfus, who he was convinced had been his brother's corrupter, and Harvard University, which had permitted this nest of perverts to operate on its campus with impunity. If he had any misgivings about his course of action before, he had none now. He would go directly to Boston and confront the scoundrel Dreyfus. Then he would visit Harvard's dean to demand action against the ring of degenerates the college harbored.

THE FUNERAL OF Cyril Wilcox took place on May 17, three days after his body was found. Among those attending was Ernest Roberts, the writer of the first letter, who was in fact a pallbearer. Roberts would later tell another student that George Thomas Wilcox, Cyril's father, approached him after the ceremony to ask if he felt that Cyril had been "abnormal." One can only speculate about the response from a man who had just written in a letter to Cyril about the "darn fun" of getting into drag and the gusto with which he would seduce his fiancée's younger brother.

More important, this exchange suggests that Lester may have said something general to his father about Cyril's sexuality, probably following the suicide. It is doubtful, however, that he showed his parents the letter itself. If he had, his father would have had to be audaciously devious to confront the letter writer, manifestly as "abnormal" as they come, and ask him to his face if he considered Cyril abnormal.

There is abundant documentation of the drama about to unfold on the Harvard campus—numerous letters, notes of meetings, testimony of principal participants—but there are also missing pieces. How Lester knew where to find Dreyfus is not recorded. It is possible that Lester accosted Roberts at Cyril's funeral and demanded to be told everything about his brother's involvement with Harvard's homosexual underworld. While this would seem an improbable conversation to take place on such a sad occasion, it is not impossible that it did, given Lester's temper and agitated state of mind. If the scene occurred in this confrontational way, it would be a bizarre landmark in postfuneral recollections about the departed.

Another possibility is that Lester tracked down either Roberts or Saxton from the return addresses on the letters, probably contacting them by telephone with the aim of obtaining Dreyfus's address and as much additional information as possible about Cyril's homosexual connection. However Lester located the two men, it is unlikely that the overwrought and volatile Lester had trouble extracting the information he sought from either. Both would have been dumbfounded, if not terrified, to find themselves confronted by their dead friend's incensed brother.

BY THE TIME he arrived in Cambridge on May 22, eight days after Cyril's death, Lester Wilcox had located his brother's lover. It turned out that Dreyfus lived at 44 Beacon Street. As Lester expected, he was about eight years older than Cyril and ran a bar called Café Dreyfus, which was notorious throughout Boston's bohemian world as a homosexual hangout. Lester recalled the reference to Harry in the second letter, the man who had "remarried" something "majory" after breaking with Cyril.

Lester found his way to 44 Beacon Street. Identifying himself to Dreyfus as the brother of Cyril Wilcox, he asked to be admitted for a conversation. Drefus was a slender, natty man—a sharp crease in his trousers, a high shine on his shoes—who was just under average height, but still a bit taller than Lester. He sported a thin mustache and wore his black hair in the well-combed, slicked-back fashion of the day's movie idols. In fact, his looks and elegant style placed him somewhere between William Powell and John Gilbert. Sitting erect, his legs crossed, he was a picture of worldly poise. It was soon to be shattered.

Wasting no time with amenities, Lester announced the purpose of his visit and did nothing to hide his loathing for a man he believed to be instrumental in his brother's death. He demanded that Dreyfus confess his relationship with Cyril and provide names of other Harvard students involved in the odious activities. Whether in shock or eager to do whatever necessary to rid himself of a madman, Dreyfus wrote out a list of some ten names, most of whom were, like Cyril, sophomores in the class of 1922. Wilcox snatched the list. Then, for good measure, he gave Dreyfus a thorough beating.

With the two incriminating letters from Roberts and Saxton in hand, and with Dreyfus's list of names, Lester Wilcox headed directly to his appointment with Acting Dean of Harvard College Chester Greenough, which he had set up before leaving Fall River. According to notes of the meeting, Lester was accompanied by Dr. Earnest Albert Hooton, a full-time instructor in anthropology at Harvard who had become a friend after Lester had taken his course.* (A 1914 directory shows the two living at the same address.) It is understandable that, when going to the dean of Harvard College to make accusations of great seriousness, Wilcox chose to take with him a member of the faculty who knew him.

After Dean Greenough read the letters and went over Dreyfus's list of names, he agreed with Wilcox that they constituted irrefutable proof of a highly active homosexual network among Harvard undergraduates. Greenough expressed deep dismay as well as gratitude to Wilcox for having brought the ugly matter to his attention. If there was the hint of a we'll-take-care-of-it dismissal in Greenough's thanks, it did not deter Wilcox from demanding that Harvard immediately set about ridding itself of this pernicious scourge. He passionately pushed his thesis of contagious evil spreading fires of moral corruption.

Greatly strengthening Wilcox's case for urgency was his brother's

---

*Hooton was an interesting character. When he taught Lester, who was only three years his junior, Hooton had been a Harvard instructor for just one year. He became an assistant professor in 1921 and a full professor in 1930. In his field of physical anthropology he became recognized as a driving force and an original thinker. He wrote a number of books for the general public starting with the popular *Up from the Ape*. Given his brief connection with Lester Wilcox and the Harvard gay purges, the subject of one of his last books is unmanageably ironic. Titled *"Young Man, You Are Normal,"* it described a four-year study of 268 Harvard undergraduates, the aim of which was "to find out what 'well' men were like and how various aspects of their individual organisms are related to function, to behavior, and to each other." (In a telling clue to his quirky eccentricity, the professor named a son Newton Hooton.)

suicide, the prime evidence of a serious crisis. Wilcox had not the slightest doubt that the tragedy resulted directly from the shame and guilt Cyril felt about his seduction by Harvard's homosexual underworld, and from despair at his inability to extricate himself from it. That this was unquestionably the cause of Cyril's suicide was entirely a supposition on Lester's part, but it was a supposition deemed plausible by Greenough and, shortly, by the other Harvard officials involved. Like many men of their day, especially those in august positions, they saw a logical link between homosexuality and suicide.

At several points in the unfolding drama, a judicious decision maker might have mitigated the outraged call for action that Lester Wilcox believed was the only appropriate response. This meeting with Greenough was one of them. From Greenough's subsequent actions, however, there can be little doubt that his alarm and dismay were sincere—not just a pose to placate the overwrought Wilcox. In fact, he was as genuinely appalled and alarmed as Lester and agreed completely that immediate action must be taken.

When Wilcox and his companion left the office, Dean Greenough sat alone for a few minutes, then picked up his phone and called the office of Harvard's president, A. Lawrence Lowell. Greenough told Lowell's secretary that he had to see the president as soon as possible.

TODAY WHEN YOU approach Route 495, the highway that circles Boston, from the north, you encounter a road sign that points one direction for Lawrence, the other for Lowell. The town of Lowell was named after the Harvard president's great-great-granduncle, the town of Lawrence after his maternal grandfather. Both men amassed fortunes in the textile business large enough to enable their descendants to lead upper-class lives of culture and refinement.

One descendant, A. Lawrence Lowell, having led Harvard since 1909, was well established as an American educational and cultural giant. A distinguished scholar, a Bostonian of the bluest blood, and a man of considerable wealth, Lowell seemed suited for little else but the Harvard presidency. The following anecdote reveals the veneration that most people in the Harvard universe felt toward President Lowell. A stranger arrived in Lowell's office and told his secretary it was urgent he see Mr. Lowell. The secretary looked at the visitor coldly and replied, "The *President* cannot see you. He is in Washington seeing *Mister* Coolidge."

In the eleven years he had been in office, Lowell had demonstrated his passion for learning, his eagerness to lure the finest intellects to Harvard, and his determination to spread the range of Harvard's educational preeminence. He had also pushed through liberalizing reforms, primarily the enlarging of optional areas in the undergraduate curriculum and the mandatory assignment of freshmen to dormitories.

Under Lowell's plan, not only were freshmen dormitories chosen by the university, their rooms and roommates were assigned as well. In this way, Lowell hoped to halt the ghettoizing of undergraduates: rich students in fancy apartments on Mt. Auburn Street, foreigners in one dormitory, Jews in another. Lowell resolved that, for at least one of their Harvard years, students would be democratically interspersed. (Lowell's subsequent espousal of minority quotas negated any reputation for liberality that his freshman-dispersal plan had earned him.)

Lowell began his career as a lawyer. He wrote several books on government, which led to his lecturing at Harvard. In 1900 he became a full professor. He married his cousin, Anna Parker Lowell, with whom he remained throughout his life, although the marriage was childless and unhappy. The antagonisms between Lowell and his wife were so frequent that he spent much of his married life living at one of his Boston men's clubs. For the most part, he was consumed by the Harvard presidency and in the role did much good. After his death, a major portion of his fortune was set aside for the establishment of Harvard's Society of Fellows, a philanthropy that has subsidized Harvard's finest minds for many generations. Perhaps unjustly, it is his mistakes that are remembered.

When he received Dean Greenough's request for a meeting, President Lowell was deeply engaged in affairs of the highest national and international importance. A staunch Republican, Lowell was also a fervent advocate of the League of Nations, the day's most pressing political issue. Since the League of Nations was established in 1919, Lowell had fought fiercely for the United States to become a member; he was glad it had become a campaign issue but distressed that his Republican side was seen as opposed to the League.

Unwilling to yield the League to the Democrats, Lowell publicly insisted that Harding opposed the League only in its proposed form, but not in principle. In private letters written to Republican colleagues in April 1920, one month before Lester Wilcox's visit to Greenough, Lowell stressed the battle they had on their hands in the months before the fall election. The letters leave no doubt that Lowell felt the outcome would determine the world's fate.

With this on his mind, Lowell was informed that a number of his undergraduates were having sexual intimacies with each other and with Boston men unaffiliated with Harvard. Given Lowell's global vision at that moment, his horrified reaction was surely combined with exasperation and anger that he should have to involve himself with such a sordid and petty business. But involve himself he did.

There was a joke around Harvard at that time that a plaque in Harvard Yard commemorated the spot where A. Lawrence Lowell once spoke to a freshman. Now, not only would Lowell be obliged to speak to freshmen, he would have to discuss with them the most unspeakable aspects of their behavior.

GREENOUGH'S MEETING WITH Lowell was another point in the progressing drama that might have produced a judicious and tempering response. College presidents of the day had been presented with similar crises, which they handled calmly, humanely, and discreetly. It is more a quirk of this particular story than a reflection of the day's mores that, far from searching for a measured course of action, the two men who might have softened Harvard's reaction, Greenough and Lowell, both regarded the student activities that Lester Wilcox had laid before them as a dangerous crisis that required prompt and forceful measures.

It turned out that, of all the men who became involved in rooting out homosexuality on the Harvard campus, none was as incensed and unforgiving as A. Lawrence Lowell.

As a member of the sixth generation of Lowells to have attended Harvard, Lowell was particularly dismayed that such outrages were happening not in a boarding school, not in the navy, not in a seedy Boston bar, but at *Harvard*. Indeed, a vision of the idealized Harvard man looms over this story and will be examined more fully later. Also, a worrying unknown at this point for Lowell and Greenough was the extent of the sexual blight among the undergraduates. An investigation was essential to assay the damage.

But there also appears to have been something in Lowell himself that exacerbated the disgust or revulsion with which many people regarded aberrant sex. In him, these feelings were raised to a near frenzy of vindictiveness. Conferring with Greenough, Lowell decided to form a committee to investigate and root out the homosexuals on campus. It would be made up of Greenough and his assistant deans, and one or two others. It would be known as the Court, and it would operate in secret. Lowell was particularly keen on the group doing its job quickly so that the entire sorry business would be behind them as soon as possible.

There is an array of clues hinting at possible explanations for the particularly harsh response meted out by Lowell and his cohorts, but none of the answers suggested by the clues is definitive. Precise explanations may be buried deep within the all-but-unknowable labyrinth of each man's sexual nature and each man's attitude toward those who are different.

WITHIN A FEW days, President Lowell had selected his court: five men, all but one on the Harvard faculty, and that one was the university's regent, charged with supervising the students' well-being and conduct. As acting dean, Chester Greenough was to be the Court's head until Dean Henry Yeomans returned from Europe to resume his post as dean of Harvard College. Greenough was much admired by the critical Lowell. Eight years later, when Lowell inaugurated the house system, the first faculty member he approached to assume the post of housemaster was Greenough (Dunster House).

When asked to head up the Secret Court, Greenough was forty-six years old. He had graduated from Harvard in 1898 and received his Ph.D. in 1904. A professor of English literature, he was on his way to becoming a leading specialist in American writers such as Melville, Hawthorne, and Henry James. He would write a number of books, among them a biography of Emerson and a book on the art of writing distinctive prose. Like many academics, Greenough was in love with his own erudition and could always conjure up a quote from Emerson or Longfellow to lend intellectual heft to his wrong decisions.

He was a pleasant, scholarly type with bland, slightly weak good looks. Black wire-rimmed glasses could not conceal a boyish countenance, vestiges of which would remain throughout his life. As the acting head of the Court, he executed his prosecutorial duties, which he hated, with an earnest desire to be fair yet thorough. His written references to the crimes under investigation as "unspeakable" and "abhorrent" show that, on the surface at least, he had mustered a level of outrage and disgust at the homosexual outbreak that was equal to Lowell's. Yet in some of his dealings with individual students, he revealed hints of compassion and misgivings about the harshness of the Court's sentences.

The regent who would serve on the Court was Matthew Luce, a prominent Boston businessman who had graduated from Harvard in 1891. The head of Harvard's department of hygiene, Dr. Roger I. Lee, who, as a physician, was the only member of the board with any background in science, was selected to bring a note of up-to-date knowledge to the group. This suggests that Lowell may have felt he was dealing not only with a moral problem, but a pathological one as well. If so, it would have been a nod to the day's most enlightened thinking: homosexuality was not a sin but a sickness. If Lawrence Lowell believed this to any degree, his "enlightenment" was subsumed by a visceral moral anger.

Given the enormous power the Court would come to hold over the lives of many undergraduates, the youth of some of its members is remarkable. Assistant Dean Edward R. Gay was only twenty-two, younger than some of the men whose fates he would be deciding.* When appointed to this post the year before, he was the youngest man ever named a Harvard dean. His father, Edwin F. Gay, had been the first head of the Harvard Business School. Shortly after his experience on the Court, Edward Gay left academia to become a newspaper editor, first at *The New Orleans Times-Picayune*, later at *The Los Angeles Express*. In 1928 he left newspapers and went into the paper-manufacturing business.

Assistant Dean Kenneth Murdock was twenty-five when he was asked to sit in judgment on the sexuality of men a scant five years younger than he. In 1916 he had graduated *summa cum laude* from Harvard and, two years after serving on the Court, he would earn a Ph.D. in English literature. He would remain at Harvard, eventually becoming the Francis Lee Higginson Professor of English Literature and coteaching a famous course, English 33, with the renowned F. O. Matthiessen. High among his accomplishments was his editing, with Matthiessen, of the notebooks of Henry James.

In 1960 Murdock was named by President Pusey to head up Harvard's Center for Italian Renaissance Studies that was to be housed at I Tatti, the lovely Florentine villa bequeathed to Harvard the previous year by Bernard Berenson. Murdock's 1920 grounding in the homosexual personality must have strengthened his perspective when working with the homosexual Matthiessen, editing Henry James's notebooks, and presiding over the art-world luminaries who flocked to I Tatti.

The final member of the Court was Henry Yeomans, who assumed Greenough's role as acting head of the group when he returned to Harvard in 1921. Even Yeomans, an experienced administrator, was only forty-four.

It would be interesting to know if any of those chosen by President

---

*The irony implicit in this name seems to have run amok in this story. The full name of Roberts's fiancée was Helen Gay Smith. Irony is followed closely by confusion. One of the implicated students was named Say, another Day.

Lowell to sit on this unusual board declined the assignment, and if so, why. Those who served may have felt they had little choice but to accept, given the veneration in which Lawrence Lowell was held. Then, too, given the obvious alarm with which both Lowell and Greenough viewed the crisis, a member of the Harvard staff would have had to be brave indeed to appear to condone the crime his superiors deplored.

Today, the sexuality of undergraduates is not considered any concern of the faculty or administration, but the view was quite different in 1920. Since four of the six men of the Court were deans—Yeomans, Greenough, Gay, and Murdock—an article in *The Harvard Graduates' Magazine* of September 1921, seventeen months after the Court's action, is illuminating about the deans' role in matters of discipline. In fact, the changes referred to may well have resulted directly from this particular scandal.

> Several factors have combined of late to bring to the office of Dean of Harvard College a new set of duties and to impose on the Dean a new leadership. Responsibility for discipline will doubtless always rest upon the Dean. As chairman of the Administrative Board he will be charged with the presentation to the Faculty of the most serious cases of student misconduct. He will have to deliver in person some of the heavier sentences and he will be called on always to answer delicate questions in the administration of justice as between the college and the individual.

This job-descriptive paragraph raises the whole issue about the degree to which university officials must serve *in loco parentis,* that is, as guardians of their students' behavior and welfare. Obviously, a university must have rules and limits for student conduct, but the boundaries of faculty purview in this regard had changed enormously at Harvard in the two and a half centuries before 1920 and have changed even more in the eight decades since.

In May 1920, none of the deans of the Court had the least doubt that undergraduate homosexuality fell squarely within the confines of their responsibilities. From the defensive tone of the redefinition of the deans' duties, however, it appears the question of jurisdiction had been raised at some point during this period, most likely by the Administrative Board. Someone apparently wondered aloud if student sexuality was any of the university's business.

ON JUNE 1, a full week after the Court's formation and with interrogations well under way, Dean Greenough and President Lowell placed the entire matter before Harvard's Administrative Board. Since this was the university's principal governing body for day-to-day operations, it is curious that they waited so long to inform the board of such an unusual disciplinary proceeding. The board was headed by the dean of Harvard College, some faculty men, and a few prominent businessmen and cultural leaders. No one knows exactly what occurred at the meeting; in fact, it was not for many years that any outsider knew that such a meeting had taken place. But the results of the meeting are well documented.

The members of the board agreed that action should be taken against the homosexual students, but *they wanted no part of it.* They may have felt that such direct involvement with disciplinary action was not their job, but this would go without saying. Lowell and Greenough surely were not asking the board for constabulary assistance, but rather that they condone, oversee, and backstop the course that was already in progress.

The actual wording, in notes of the meeting taken by one of the deans present, was that the Administrative Board "would not touch it." This expression indicates several other possibilities. The board recognized how incendiary the topic was, how disputable the level of sin involved, and how prone the issue was to newspaper scandal. They may have felt that only the most experienced professionals should handle a problem so rife with pitfalls and, on that basis, declined involvement. Or, in the most charitable view, they may have been reluctant to weigh in on something about which they had moral and ethical qualms. The true explanation for their sidestepping the entire matter was probably a combination of both. Even if it was the latter, they could see their president was in no mood for fuzzy scruples.

The board agreed to President Lowell's plan, to the formation of a committee to investigate the charges, which none now doubted, and to the men selected, who would interrogate the accused with the aim of establishing guilt and also of learning the names of others who were equally guilty. But they made it very clear to Lowell that those appointed to the Court would report their findings directly to the president, bypassing the Administrative Board entirely. Without oversight from anyone but Lawrence Lowell, the Court had its marching orders: to quickly rid the university of this hateful eruption of the most despicable behavior, behavior that was unthinkable for Harvard men.

3

A Walk Along the Charles

———◆———

AS NATHANIEL WOLFF walked across Harvard Yard early one mild evening in October 1919, seven months before the formation of the Secret Court, he spotted a junior he had met at a Dramatic Club get-together. He remembered him as pleasant and bright. Good-looking, too; the Arrow Shirt man's younger brother.

"Smerage," he called out, then as he drew closer, "Nice evening for a stroll, don't you think?"

"Very nice," Keith Smerage answered somewhat tentatively. "Wollf, isn't it?"

"Yes, Nathaniel Wollf. Slogging away at my final year. And you're Keith, right?

"Right."

"Care to walk with me a bit?" Wollf said offhandedly and with a hint of the condescension of a senior.

"Yes, that would be nice. I wasn't going anywhere in particular. And we share an interest in theater."

They headed for the Charles River, which looked particularly lovely in the dimming light, trees along the banks burnished with yellow-green buds, the setting sun sending back flashes of light from the windows of office buildings in distant Boston. The two young men discussed their courses, their lives at Harvard. Turning to their backgrounds, Wollf said his father was a successful banker in Buffalo who had sent Wollf to Exeter, then to Harvard. Presently premed, Wollf would be entering Harvard's medical school in another year.

Smerage thought he looked like a banker's son—starched white collar, natty bow tie, a nonchalant air. A fullness in his lower face kept him from being classically handsome, but expressive eyes and full lips combined for a simpatico appearance. He seemed almost too much the dandy to become a doctor.

Smerage said his family owned a country inn about an hour north of Boston, in a historic Massachusetts village named Topsfield. As he described his earlier life, he repeatedly mentioned his mother, who managed the inn. She had nursed him through two years of bad health and insisted he go to Harvard although money was tight. She was his closest friend and confidante.

Wollf finally asked, "Is your father deceased?"

Smerage looked startled. "No, but he was in a bad accident a few years back and hasn't been himself. My mother runs the inn, runs the show, really."

"Confidante? You tell her *everything*?"

Smerage appeared confused, then looked directly at Wollf. "Of course, not everything."

Wollf gave his companion an appraising glance. Medium height, light brown hair neatly combed, well-etched features, a worn tweed jacket, soft white shirt, a drab four-in-hand necktie. Probably his father's.

"Look here. When I ran into you, I was on my way to get a little dinner. Would you care to join me? My treat."

Thanking him, Smerage agreed, and they turned back toward Mt. Auburn Street. On a side street, Wollf entered a small door and led them up a narrow staircase. At the top was a brightly lit, richly colored Italian restaurant, most tables full of animated diners. They were greeted by a handsome young waiter.

"Good evening, Antonio. Give us your quietest table in a corner, *per favore*."

When they were settled, Wollf snapped his napkin onto his lap. Lowering his voice, he said, "I always insist on Antonio when I dine here. It is his face. He could have posed for Donatello's *St. George*, don't you think?" Without waiting for Smerage to reply, he said in a normal voice. "So you're interested in the theater? You must be, if you're in the Dramatic Club."

"I haven't been accepted yet. I want it very much. Are you in?" Smerage tried not to sound desperate.

"Yes, been a member for two years. Great fun. Maybe I can help. Some of the fellows who decide these things are friends of mine."

"Oh, that would be wonderful! I did my freshman year at Tufts, but transferred to Harvard mainly because of the Dramatic Club."

When the waiter approached with menus, Wollf said, "Antonio, do you still have that brown bag I left here the last time?"

"*Sì, sì*, Signor Wollf. I bring it right away."

"And two coffee cups, if you don't mind."

When the waiter returned, he handed Wollf the bag and placed a cup before each man. When he left, Wollf said to Smerage in a near whisper, "Take your cup and hand it to me under the table." Wollf reached for the cup. Then, leaning toward the side of the table away from the room, he poured something from the bag into Smerage's cup, then into his own.

Wollf drank, then said, "What an odd country we live in, don't you think? I mean, in France and Italy, eight-year-olds are allowed to drink wine, but in this country, no one of any age is allowed so much as a sip."

They talked more about the theater.

"I hope to get down to New York before too long," Wollf said. "Some plays I want to see. I hear the new *Follies* is excellent. Fanny Brice is said to be great. Irving Berlin wrote the songs."

"Yes, everybody's singing 'A Pretty Girl Is like a Melody.'"

"Not everybody," Wollf said pleasantly and without innuendo.

Smerage ignored the comment. "I've heard that the great composer Giacomo Puccini has approached Berlin about writing an opera with him."

Wollf put down his cup of wine. "Now listen to me. If I am going to try getting you into the Dramatic Club, you must temper the more outlandish rumors you hear."

"It's true. I heard it from a very good source. An older man quite familiar with the classical music world."

Wollf was quiet for a minute as he studied his companion. Finally he said, "You are very sweet."

"Thank you," Smerage replied awkwardly. "I am enjoying our conversation."

"So am I."

When their dinners arrived, Wollf said how much he loved Puccini, an oblique apology for his abruptness over the Berlin-Puccini collaboration. "When I next get back to Europe, I hope to visit his home in Torre del Lago."

"You've been to Europe?" Smerage tried not to sound overly impressed.

"Twice. Once with my parents, once in the military. I yearn to go back on my own . . . or with a friend my age. There is still so much I want to see. After I've seen everything in Europe, I want to travel through Asia. South America, too."

Smerage sipped his wine. "You seem too adventurous to become a doctor. Don't doctors get trapped by their patients—or by hospital duties?"

"Not necessarily. Have you heard of Wilfred Grenfell? He abandoned a successful medical practice in England to help destitute fishermen in Labrador. For many of those poor families, Grenfell brought them the first professional care they had ever seen."

"So you have an altruistic side?" Smerage said.

"I'd say I do. Doctors are needed everywhere. I do not plan to stay at home treating the imaginary ailments of bored rich people. What about you?" Wollf asked. "Do you have a grand plan?"

"Not so grand," Smerage responded with a slightly derogatory laugh. "My thoughts about my future are more selfish than yours. I think I have talent, but I'm not sure where it lies. I play the piano and sing. I love acting. I also love to write. As you can see, I'm all over the ballpark. Right now my energies are aimed at finding my strong point, then working like hell to develop it."

"That is not so selfish. If I felt I had a special talent, I'd think the same way."

Tentatively, then with increasing enthusiasm, Smerage told of his dream of going on the stage. Wollf was encouraging. There were a few moments of silence, but both boys were now sufficiently comfortable with each other and felt no embarrassment. Wollf got the check.

Impulsively, Smerage said, "You are so much more traveled than I, more experienced . . ."

With a sly smile, Wollf said, "One doesn't have to travel to be experienced."

Smerage said nothing.

Wollf persisted. "With your good looks, I am sure you have had many interesting . . . *experiences.*"

Smerage understood fully what Wollf was hinting at, so as they were leaving the restaurant and Wollf asked him to stop by his dormitory room, Smerage accepted, knowing what would happen. He liked Wollf but was not sexually attracted to him. Nevertheless, he had a strange sense that, sharing these impulses, he was obligated to accept Wollf's overture. Honor among criminals perhaps.

When they entered the dormitory room, Wollf switched on a reading lamp that stood behind an armchair by the fireplace. The room remained quite dark. The décor was slightly richer than in the average student's room—well-framed hunting prints, a bronze statue of a stag, a silver cigarette box, heavy fringed curtains—but none of the arty décor that proclaimed the eccentricities of the more bohemian students. Wollf turned to Smerage, who was still standing awkwardly by the doorway. He put his arms around him and kissed him on the mouth. Smerage did not recoil, but he did not respond, either.

Wollf chuckled and walked to a makeshift bar on a dresser top. "You hold yourself so rigid. Did that bother you? Surely you have been kissed by a man before."

Without responding, Smerage said, "But right here? On the Harvard campus? It seems wrong."

"I know what you mean," Wollf said to Smerage's surprise. "At Exeter all the boys were misbehaving. If I'd had no taste for the sport before going to that venerated boarding school, I would surely have developed it quickly. Here at venerable old Harvard, however, I planned to give it up. But seeing you walking across the Yard tonight, I thought maybe I had found a kindred spirit."

Smerage looked very serious. "I do not pretend that I have never had"—he paused—"an *encounter,* but I strongly believe that I must not give in to that side of my nature, not now that I am at Harvard. We should both give it up."

"You're right," Wollf said, handing him a glass of sherry. "But let's give it up tomorrow."

For the first time since leaving the restaurant, Smerage smiled.

ABOUT A WEEK after their one night of lovemaking, Wollf dropped by Smerage's room, saying he had been on a stroll and, on an impulse, decided to pay a visit. For a while they sat and talked, then Wollf suggested that Smerage join him as he continued his stroll. They set out, but it was soon clear what Wollf wanted: he persuaded Smerage to come to his dormitory room, where they again had sex. This time, however, Smerage made it clear he did not want it to happen again. Smerage explained to Wollf that he really was trying to straighten himself out. The two men said goodnight on amicable terms.

As Smerage was going out the door and in the corridor, Wollf called after him, "I won't forget about putting in a word for you at the Dramatic Club."

MOST OF THE school year Smerage was preoccupied with his courses, being determined to present his struggling family with good grades. Weekends he generally returned to Topsfield to help his mother with the inn. Even with these frequent contacts, he wrote her long letters during the week. On May 23, as he was heading into the final exams of his sophomore year, Smerage wrote his mother a letter that reads like a status report on his state of mind. With a tone that bounces between joviality and reflection, he struggles cheerfully toward the conclusion that he is finally pulling his life together.

He tells her of his shock on learning of Cyril Wilcox's suicide and links it to the suicide of another friend of his who was not connected to Harvard in any way. "Ye gods! Another! Seems like if things [keep] going as they are at present I won't have any of last year's 'cronies' left to haunt me—in person at least; but it is quite frightful to see them all go the same way. There is perhaps a lesson in it all—but, oh what a lesson!—better unlearned I should say."

He makes the usual student request for more money ("I have to eat"), then talks enthusiastically about his satisfaction in acting a small part in a well-received student play, *The Governor's Wife*. For Smerage, who from a young age had dreamed of life as an actor, the experience had given him "a spirit of confidence, a sense of equality, a 'terra firma' for future endeavor, as well as inspiration. You know well that a lack of confidence is, or has been, my stumbling block hitherto, but I intend to make things different now."

He reflects on mistakes he has made in the past. "I hope it is not going to prove all loss. Meeting up with all sorts is part and parcel of life, and through mistakes we learn our best lessons. The things I have seen and been in may give me a foundation to do real good to society some day."

The very next day Smerage wrote his mother an even longer letter. The tone was ecstatic because he had just received word that he had been elected to the Dramatic Club. Acceptance into Phi Beta Kappa or the Porcellian Club, the top final club for socially prominent Harvard undergraduates, could not have evoked more triumphant joy, and the entire letter is a soaring aria of youthful elation. The club acceptance has infused him with a thrilling sense not just of his own worth, but the worth of life itself. In his burst of happiness, he alludes to his writing ambitions, then brings up one subject that will be his downfall.

> *I am full beyond words. And as is usual with me, I wept just a little. It's silly weak, kiddish and all that, but, gee, to have done something real . . . One* can *if one* will. *Now I know it. We measure by material accomplishments, that is, in the eyes of society. . . . I think I am registering a comeback, to employ the vernacular. Now to burst into print and to begin—not to*

shine—but to show phosphorescent tendencies that may assemble into a little glow. Big fires from little sparks grow. You're with me, dad's with me; and there are many I rather feel will jump on top when my bus gets going. I have youth; I am acquiring faith, i.e. courage, confidence, right's might: I am learning every day and developing every hour. . . . Fool that I am, I'd like to cry for a week, just from sheer happiness. . . . This year I am sure is the most glorious in my college so far after all.—If only I could find a girl, now. That is a big problem for me to thrash out— and it must be for myself, by myself, and with no other source or guide, less perchance it be Experience. I have so long avoided and put off telling this to you: but you must see it. After Emma, I have lost faith in your sex. That affair you never knew in detail. I can tell you of it some day, but not here and now. . . . Why I write this, I cannot say. I don't know. But as I see engagements about me by the score—not that I think it even tolerable in one so young—but because I realize that I of equal age (in years) do not feel the slightest attraction or inclination to . . . (page missing)

The missing-page reference is puzzling. The above is quoted from what surely is the original letter. It is written on a typewriter and is full of typos and ink smudges, about which Smerage jokes. Yet the "page missing," which is in the same type, comes about three lines into the letter's second and last page. It certainly appears to have been typed into the text by Smerage himself. Coming just as he is about to make a major confession to his mother, it is provocatively mysterious.

He says enough, however, to make clear to his mother that he is not attracted to women and feels that the right girl would change that. "Page missing" could stand for all the emptiness and despair that consumes the inchoate homosexual when he realizes he does not feel what society demands he feel. In Smerage's case, however, the "page missing" insertion may be nothing more than his joking way of telling his mother, "There's much more to say about all this, but for now, I've said enough." Indeed he had.

Despite this dark allusion at the letter's conclusion, most of the text is extremely upbeat and happy. In fact, his willingness to broach such a painful subject with his mother can be seen as an indication of his optimism and newfound confidence. No problem was unsolvable. The pieces of his jumbled adolescence were coming together. Every indicator pointed up. Only a few days after writing this ode to youth, joy, and promise, Keith Smerage received a note from Dean Greenough summoning him before the Secret Court.

4

A Rare Outbreak of Evil

———◆———

IN THE DAYS immediately following Lester Wilcox's visit, Dean Chester Greenough made some inquiries and quickly learned that Ernest Roberts was notorious as a ringleader of a vibrant homosexual subculture on the Harvard campus. Roberts's renown may have explained why the dean and the Court were so quick to assume he was *the* ringleader, rather than one of several—or many. This was one of a number of precipitate assumptions that skewed the Court's thinking in the first days of the investigation and launched it so resolutely on its shaky course.

The members of the Court seemed gripped by the idea that, under normal conditions, Harvard was totally free of such disgusting behavior. On several occasions they referred to the deviant group they had stumbled upon as "an outbreak." This comforting assumption led to a strategy of a few interrogations that would uncover all manifestations of this anomalous eruption and enable the Court to rid Harvard of homosexuality. Had they not believed this, their dogged pursuit of only one of many such groups would have been a sizable injustice, one that many might feel outweighed the Court's need to punish and expel the group they had uncovered.

It does not seem to have occurred to President Lowell or the men of the Court that the university might harbor many sorts of homosexuals—social groups, pairs of lovers, predatory lone wolves— not just in the hapless class of 1922, but in the three other classes of undergraduates, in graduate schools, among the faculty and university employees. They were convinced that a most egregious and exotic form of vice had broken out in the sophomore class of Harvard College in the year 1920 and nowhere else in the university and at no other time. If there were other active homosexuals at Harvard—and surely there were—it is interesting to speculate on how they viewed the brutal witch hunt that was about to devastate this one group.

Even if Harvard had many such cliques and ringleaders, Roberts was surely a standout. While he must have known that many, if not most, people abhorred his exotic lusts and appetites, he pursued them zestfully and openly, with no discernable fear of censure. His dormitory room, number 28 Perkins Hall, was the scene of frequent parties, some of which, even by today's standards, are remarkable for the unabashed outrageousness among college undergraduates: boys in makeup and women's clothes, women in men's clothes, sailors in uniform from the streets of Boston, male and female prostitutes. Roberts made no move to restrict the guest list. Anyone who cared to wander into the room could see town boys and Harvard students dancing, kissing, and engaging in erotic interplay. For lordly arrogance, Harvard had met its match in Ernest Weeks Roberts.

Regardless of how many homosexual groups were active at Harvard in the early 1920s, there is little doubt that the homosexual milieu created by Roberts was singularly blatant, as well as daring to a defiant degree. Even if Harvard's administration took a benign, look-the-other-way approach to homosexuality per se—and ample evidence says it did not—the deans might well have been moved to disciplinary action against the unrestrained saturnalia in Perkins 28.

One wonders how such flagrant behavior could have progressed for so long on a college campus without attracting the attention of university authorities. Like most colleges, Harvard had a system of proctors, often graduate students who were given free or reduced-rate dormitory rooms in exchange for monitoring student activities in those dormitories. To Greenough and his cohorts, the proctor of Perkins Hall had clearly let the university down quite badly. A system of overseeing students that had worked well for over two centuries had now broken down egregiously, and Greenough was furious.

At the outset of his investigation, Greenough summoned to his office the Perkins proctor, a graduate student at the Harvard Business School named Windsor Hosmer. Absorbed by his work for an MBA, Hosmer admitted to Greenough he was aware of odd happenings in room 28 of Perkins, but was not aware of any activity that broke university rules or caused a disturbance to the other residents.

Curbing his exasperation, Greenough instructed Hosmer to keep number 28 under constant scrutiny and record in detail everything he saw there. The dean particularly wanted the names of all students Hosmer observed visiting the room at present and of those he recalled having seen there in the past. He wanted the information in three days.

The day Greenough expected his report from the proctor, May 26, he received a report of a different sort: an anonymous and unsolicited letter from a student who poured out to Dean Greenough his disgust with the homosexuality he claimed was rampant on the Harvard campus and who urged the university to put a stop to it.

The letter opens with a statement of the basic facts about Cyril Wilcox's suicide, the writer noting that Wilcox "was registered in the College this year as a 1st year student but he should have been registered as a 2nd year man as he entered college a year ago last Fall." With total confidence in his information the writer goes on to tell the dean why Wilcox had taken his life: he had met students during his freshman year who had induced him "to committ [sic] on them 'unnatural acts' which habit so grew on him that realizing he did not have the strength of character enough to brake [sic] away from it concluded suicide the only course open to him."

The letter names Ernest Roberts as the leader of the depraved group and says that the parties in his Perkins Hall rooms "beggar description." Among those attending were sailors in uniform who had been picked up from the streets of Boston by Roberts and "his friends of his type . . . to be used for [their] dirty, immoral purposes." The writer also tells of non-Harvard young men from Boston, calling them "degenerates" and giving their names. Some of these town boys dressed as women and "appeared in the public hallways and entries of Perkins so dressed."

Among the students present at the parties, the letter writer mentions Kenneth Day, Edward Say, and others whose names he does not recall. In addition, he specifies dental student Eugene Cummings, whom he incorrectly places in the law school, and Harold Saxton, an independent tutor to Harvard students. All of these people were in regular attendance at Roberts's parties, where "the most disgusting and disgraceful and revolting acts of degeneracy took place openly in plain view of all present."

The letter ends with a strident call to arms aimed at stirring the most complaisant dean to forceful action: "Isn't it about time an end was put to this sort of thing in college? If you will look into the above you will find the charges are based on facts. Very truly yours,   '21."

The letter leaves no doubt that the writer's disgust stemmed from an intimate knowledge of this aspect of undergraduate life. He signed his letter only " '21," for the class of 1921, which meant he was a junior. He therefore could have lived in Perkins, close to ground zero of the activity he deplored, and could have acquired his familiarity from unavoidable spectacles in the public corridors and perhaps acquaintance with some of the participants. Although the writer shows close knowledge of the gay group, at the same time he makes mistakes such as placing Cummings in the law school rather than the dentistry school.

The letter arrived only a few days after Lester Wilcox's initial visit to Dean Greenough, the meeting that launched the Secret Court. It was written on the same day as the first interview. At the time, few people knew about the campaign against homosexuals that was just beginning, and the letter indicates no awareness of this campaign. Yet it strains belief to think that just as Harvard officials were launching an unprecedented campaign against homosexuals, someone just happened to send the dean a letter denouncing rampant campus homosexuality.

The letter contains many curiosities. First is the writer's great care in maintaining his anonymity. He typed the letter, including the closing, suggesting a fear that his handwriting might reveal his identity. But if he believed that the outbreak of homosexuality was a dangerous evil that had to be eliminated, why would he be so intent on anonymity? The simplest explanation is that, if he lived close to

Perkins 28, he would be forced to encounter the group he was denouncing and endure their hostility.

The letter writer has detailed knowledge of Cyril Wilcox's suicide, which is not surprising, since the death caused a sensation on campus. But he also knew more than a casual acquaintance would have known of Cyril's student status. For instance, he points out that, in newspaper stories, Wilcox was designated a first-year student when "he should have been registered as a 2nd year man as he entered college a year ago last Fall." It is odd that one writing to demand Harvard rid itself of rampant sin and depravity be so intent on correcting a minor error about which class a deceased student had been in.

Even odder is the letter writer's presumption that he knows exactly why Cyril Wilcox committed suicide. Without allowing for other possible explanations—deteriorating health, failing grades, the squandering of a rare educational opportunity—the writer boldly announces the sole reason why Cyril took his life: his homosexuality. Not only did the writer know why Cyril killed himself, he knew the specific sexual activity that led to his death, including who did what to whom.

All of this detail, especially the certainty about the reason Cyril killed himself, would suggest the letter might have been written by Lester Wilcox himself. The nit-picking about Cyril's Harvard year bespeaks an irrelevant fastidiousness that was typical of Lester. His unequivocal assertion that Cyril's homosexuality prompted his suicide fits with Lester's certainty on the point. Few others would have ventured such a strong opinion at that early date. Lester could have learned names of the town boys and details of Roberts's parties from his meeting with Harry Dreyfus.

While these aspects of the letter point toward Lester, many other things point away from him. The letter contains more detailed information about the extent of gayness at Harvard than it was likely for Lester, an outsider in two senses, to have possessed—or, for that matter, for Harry Dreyfus to have been in a position to tell him. The writer goes into more detail than necessary about Cyril Wilcox's gay activities. This seems an improbable smearing of a beloved brother whose loss Lester was still grieving. Lester graduated from Harvard in 1914. Why would he name himself " '21"? This letter and a subsequent one from the same source contain glaring mistakes in spelling and syntax. "Brake out" for "break out," "committ" for "commit," and so on. As Lester's later writings and his linguistic abilities proved, he was meticulous about language.

It also makes little sense for Lester to write an anonymous letter to a dean whose ear he already had, to whom he had related the most shocking details, and in whom he had instilled appropriate dismay. One could conjecture that Lester did it to strengthen his charges—a second opinion, so to speak. But this would clearly have been unnecessary: Lester, without any outside help, had already roused Greenough to forceful action.

The more one analyzes the letter's information and concerns, the more the suspicion grows that it was written by a student who had been a full participant in the group and become disaffected to a vengeful degree. Or the boy may have been disgusted by his own slide into depravity and, like a vindictive Brünnhilde, sought to bring destruction on his former cohorts in crime.

The writer's identity was never established, but whoever he was and whatever his motivations, the information he provided jibed neatly with the information already in Greenough's possession. The letter also expanded on it sufficiently to reinforce Greenough's belief in the accuracy of Lester's accusations and the spreading nature of the problem. By focusing on the infamous dormitory room of Ernest Roberts, the writer also confirmed the Court's belief that this one open sore would reveal all deviant infection on the Harvard campus.

THE SAME DAY Greenough received the anonymous letter, May 26, Proctor Hosmer delivered his report. Considering the more than twenty men who would eventually be named as regulars in Roberts's rooms and at his parties, it was a puzzlingly short list. Hosmer first presented the obvious name of Roberts, as if to pad his meager tally. He then named Kenneth Day and a class of 1921 student, Keith Smerage. After both names, Hosmer wrote in parenthesis "often." He named Eugene Cummings, also named by Dreyfus, whom he correctly placed in his final year at the Harvard School of Dentistry. Other undergraduates were named, including Nathaniel Wolff, a premed student from Buffalo who was in his final year, and two other boys. After the latter names Hosmer wrote that he was "inclined to think that neither is part of the group that has centered around Perkins." Unlike the anonymous letter writer, Hosmer said nothing about town boys, drag queens, or sailors.

Three days later, Hosmer returned to Dean Greenough's office to report that he had had a visit from the two boys on his list. They had spoken to Hosmer at length about the injustice of having been included and convinced him that their names should be removed. He had been mistaken, Hosmer told Greenough, and wished the two names to be removed. In his notes of that meeting, Greenough wrote that Hosmer's change of mind resulted from the two students' visit, then added, "The others don't speak to him."

It is one of the many mysteries surrounding these first days of the Court's activity that the two students who felt themselves wronged had so quickly learned of the accusation against them and its precise source. Perhaps Proctor Hosmer, inexperienced at detective work, had made inquiries in such a way as to reveal exactly what he was about. However the two students acquired their knowledge, they found out immediately that the proctor was compiling a list of suspects and that their names were on it.

The students' quick move for exoneration is indicative of the speed with which word spread about the "Secret" Court and its unprecedented mission. To be sure, the Court was issuing curt notes of summons to the students it wanted to interrogate, but the notes said nothing about a court or the issue to be discussed. They were simply orders for the boys to present themselves at the dean's office at a certain time. Students may have figured what it was about merely by the reputations of the boys who received the summons. It is also likely that Harry Dreyfus had warned student friends about Lester Wilcox's rampage.

However the students found out, word of the impending inquest shot through the undergraduate gay network, causing shock waves of fear. In a later letter, the anonymous writer spoke of "excited conferences" by phone and in person of the twenty or so students who knew or feared they would be implicated. As the summonses were issued, it became clear that it was not only the actively gay who were being called in, but anyone who was friendly with gays or happened to be assigned a gay roommate. In the deans' view of guilt, a student did not have to be an avowed homosexual; contamination could occur in many ways. To expunge the insidious blight, Harvard was setting very broad standards of culpability.

It is not hard to envision the fear that gripped those boys who knew they were in danger. Frantic phone calls, late-night visits to one another's rooms, warning phone calls to boys off campus. A panic had swept the university's homosexual community. Since panic is not the best state of mind for keeping secrets, it is more than likely that the entire student body was aware of the sexual crackdown that was about to shatter Harvard's ivied tranquillity.

ONE STUDENT TOLD friends that when he had been called in by the Court, he had been seated in a darkened room with only one light burning. Since the interrogations occurred during daylight hours, the Court must have drawn curtains and reduced artificial light to a minimum—or possibly found a room with no windows. It is odd that Harvard University would resort to the intimidating tactics of a second-rate detective film, but the intention may have been to underscore the grave and exceptional nature of the interrogation. The Court was also determined to discover exactly what had happened and to obtain tidy, easy-to-act-upon confessions of guilt.

From the outset of the hearings, the Court kept careful notes on what each student said. They were handwritten, usually by Dean Greenough, and set down in a telegraphic, almost shorthand style. The majority of the descriptions that follow are based on these notes but are expanded on by comments, in letters and conversations, from the students themselves. Whatever dangers may lurk in relying so heavily on the report of one side of this battle are mitigated by the Court's certainty of the rightness of its action. While the members of the Court had little reason to believe the record of their proceedings would ever come to light, they felt no need to conceal or doctor the record of their investigation. The only concession they made to secrecy was in giving the students code names: S1 for Roberts, S3 for Day, D1 for Cummings, and so on.

The Court records make no mention of which Court members were present during the interrogations. In a few instances, the notes mention the presence of President Lowell, but that is only in the case of two accused men who relied on Harvard for their livelihood. One was an assistant professor, so a university employee; the other tutored Harvard students. For all the other interrogations, it is safe to assume that every member of the Court was present: the three deans— Greenough, Murdock, and Gay—plus Dr. Lee and Mr. Luce.

It is a rare and serious matter for a student to be called before one dean, but each of the boys summoned had to face three deans, a regent, and the head of the university's health department. Not only did they face a battery of academic power, they were submitted to the most excruciating and intrusive questions about their sexual histories with both men and women, the extent of their friendships with other students, the degrees of involvement with town boys, the sleepovers in off-campus apartments.

The members of the Court did not limit their questions to interactive sex. For some reason, they were intent on knowing whether or not each boy masturbated and, if so, how often. This may simply have been an effort to find out how highly sexed each student was, but the frequency of the question suggests they subscribed to the theory of a connection between masturbation and homosexuality. Topping these humiliating questions, the deans demanded to know if the student had had "immoral relations" with men while at Harvard.

The Court clearly felt that the behavioral crisis it confronted was of such magnitude that the most rigorous, unflinching probing was justified in order to unearth the extent of the damage and, of course, the degree of each student's guilt. The picture approaches the comic when one contemplates these eminent Harvard deans and officials, men who had renounced the outside world's squalid strivings and maneuverings in favor of the cloistered refinements of ivy-draped academia, having to ask students how often they masturbated and when they were last with a woman. It is less comic when one realizes that they were seeking confessions that would lead to summary expulsion from Harvard.

OF THE TWENTY or so boys interrogated, few confronted the Court encumbered with as much damning evidence as Ken Day. He had been named on the list Dreyfus had given Lester Wilcox and by the proctor, Windsor Hosmer, and the anonymous letter writer. Even more incriminating was Ernest Roberts's letter to Wilcox, which stated that Day "is being sucked foolish by anyone and everyone he can lay hold of." If, in the homosexual circle, Roberts was the most socially active, it appeared Day was the most sexually active.

Day's wide trail of incriminating evidence may say more about his innocence and naïveté than his gay prowess. He was unlike most of the others under suspicion in that he was thoroughly masculine and showed no leanings toward bohemianism or artiness. He was a diligent student, and his nonacademic enthusiasms centered on athletics. Since arriving at Harvard he had distinguished himself as both a runner and a boxer. He used none of the gay jargon common to the other members of Roberts's circle and had even shown hostility to the effeminate types with whom he came in contact.

From all previous and subsequent evidence, Kenneth Day appears to have been a heterosexual who, lacking other sexual outlets, availed himself of the services of the resolutely homosexual students. In deciding which students were "guilty," this turned out to be a subtlety of no importance to the judges on the Secret Court.

Kenneth Day had been born to an old New England family with a tradition of gentility and education, but no great wealth. His parents died when he was very young, and he was raised by his grandmother, who would raise five other grandchildren. The closest in age to Ken was his first cousin, Homer, who, although several years older, developed a stronger bond with Ken than that shared by most brothers. When it came time for Ken to attend college, it was obvious to the Day family that Ken—with his brains, good looks, and mature sense of responsibility—had a bright future, so various family members pooled resources to put him through Harvard.

The warm relationship between Ken and his cousin is established in a letter Ken wrote to Homer a year before the gay scandal broke. Then a freshman, Ken thanked Homer for sending him an overcoat and some neckties, saying, "You are a peach all right." The letter went on to describe problems Ken was having with his roommate, Cyril Wilcox, who so disgusts him that he cannot bring himself to speak with him. He tells his cousin he fears that "some day I will give him what he deserves."

He alludes to Cyril's lover, Harry Dreyfus, as "that terrible wreck you saw Sunday" and mentions that Dreyfus had slept in their room for several nights and that Cyril would then leave to sleep at Dreyfus's place. Thoroughly fed up with his roommate's behavior, Ken tells Homer: "It makes me so damn mad I could kill him." Ken decides, however, he can put up with the situation for two more months, "then never again. I'll room alone or know whom I'm getting." He ends the letter with a cautious parenthesis and underlines the words "(<u>This is all confidential.</u>)"

The letter boasts of Ken's track meet showing—he finished fourth in the 100-yard dash—and closes by saying how much he enjoyed Homer's recent visit. He signs the letter "Yours with love" and adds in parentheses "(Give my love to grandma.)" About two weeks later, Ken wrote Homer another letter in which he says that Cyril had left him an apologetic note, so perhaps wasn't as bad as he had thought. Although the roommates hadn't spoken for two weeks, Ken says he "couldn't help but shake hands with him." He tells Homer that they went to church together and that Cyril was so happy to be friendly again, he nearly broke down. Ken concludes: "So I guess he must be all right only perhaps he can't help being a little queer. Of course I won't get too pally with him, but it is so much better to be at least on a speaking basis."

The letter switches to his studies, and he crows about getting an A– on an English test ("glory of glories") and says that doing well on that test had been his "ambish." He then discusses his curriculum for his sophomore year and asks Homer's advice. He was leaning toward a combination of government, economics, and history "with the principle [sic] stress on government."

The letters also make clear that Ken Day was at Harvard on a very taut shoestring. If he had to rely on his cousin's cast-off clothing, he clearly did not have the extra money needed for dating girls. This simple economic fact, coupled with a highly active libido, may say a great deal about the disastrous trouble he found himself in at Harvard.

When Kenneth Day was ordered to appear before the Secret Court, he was still one of Harvard's, if not the nation's, favored. He was flourishing at Harvard and could only look to an auspicious future. A good student and talented athlete, he was handsome, popular on campus, and graciously forgiving of his "queer" roommate. He was the embodiment of the Harvard ideal—physically and mentally proficient, serious, manly, loving, even compassionate. He was the well-rounded prototype of meticulously honed masculinity that Emerson, James, and Eliot had envisioned. Having been named by four different sources, he was, in the Court's eyes, a standout culprit and the first to receive the neatly typed summons.

LIKE ALL WILY interrogators, the Court began with a few routine questions about Day's home address, family, and previous schooling, then jumped into the business at hand by asking Day how well he had known Cyril Wilcox. This was disingenuous, as they knew Day had been Wilcox's roommate the previous year. They asked if he recalled anything unusual about Cyril. Day told the Court that, while they were roommates, "funny-looking fellows" had visited Wilcox in their room.

"Was a man named Harry Dreyfus among them?" Dean Greenough asked, looking over the top of his spectacles.

"Yes," Day replied evenly.

"Did you know what was going on?" Murdock shot at him.

"You mean between Dreyfus and Wilcox?"

"Yes. That is what I mean."

"I guessed."

"How often did Dreyfus visit the room?" Dean Gay asked.

"He came by maybe six, maybe seven times."

"Did you see Dreyfus elsewhere?" This from Dr. Lee.

"Yes, Dreyfus also attended a few parties in Roberts's rooms."

The deans brought up Dreyfus's apartment and the fact that he lived alone. They asked if Day had been to his apartment.

"Yes, but only once."

"Did you ever spend the night with him?" Greenough asked.

"No, never."

"Mr. Day," Dean Murdock broke in, "have you ever visited a restaurant in Boston called the Lamp?"

"Yes, I went there with Ernest Roberts and some others." The deans exchanged glances.

Day told them about the row he had with Wilcox; even though roommates, they had not spoken for several weeks. Day acknowledged that he was a good friend of Roberts and visited his rooms almost every day.

"Mr. Day," Mr. Luce asked, "have you ever had improper relations with any man?"

His body went tense in the chair. "No. Never."

"Do you like women?" Dean Gay said, as though asking if Day liked Hawthorne.

"Yes, I was with a woman maybe two years ago."

"How often do you masturbate?"

"I have not masturbated for seven years."

"These people you were seeing here at Harvard, the men in your circle, you knew what kind of people they were, did you not?"

"Yes."

"Yet you kept on associating with them?"

"Yes."

They asked if he knew certain town boys: Harold Hussey, Ned Courtney, and Winn Adams. He said he knew them only very slightly.

He admitted to knowing Cummings and Saxton and spoke again about having gone into Boston with Roberts. They asked if he had attended parties in Roberts's dormitory rooms.

"Yes, I went to a few."

Dean Greenough asked him to describe them.

"Well, they were just like parties in students' rooms."

"Nothing unusual?"

"At one there was a man in women's clothes. Once there was a woman in men's clothes." Day squirmed uncomfortably.

Greenough read him a list of ten names. Four were unknown to him, he said. But he did not hesitate to reveal what he knew about the other six. One was "innocent" and five were "guilty"—Edward Say, Eugene Cummings, Harold Saxton, and two town boys, Courtney and Hussey. He had been told about this homosexual group by Cyril Wilcox and "various other people."

"Have you yourself been approached, Mr. Day?" Dean Murdock asked.

"Yes." Then suddenly becoming animated, he said forcefully, "But the statement in Roberts's letter about my promiscuity with men"—his voice rose—"is a lie out of whole cloth."

Ignoring his outburst, Greenough said calmly, "Even if you are not as active as Mr. Roberts says, you will admit to a certain degree of guilt in this sort of crime?"

He hung his head. "I guess I have become a little . . . *tainted.* Maybe it's true that my mind has been poisoned." Rallying, he added, "But I have cut it all out since thinking it over."

"Are you telling us, Mr. Day," Greenough said, "that you have had sexual relations with men?"

Day now appeared thoroughly disoriented. "Yes, I have, but only with one."

"Who was that?"

"Roberts."

"When?"

"The first time was this year, near the beginning of the year. The last time was over a month ago."

"Thank you, Mr. Day. I think you have told us enough."

Knowing he had said more than he should have, pretty sure he had hanged himself, Day somewhat pathetically insisted on his moderation.

"It never has been so," he said with all the indignation he could muster, "that I had immoral relations with everyone who came along."

Day's complete reversal—from denying ever having had sex with any man to admitting to sex with Roberts a number of times—indicates that considerable pressure was exerted on him. This pressure had succeeded in unnerving Day and eliciting a confession that he had every reason to suspect would have dire consequences for his immediate future. As it turned out, the consequences would last throughout his life.

From the Court's point of view, it had done quite well with this early witness, winning an admission from a popular student and promising athlete that he had been guilty of the kind of abhorrent sexual activity the Court was seeking to expunge from Harvard. It had also induced him to incriminate five others. He may not have admitted to being as insatiable for male sex as Roberts claimed in his letter, but to the Court, degrees of guilt were as irrelevant as degrees of pregnancy. Day was expelled from Harvard, and the Court was in full swing as it sought to rid the campus of the scourge of homosexuality.

5

Harvard and the Homosexual

———————

ONE OF THE most puzzling aspects of Harvard's Secret Court is the shock and horror of the judges when they discovered that such infamy existed so close at hand. They seemed to feel that the behavior Lester Wilcox reported was a rare and exotic form of vice that existed in depraved sinkholes of urban slums but nowhere else. To be sure, homosexuality was far less apparent in the 1920s than it is today, but it was a long way from invisible. It is very difficult to believe that the five members of the Harvard elite—urbane, well-traveled, educated men of the world—would not know that, in 1920, homosexuality was rampant in all social strata of Europe and America.

Havelock Ellis, the pioneer chronicler of aberrant sex, quotes a correspondent in the 1915 edition of his landmark book, *Sexual Inversion*. "The great prevalence of sexual inversion in American cities is shown by the wide knowledge of its existence. Ninety-nine normal men out of a hundred have been accosted on the streets by inverts, or have among their acquaintances men whom they know to be sexually inverted. Everyone has seen inverts and knows what they are."

The men of Harvard's Secret Court must also have known that there was a growing body of intellectual thought that considered homosexuality a medical anomaly that could be treated. However misguided such thinking proved to be, it represented a considerable advance over the long-held view that homosexuality was an unspeakable sin, an offense against God, immorality of the worst sort. Yet the men of the Court seemed to embrace such extreme Old Testament judgments, which could come only from individuals oblivious to the benign presence of homosexuality at every level of society.

This awareness, however unwanted, would have been imposed on them in many ways. Surely they were acquainted with the homosexual tradition of New England boarding schools, which these men either attended or knew well. They were undoubtedly well versed in classical literature and knew the high regard of the greatest Greeks and Romans for man-boy or man-man sex. The great literature of Melville and Whitman and Henry James was peppered with both open and thinly veiled allusions to same-sex erotic relationships. Every city, particularly Boston, had bars and restaurants notorious for their homosexual clientele. The more flagrant male denizens did not confine themselves to such places but, in androgynous clothing and touches of makeup, spilled over into respectable theaters and restaurants. The righteous could cluck their tongues, but they couldn't claim to be unaware.

The very conspicuousness of some homosexuals provided solace to the straight world in that it made the problem seem easy to identify and therefore confine and handle. Ironically, these misconceptions about the rarity of homosexuality and the flamboyance of all homosexuals undoubtedly contributed to the Court's "dealing with" the problem in such an overheated, disproportionate manner. Most of the students involved were not recognizably gay, and that was not playing by the rules.

The 1920s had other driblets of knowledge about sex among males. Most adults had heard the gossip about sex in prisons, about hobo-camp liaisons, or about the venerable naval tradition of sailors at sea—an outlet either tolerated or enjoyed by officers. Although the Oscar Wilde trials had occurred twenty-five years earlier, they still reverberated powerfully among the educated classes and served to remind the resolutely oblivious that homosexuality was not the exclusive domain of a pathological fringe but permeated even the loftiest walks of life. Then there were the newsworthy scandals—the molesting scoutmaster, the police roundups in public toilets, and, one year earlier, the U.S. Navy's gay scandals in Newport, which became a national cause célèbre that will be examined in some detail in the next chapter.

With so much evidence of homosexual activity throughout American society, it is hard to understand the panic and shock of the five Court members when they discovered this vice also existed at Harvard. They acted as if the gay activity they had uncovered on campus was a spontaneous combustion of hellfire in 28 Perkins Hall, a bizarre anomaly that fate had chosen them to stamp out.

In the face of so much evidence of homosexuality in the world beyond Harvard Yard, how could the Court maintain its stance of shocked outrage? One reason is that much of their knowledge was gleaned from public scandal, which meant they saw only the most outrageous tip of the gay iceberg—gender-crossing transvestites, child-molesting perverts, sex-starved sailors. This made it possible for the judges to relegate homosexuality to a depraved and psychotic fringe of society. That such criminality could exist on their campus shattered their comforting vision of such abominations being confined to squalid precincts on the wrong side of the Charles River.

Even if they knew how widespread homosexuality was, they undoubtedly felt that Harvard was a bulwark against such expanding sin. The same mechanism can still be seen at work in professional sports. The David Kopays, Billy Beans, and Esera Tuaolos, players brave enough to proclaim their gayness, encounter greater criticism because they are in a field that many consider a bastion of normalcy against the perversions that pollute the rest of the world. These exceptions are seen as the Trojan horses that will bring down the remaining holdouts against the broader society's capitulation to moral anarchy.

With Harvard, it may not have merely been the arrogance and elitism of a great institution that felt itself above such sordid vice, but the zeal of crusaders who felt that if the vice couldn't be stopped at Harvard, it couldn't be stopped anywhere.

So the irony deepens. On one side are people who think the Court's excesses were more egregious because one expects more compassion, tolerance, and understanding from a great university. On the other side are reasonable, intelligent men, probably even kind men, reacting in such a brutal way precisely because they see themselves as safeguarding a mighty university's moral standards.

So much of it seems to come down to the specific attitudes toward homosexuality of each member of the Court. To be sure, the instigator of the entire affair was the hotheaded Lester Wilcox, who demanded that Harvard's dean take action against the gay ring he had discovered. But Wilcox's crusade would probably not have met with such success had it not found a powerful response on the Harvard side. And of all Court members, none were so exercised and outraged as President A. Lawrence Lowell. And here the irony that abounds in this story reaches its greatest intensity.

To the above list of possible sources of information about homosexuality that could prod the straight world into awareness, there is one more entry. Few people then, as now, do not have a family member, friend, or associate who is not either obviously gay or openly involved in a same-sex union. In even the finest families, there is a maiden aunt or bachelor uncle who has lived with the same partner for years. Ironically, these unions among women were called "Boston marriages." Everyone knew of these situations, but they were never discussed. When Henry James wrote about a Boston marriage in *The Bostonians* (1886), the public ignored the novel.

A. Lawrence Lowell—aristocrat, scholar, national figure, confidant of U.S. presidents, prime mover of the Secret Court that would purge Harvard of homosexuals—had at home a younger sister who was extremely fat, smoked cigars, and wrote and published love poems to her live-in female secretary. She was the soon-to-be-famous poet Amy Lowell. At the time, she was known only as the sister of Harvard's president; in recent years he has come to be known mainly as Amy Lowell's brother.

Amy was born in 1874, when Lawrence was seventeen and a Harvard undergraduate. She venerated him and saw him as a father figure. For his part, he was fond of Amy and protective of her. When she was in her teens, he made himself a family hero by rescuing his sister from a runaway horse. The family was close. Dinners at their Brookline estate, Sevenels, were animated by lively discussions on a wide range of topics.* When Lawrence was starting out as a lawyer, the family would have mock trials at the dinner table. One evening the topic was the Lizzie Borden murders. Lawrence presented a brief proving the murders had been committed by the ax, which had then buried itself in the garden.

As Amy became more eccentric and Lawrence more august, his attitude changed to one of thinly concealed embarrassment. When Lawrence became president of Harvard in 1909, the entire family came under public scrutiny, and the newspapers began making raised-eyebrow references to Amy, especially to her fondness for cigars. When people close to Lawrence gingerly raised the subject of her eccentricities, he would register his disapproval in the most general terms. On her cigar smoking, for instance, he told a friend, "I do not approve of women smoking in public." Smoking women were the problem, not lesbian sisters.

The effort at a brave face was made more difficult by Amy's refusal to keep a low profile. She bought herself a maroon Pierce-Arrow and outfitted her chauffeur in maroon livery. Every summer, she and her companion, Ada Dwyer Russell, traveled to Europe and shipped over the car and its matching chauffeur for their conspicuous tours.

Back in America, the two women were also fond of taking long drives in the countryside beyond Brookline. One day the Pierce-Arrow broke down and was towed to a mechanic. After the car was repaired, the man told Amy she owed him $230.

Airily she said, "Just send me the bill."

The mechanic protested, saying he didn't know her.

"I am Miss Amy *Lowell*."

*Lawrence and Amy had an older brother, Percival, who would become a highly distinguished astronomer and was once referred to by Lawrence as "the most brilliant man I ever knew." Percival founded the Lowell Observatory outside Flagstaff, Arizona, where he spent a good part of his life studying Mars. He was the first serious scientist to advance the notion that life had once existed on Mars, and he was convinced that there was a ninth planet beyond Neptune (Pluto was discovered fourteen years after Percival's death in 1916). Such big ideas were common currency at Sevenels.

The mechanic looked blank, so she added slowly, "My brother is president of Harvard."

"How do I know he's president of Harvard?"

"Just telephone him."

The mechanic dialed Harvard, got the president's office, and said he was calling about the president's sister. He was put right through.

"I've fixed the car of a very fat lady who owes me $230. She says she's your sister."

"What is this fat lady doing right now?"

"She's sitting on a wall across the road, smoking a cigar."

"That's my sister. Your bill will be paid."

Lawrence Lowell always maintained an affection for his sister and took some pride in her growing fame. He even showed occasional humor about her oddities. But he would stiffen each time her name was mentioned and, according to the biography of Lowell by his protégé, Henry Yeomans, he disliked Amy's poetry and her "eccentric habits." This and other evidence suggests that, for this imperious, stiff, oh-so-proper Bostonian, his flamboyantly peculiar sister caused considerable mortification and pain. There may be a connection between his forbearance and tolerance toward a gay sister he loved and his implacable cruelty toward homosexual boys he did not know, students who happened to be in his charge.

This contradiction is underscored by a story about Lowell that found its way into several Harvard histories. An elderly professor on Lowell's faculty was exposed in a highly public homosexual scandal. Called into Lowell's office to be dismissed, the man pleaded that he was old, had been at Harvard his entire career, and knew nothing else. What could he do?

"If I were you," said Lowell, "I would get a gun and destroy myself."

It is difficult to believe that a man with a gay sister could have such a fierce attitude toward gayness or that he and the five Court members could be so unaware of the prevalence of homosexuality. Even without gays in one's own family, the sources of information about homosexuality were plentiful and unavoidable, even for the most protected, ivory-towered recluse. Yet Lowell and his deans seemed to attack the problem they had been forced to recognize with a degree of naïveté and ignorance that is hard to understand.

ANYONE READING HISTORIAN Douglass Shand-Tucci's richly detailed history of homosexuality at Harvard, *The Crimson Letter,* in which the above story is found, would wonder if Lowell and his tribunal were part of the same university that the historian describes. Starting with the favorable impact on Harvard of visits from Oscar Wilde and Walt Whitman in the latter years of the nineteenth century, Shand-Tucci traces a century-long procession of illustrious homosexuals through Harvard. Some of these men were deeply closeted, others as open as the times permitted. Some, such as philosopher George Santayana, became familiar names to the outside world; others were legendary figures for decades in Harvard Yard. But they were all either known as homosexuals or highly suspected as such and were nonetheless proudly pointed to, in their day, as emblematic of Harvard's prestige. It is hard to understand how Lowell and his Court could be so aghast that this aberrant form of sexuality, which Shand-Tucci portrays as something of a Harvard tradition, could exist on their campus.

Edward Prime-Stevenson, a popular writer of Horatio Alger–style boys' books, who also wrote homoerotic fiction under a pseudonym, stated that homosexuality flourished at Harvard and Princeton in 1908. He also said that Boston was the second most active of eight "homosexual capitals" in the country. Outstanding among the Harvard luminaries to win space in Shand-Tucci's gay tally were Professor of Medieval Art History Arthur Kingsley Porter, who invited a young male lover to live with him and his wife, and the "now obviously homosexual" English professor Charles Townsend Copeland ("Copcy"), a much-loved professor of English literature, who "held court between 1904 and 1932 in Ralph Waldo Emerson's old room."

James Mills Peirce was Harvard's dean of faculty from 1895 to 1898 and cofounder with President Eliot of the Graduate School of Arts and Sciences in 1872. Peirce, a lifelong bachelor, wrote warm letters to

John Addington Symonds supporting his courageous pioneering efforts on behalf of homosexuality. Peirce also anonymously wrote an essay extolling the beauty of male love. Another highly likely homosexual among Harvard's most eminent figures was George Pierce Baker, who taught playwriting at Harvard (to Eugene O'Neill, Philip Barry, and Thomas Wolfe, among others) and who was instrumental in founding the Yale School of Drama. Although married, Baker hired an assistant, an attractive and gay graduate student, who accompanied him on several summer trips to Europe while the professor's wife stayed home.

Of particular interest among Shand-Tucci's characters is the group surrounding financier A. P. Andrew, a professor of economics at Harvard during the twentieth century's first decade. That Andrew had a major influence on American society is beyond question. As assistant secretary of the U.S. Treasury, he was instrumental in setting up the Federal Reserve system and—with his probable lover, Henry Sleeper—Andrew founded the American Field Service, whose heroic work during World War I was well chronicled by Ernest Hemingway, e. e. cummings, and others.

Some of the most gaudy gay personalities had only a slight official connection with Harvard but were integral to university life. Orientalist William Sturgis Bigelow was a wealthy art patron who entertained sumptuously at his Beacon Hill home, was host to his good friend Theodore Roosevelt on his visits to Boston, and, from time to time, lectured at Harvard on Japanese art. But it was on his estate on the island of Tuckernuck, just off Nantucket, that Bigelow threw caution— and clothing—to the winds.

A lifelong bachelor, Bigelow entertained Harvard students and other young men at this paradisiacal retreat where the dress code was nudity during the day, black tie at dinner. Although Bigelow's establishment dominated the island, there were enough other summer homes to guarantee gossip about the all-male revels. When this notoriety was further spread by subsequent reports from Bigelow's guests about how they spent their summer vacations, it is all but impossible that the Harvard powers did not hear of his island bacchanals.

Shand-Tucci does a painstaking job of tracing large numbers of the outright gays—or highly probable gays—who made substantial contributions to Harvard's glory. Given the ample evidence of such a constant presence of homosexuals among Harvard's most distinguished figures, the Secret Court's response to a small amount of homosexuality among undergraduates is all the more perplexing.

In spite of enough noteworthy Harvard homosexuals to fill a 356-page book, a record covering the 150-year period prior to the book's publication in 2003, President Lowell and his five-man court treated the homosexual circle they discovered in *one* year, centered in *one* class and in *one* dormitory, as a rare outbreak of wickedness, a unique anomaly, the elimination of which would, once and for all, rid Harvard of homosexuality.

IT SEEMS UNAVOIDABLE that, prior to Lowell, the Harvard presidents and deans had been aware of homosexuals among the faculty and students but had chosen to look the other way, perhaps in the hope that none of the afflicted would have the temerity to act on their shameful condition. President Charles William Eliot was known to dislike George Santayana, one of his most renowned faculty members, saying to a colleague he thought Santayana "abnormal." But as far as is known, Eliot went no further in impugning his illustrious philosopher's sexual orientation. More important, he did not obstruct Santayana's advance in the academic ranks. The rule seemed to have been: Be what you will, but keep it private, Harvard's version of Don't Ask, Don't Tell.

Even this was a sizable concession to deviance, and it did not reflect a like permissiveness among the privileged classes. The hard fact is that, throughout the nineteenth century and the first half of the twentieth, overt homosexuality carried serious consequences in any level of society, as was so tragically demonstrated by the Oscar Wilde trials of 1895. One could be "a confirmed bachelor," "a man's man," "a bohemian," "an aesthete"—any one of a score of euphemisms for a man who showed little interest in women and who appeared to prefer his own sex. But as soon as there was the slightest evidence that this quirkiness crossed the line into physical action, the roof fell in.

There is no better evidence of the fear that gripped all homosexuals in the latter part of the nineteen century and the first half of the twentieth than the correspondence, so ably documented in Jonathan Ned Katz's *Gay American History,* between Walt Whitman and the English author and gay pioneer John Addington Symonds. For the twenty-five-year-old Symonds, Whitman's Calamus poems, his most openly homoerotic work, were an epiphany. In 1871 Symonds began a twenty-year correspondence with Whitman, which was dominated by a campaign to elicit an admission that the poems were referring, explicitly and unambiguously, to homosexual passion.

Remarkably, the groundbreaking Whitman, so forthright and courageous in his poems, was doggedly coy and evasive with Symonds. And his refusal to own up to the poems' meaning was not just the denial of candor to an annoying fan. Whitman liked and admired Symonds and once referred to him as "a royal good fellow." In 1890, after nineteen years of deferential and oblique questions to Whitman on the true import of the Calamus poems, Symonds came out and asked the question directly: is Whitman, in these poems, referring specifically to physical love between men? His back to the wall, Whitman denies his poems have any homosexual content and claims to have six children.

That Whitman was not just a homosexual but an exuberantly active one is now beyond question. His craven and dishonest denial is a strong indication of the fear in which homosexuals lived, and this letter was written five years before the Wilde trial. Ralph Waldo Emerson was just one of a number of admirers and well-wishers who warned Whitman about the dangers to his career in publishing such sexually transparent poetry.

Whitman's blatant falsehood in a correspondence he had good reason to believe would endure (both men were then well known) must be seen as a capitulation for survival. An announcement of his homosexuality, not in fanciful flights of ambiguous lyricism, but in crystalline prose, must have seemed to Whitman a reckless courting of ruin. Symonds's terrierlike persistence and Whitman's two decades of prim evasions could be seen as Victorian high comedy, had the standoff not been caused by a realistic fear of a dangerous, hostile world.

SO HARVARD'S LOOK-THE-OTHER-WAY tolerance in the latter years of the nineteenth century was not the predictable permissiveness of a worldly elite. It probably stemmed from the confidence that no Harvard man, no matter how "odd," would ever sink to such unspeakable behavior. This thinking was only possible if one did not look too deeply, which was exactly the course adopted, with gentlemanly resolve, by the Harvard hierarchy.

Even this level of tolerance was remarkable, considering the university's origins as primarily a theological institution. It had come into being in 1636, 140 years before the American Revolution, 20 years after the death of William Shakespeare, and a scant 16 years after the *Mayflower* landing. This placed its birth in the midst of New England's most virulently puritan, Taliban-like years, when government critics lost an ear, adulterers could be executed, and a law was considered that would have made it obligatory for women to wear veils.

In 1642, six years after the inception of Harvard, William Bradford, governor of the Plymouth Colony, wrote of his consultations with theological authorities in the area about the proper punishments for various crimes. The consensus was that adultery, rape, abortion, incest, bestiality, and sodomy—which one clergyman described as "this unnatural art of more than brutish filthiness"—all deserved death sentences. Writing of that year in his history of Plymouth Plantation, Bradford noted that "even sodomy and buggery (things fearful to name) have broken forth in this land oftener than once." Later the same year, Bradford presided over the execution of a teenager, Thomas Granger, who was caught in an act of buggery with farmyard animals.

In spite of the climate from which Harvard sprang—or perhaps because of it—the college, from its earliest days, struggled for independence from the oppressive scrutiny of the church and the region's governing body as well as from the school's founder, the Massachusetts General Court. Still smarting from the tyranny they had fled in England, the men in charge of the new college refused to require students and faculty to swear an oath, making Harvard, for many years, the only New World college without this requirement. When Harvard announced in the late 1600s that it was issuing a translation of Thomas à Kempis's *Imitation of Christ,* the General Court forbid publication on the grounds that the book contained ideas that would "be unsafe for the people of this place." The episode made clear to at least some administering Harvard the need to distance the college as much as possible from the local government and the church hierarchy.

The struggle reached a climax during the years of John Leverett, Harvard's president from 1708 to 1724. The religious sectarian faction, led by the querulous Cotton Mather, deploring what they saw as Harvard's secular tendencies, pushed hard for the college to be nothing more than a divinity school for their rigid sect. Fortunately, many people of influence had broader hopes for Harvard. With their backing, Leverett won out against the rigidly orthodox group (whose power had been weakened by the excesses of the Salem witch trials) and created a college that, while religious, was not under the control of one strict denomination. Harvard historian Samuel Eliot Morison summed it up: "Leverett, in a word, founded the liberal tradition of Harvard University."

Later presidents also had their battles for independence. President John Thornton Kirkland (1810–28) withstood a concerted attack on Harvard for its "aristocracy and atheism," and Josiah Quincy (1829–45) eloquently reiterated the necessity of academic freedom. Early in the nineteenth century, Harvard broke free from a major source of potential interference. Since the university's finances were on a solid footing, the Massachusetts General Court ended its practice of contributing funds each year. Then, in 1866, the state quietly relinquished its seat on Harvard's Board of Overseers. From then on, Harvard had no direct ties with the Massachusetts government.

By the time Charles William Eliot ascended to the presidency in

1869, the church had retreated in the face of Harvard's now-massive prestige (and perhaps its good-enough morality). The government, however, continued its attempt to influence the school and has continued to do so pretty much up to the present by such means as dangling or withholding federal grants. But these efforts have been paltry compared with the early demands of the clerics and the General Court. The U.S. government's intrusions appeared to have been feeble attempts to get for their money some small influence, not all-out assaults on academic freedom. (In the ROTC debate, the efforts to influence have gone the other way. Harvard banished the officer program in 1970 as protest against the Vietnam War and now is resisting a movement to bring it back because of the military's antigay policy.)

Although the government scaled down its meddling and the church quit the field altogether, Harvard was left with its alumni who, in three hundred years, have never ceased their efforts to block change and to launch attacks on any president who harbored faculty members noisily at war with the status quo. Some of the greatest challenges to Harvard's academic independence—and, more specifically, to its determination to have all views represented on its faculty—came during the presidency of Lawrence Lowell. In most ways a conservative, Lowell was ferocious in defending the rights of his faculty to voice the most unpopular views and heroically withstood cries of outrage from both alumni and his Board of Overseers at the public utterances of various professors.

Harvard's noble battle for independence has bearing on the formation of the Secret Court in 1920. Having freed itself from external oversight, it felt a greater need to keep its house in unassailable order. While striving to become great, Harvard also strived to remain blameless—for its own high-minded reasons, to be sure, but also to hold at bay the yahoos in political power. Moreover, it had its own ideas and methods for doing this. Its early struggles with religious rigidity, its brushes with governmental pressure, and its resolve to become the nation's preeminent educator all led to an institution of fierce independence and formidable power. It gradually transmogrified into an imperious city-state operating with haughty autonomy within a sovereign, but less tidy, nation.

*   *   *

HARVARD'S HARD-WON INDEPENDENCE had little immediate effect on its students, for whom authority was authority. At the same time, the institution's pride and insularity invariably rubbed off on students, who considered themselves special, elite, and invulnerable to the strictures of the outside world. Undoubtedly, this borrowed arrogance played a substantial role in the cavalier recklessness of the gay men in 1920.

In most ways, the life of a Harvard undergraduate was not very different from that of other college students of the day. For all its prestige, Harvard was not difficult to get into. This was true throughout most of its history, although for many years it had its own entrance examinations and the surrounding area teemed with tutorial schools aimed at prepping students for Harvard acceptance. But according to E. J. Kahn in his 1969 book *Harvard Through Change and Through Storm,* until the 1960s it was as easy to enter as any other college. A case in point would be Cyril Wilcox, who had no trouble being admitted although at Exeter he had barely managed to maintain a C average.

Like most colleges in the eighteenth and nineteenth centuries, Harvard imposed firm rules of behavior on students. Generally the rules were adhered to, except for occasional student uprisings. But these were more in the nature of Victorian panty raids than the full-scale campus takeover of 1969. At times the rules for students were petty, even prissy. In the 1870s, a student could be punished for shouting a greeting from a third-floor dormitory window to a friend spotted in the Yard below. Even though crippled with arthritis, President James Walker (1853–60) maintained the presidential tradition of patrolling the Yard each night to make sure the students were safely confined to their rooms.

By 1920 the university administrators relied on dormitory proctors to see that student behavior stayed within acceptable bounds. It was rare that a student would be so much as suspended on a behavioral matter, and expulsions for any reason other than consistently poor academic work were rare. Warnings were sufficient to correct most problems; in serious cases, students were suspended. Little was considered serious enough for summary expulsion.

ANOTHER PRESSURE ON Harvard in the first decades of the twentieth century may have exacerbated the harsh reaction of President Lowell and his deans to the presence of an active homosexual group on campus. Around the turn of the century, Harvard found itself inundated with applications from worthy candidates who in no way fit the stereotype of the consummate Harvard man. With increasing frequency, children of Irish, Greek, Italian, and Jewish immigrants presented themselves for admission and proved qualified. A few black students were also admitted, most notably W. E. B. Du Bois and Alain Locke, who became a highly influential scholar and educator. While Harvard wanted to prove its ecumenical openness and its progressive, democratic spirit, it had trouble with the violation done to the prototype that had been so many years, even centuries, in the honing.

In his interesting 1996 book, *Manhood at Harvard,* historian Kim Townsend traces the visions of Harvard administrators and leading thinkers about the sort of young men Harvard should be turning out. Scholars? Intellectuals? Political leaders? Captains of industry? Or merely that vague creature, the well-rounded gentleman, who, though lacking utilitarian value, would bring credit to his elevated social class.

Harvard leaders were far from alone in asking what a man should be. Burdened, however, with a reputation as the foremost crucible for molding outstanding American manhood, they pondered the question perhaps more earnestly than others. In wrestling with his unwieldy subject, Townsend makes one point clear: the ideal Harvard man was a concept that preoccupied the deans and presidents throughout the university's history.

More than others, university presidents were obliged to possess a well-etched vision of the young men their institutions were trying to fashion. According to Townsend, however, it was Harvard's strong intellects and forceful personalities who contributed most tellingly to this dialogue. Men like William James, Emerson, Theodore Roose-

velt, Oliver Wendell Holmes, Henry Adams, and countless other emi-
nences all had their checklists of traits that they would like to see in
the well-rounded Harvard man.

The virtues they catalogued now sound like manhood goals out-
lined in the *Boy Scout Handbook*. Moreover, Harvard cannot be cred-
ited with discovering the desirability of such qualities as honor,
intelligence, courage, strength, honesty, serenity of spirit, piety, compassion, and all the other virtues bandied about by the Cambridge
thinkers. Moreover, it is likely that admiration for these qualities goes
far deeper in the human species than the idle constructs of Harvard
intellectuals.

One of Harvard's visionaries went somewhat overboard in his
struggle to verbalize the ideal Harvard male. Dudley A. Sargent, forty-
year director of the university's Hemenway Gymnasium, in 1883
wrote an article about the goals Harvard set for its students. Comparing the men at Harvard to those at Yale, Sargent was transported by
his eye for detail: "In the Harvard man there is a greater development
of the chest muscles; while the Yale man has a larger chest-girth,
though the lower border of the chest-muscles is hardly discernible."
He appears to be comparing Praxitelean perfection with barrel-
chested oafishness, leaving open the question of whether the exquis-
ite Harvard pectorals were the result of his athletic program or of
some sort of genetic selection going on in the admissions office.

While the director's observation may sound like the rumination of
the art director of *Penthouse* magazine, it was in fact from a university
administrator exciting himself about the finished product to roll off
the Harvard assembly line. Sargent also sounds like an educator of
young men whose enthusiasm for his work might spring from deep-
seated drives that his colleagues would have deemed unacceptable.

While all of the soul-searching and philosophizing brought forth
many variations on the prototype, they all had one thing in common:
an assumption that the raw material Harvard had to work with would
be intelligent, somewhat educated, white male Protestants whose an-
cestors were, if not English, at least northern European. They were
men who would marry, have children, and be leaders in their commu-

nities. This vision definitely did not include young men who lusted after their fellow students and whose sexual nature condemned them, if
not to disgrace, at best to bleak lives of suspect bachelorhood.

In the midst of the ongoing quest for the qualities Harvard wanted
to instill in its students, the influx of new races and nationalities
forced the university to alter drastically its concept of the raw material.
And looming ever more ominously over the melting-pot pageant was
another group that would be perhaps the biggest threat to the time-
honored image of the ideal Harvard man: *women*. With the founding
of Radcliffe in 1879, women became an increasing presence on the
Harvard campus, and the march toward gender integration was
clearly under way.

By 1920, When Lester Wilcox stormed into the office of Dean
Chester Greenough, administration elders were still struggling to rec-
oncile the polyglot reality of incoming freshmen classes with traditional notions of Harvard students. They were in no mood to extend
their embrace to practicing homosexuals, a group that most administrators considered little more than a criminal element. It is not difficult
to view Harvard's ham-fisted action against the gays it found in its
midst in 1920, at least in part, as a reaction to the strained push for in-
clusiveness in those first decades of the twentieth century. Having accepted A, B, and C, the administrators drew a righteous, indelible,
nonnegotiable line at Z.

6

America's Gay Dossier

———◆———

WHILE HARVARD, FOR three centuries, was fighting back external threats, homosexuals were creating their own furtive struggle for existence in a nation that was consistently hostile to them. Only recently has this history been coaxed from the shadows and traced in a number of excellent books. Standouts among them are John Loughery's *The Other Side of Silence* and Jonathan Ned Katz's *Gay American History*. The books tell a remarkable story of courage and spirit in men and women who, throughout their lives, were forced to mentally link fulfillment, joy, and physical bliss with guilt, fear, and disgrace.

The latter part of the nineteenth century brought forth letters and memoirs from which historians could form an accurate picture of homosexual life in that period. For the earlier history—the colonial period and before, so admirably addressed in *Gay American History*—authors have had to rely on criminal proceedings and tabloid news stories, which told only the most sensational tales of extreme behavior and so presented a distorted picture. We see nothing of the countless men and women who, throughout the nation's first century, quietly enjoyed same-sex relations. We know they existed because occasionally one of these relationships erupted into a suicide or scandal that propelled it into the public record. It would be a mistake to assume that every gay relationship ended up in the pillory or the newspapers.

For researchers of gay history, the problem is a little like seeking a complete picture of Cambrian life on earth from the fossil record when the period had billions of boneless creatures that left no trace of their existence in the primeval silt. Still, eighteenth-century America had enough of these eruptions of errant gayness among humans to indicate a good amount of invisible, but hardly spineless, sexual activity.

Even with this large blacked-out area, the gay histories present a considerable degree of open homosexuality in America's larger cities throughout the second half of the nineteenth century. The seamiest parts of these towns invariably had a few bars that catered to an array of outcasts: dope peddlers, underage drinkers, and prostitutes and their clients. Most of the prostitutes were female, but the lowest bars also had boys and adult males for sale.

The police, generally paid to look away, made sporadic raids on the low-life bars. These crackdowns were not frequent enough to affect the flourishing of sin, just frequent enough to ensure that the bourgeoisie across town knew such places existed (and that the police were doing something about them). Large cities also had periodic drag balls in which young black men were usually prominent. Often these parties were held in black sections of the city but were patronized by many whites as well. The drag balls also resulted in a few arrests—often on trumped-up charges to appease public indignation—so accounts of the parties reached the newspapers and further alerted the general public to pockets of unnatural sin and debauchery.

With all of these nineteenth-century surfacings of homosexual activity, it was always the most outrageous gay behavior that got noticed. The historical documentation therefore creates the flawed impression that homosexuality in earlier times existed only in a rank demimonde of drag queens and boy whores. It is safe to assume that then, as now, these people represented a small percentage of homosexuals. They were simply the only ones fearless enough to broadcast their sexual nature. They alone made it into the history books, and they alone won the appalled notice of the day's respectable folk.

For all the scattered hubs of gayness and for all the straight world's belief in the contagion of homosexuality, it is not a behavior that requires a gay culture for its spread. From the individual stories that eventually emerged, we know that throughout America, in every corner of the country and in every level of society and at every time in history, two men or two women would look at each other with silent understanding and, once again, homosexuality was invented.

AS THE SUBJECT of homosexuality became somewhat less "unspeakable" than it had been through Victorian times, tales began to emerge of a different kind of gayness. There were reports of male relationships in logging camps and hobo jungles. Shipboard activity in the navy and merchant service had always been known, as had homosexuality in prisons. But this sort of sex in womanless worlds was seen as *faute de mieux* expediency and was easier to dismiss. But all the homoerotic reports and rumors contributed to the dribbles of gay lore that seeped into the straight consciousness.

If the public had vague notions of a gay underworld, the occasional glimpses gave no idea of its extent. This myopia may say a great deal about the alarmed reaction of Harvard's Secret Court. Of course, Lawrence Lowell and his deans knew of the existence of homosexuality, but it was a pestilence that occurred across the Charles River, in sections of Boston no respectable person would enter. To the good men of the Court, male-male sex spoke of depravity, immorality, corrupt character, and a wanton absence of morals. Surely systems were in place to bar men with such qualities from Harvard—just as criminals, lunatics, and the diseased were barred. That the carriers of this dread infection slipped so easily into Harvard filled the deans with horror. That, once admitted to the college, the degenerates flaunted their perversions so openly filled them with anger.

Much about the Court's reaction indicates that the judges thought of overt homosexuality not as just any disease but as a highly contagious one. If this was their attitude—and the thrust of the Secret Court's interviews suggests that it was—it contains the faint outlines of an endorsement of the joys of gay sex. The underlying assumption seems to have been that *all* boys would like to partake in these pleasures but are prevented from doing so by sheer strength of character and moral fiber. These virtues might not be able to withstand such strong temptations, and temptations so close at hand.

It is a commonplace among gay theorists that the greatest homophobes are usually those who, deep in their subconscious, share the same desires. Perfectly normal men, the thinking goes, unthreatened by homosexuality, are not upset by it. While this theory, which is discussed at greater length in Chapter 19, surely explains some of the more ferocious antigay types, it certainly doesn't explain all of them. But always lurking in much of the hostility—from whatever motivation—is the interesting belief that the forbidden pleasure is indeed a pleasure.

WHILE THE 1920S became known as a period of sexual liberation, the new freedom was for young women and did not apply to homosexuals. In the years immediately following World War I, the period of the Harvard purge, a backlash occurred against America's gay underworld: police sweeps of notorious bars, bathhouses, and movie theaters. Apart from official hostility toward overt homosexuality, the small advances made toward tolerance among the more enlightened public were pushed aside by the strident demands of the flapper.

The spectacle of America's young women thrusting off the stultifying confines of Victorian corsets and rejoicing in full-throttle enjoyment of liquor and sex was a momentous change in the national scenario. Gays had no part in the seismic moral shift, however. In fact, from the midst of the day's heterosexual festival, they were looked on with even greater disdain than before. In novels and films of the time, gays were inevitably portrayed as laughable sissies. If the new freedom did not include gays, that fact seems to have been lost on Ernest Weeks Roberts and his more outrageous friends.

In the 1920s, whatever knowledge the vast public had about homosexuality was derived from tabloid gossip and dirty stories. Freud, Havelock Ellis, Sir Richard Burton, and others who wrote seriously on the subject were known only to the highly literate or highly bohemian. Popular writers on the problems of young people did not address the issue. Loughery quotes a 1931 book, *Piloting Modern Youth,* by a Chicago doctor, William Sadler. "Every father should instruct his adolescent sons regarding homosexuality. . . . Young men should be told frankly that they will come into contact with men who are a bit queer sexually . . . who want to fondle them."

Loughery follows this with a comment that characterizes the period of the Secret Court. He writes that this was "not a statement that would have found its way into the literature of family life ten years earlier." He also observes that the advice was entirely directed at the fathers of *straight* boys: "No mention is made . . . of dealing with a son's desires should he be the one who wants to fondle his male friends." Pop psychologists and gays were not yet on speaking terms.

The 1895 Oscar Wilde trials jarred the public's tidy relegation of homosexuality to urban sloughs of depravity. Many people who probably preferred not to know learned not only that male-male sexuality could occur at the highest levels of society, but that there were many young men of the educated and working classes who either shared these sexual tastes or made themselves available to those who had them.

Another gay scandal was perhaps even more of a sensation in America because it involved the U.S. government and very young servicemen. It was on front pages of every major newspaper and culminated in a Senate investigation. As it occurred in 1919, just one year before the formation of Harvard's Secret Court, it has particular resonance for this story.

IN 1917 THERE were two thousand sailors stationed in Newport, Rhode Island. A year later, mobilization for World War I had brought the number up to twenty-four-thousand, and the navy had its hands full in maintaining a semblance of order during the servicemen's off-duty hours. Yet both the navy and Newport's mayor congratulated themselves on keeping the town relatively "clean." This complacency was shattered by a chief machinist's mate named Ervin Arnold.

While recuperating from a rheumatism attack in the station hospital, Arnold overheard orderlies talking about the town's rampant gay activity, particularly between town boys and sailors. The forty-year-old Arnold was appalled, and the revelations triggered his constabulary instincts, already well honed from eight years as a detective who specialized in tracking perverts. Feigning a sympathetic interest, he encouraged the navy medics to fill him in on Newport's wide-open homosexual carnival. Sensing a kindred spirit, the young men regaled Arnold with tales of sexual traffic in the public parks, the army and navy YMCA, and other pick-up places. They also told him of sexual superstars, well-known "marriages" between town boys and sailors, and older Newport men who lined up to pay sailors for sex.

Arnold recorded the information, getting names when he could and eventually taking his findings to the base's top command, who agreed that they had a serious problem on their hands. They formed a four-man court to investigate immorality in Newport. This was to include female prostitution, drugs, and illegal drinking, but the principal target was clearly the town's gay underworld. The investigation got a hearty endorsement from the assistant secretary of the navy, Franklin Delano Roosevelt, who was running the department in the secretary's absence. Roosevelt would later deny any direct knowledge of the methods used in the crackdown.

Arnold convinced the navy that an undercover operation was the only way to obtain thorough information. He was told to proceed. Clearly knowing his prey well, Arnold recruited good-looking sailors, a dozen at first, all in their late teens, and sent them into the YMCA and parks as decoys to entrap homosexuals. With steely get-your-man determination, he told his recruits "to go the limit" if necessary to obtain evidence to convict. Should their sleuthing involve breaking a few laws, they themselves would be immune from prosecution. They were free to decline the assignment.

What followed was a high comedy that could make a splendid musical (*Hit on the Deckhand? The Keystone Kops Go Queer?*). The deputized sailors threw themselves into their work with a worrying enthusiasm, maybe on the assumption that being serviced by homos was preferable to swabbing decks or cleaning engines. "Sting operation" doesn't seem the right term for such sensuous work, but that's what it was.

Thanks to Arnold's plan, U.S. sailors were serviced regularly in the public parks and on Newport's Cliff Walk, all in the line of duty. But they were also going to the clubs and bars and forming friendships with their gay targets, again with the approval of their superiors. Sometimes this infiltration would involve quiet restaurant dinners and sometimes overnight stays at a suspect's home. Arnold seemed to feel that merely prompting advances from the suspects and obtaining their names was not adequate evidence. He insisted his decoys go all the way.

Picking up on the diligent spirit of the investigation, the undercover sailors quickly agreed that mere penetration was not sufficient to nail down their cases; they had to see the matter through to orgasm—sometimes more than once, if they felt it necessary for a solid case. Aspects of the resulting testimony suggest a degree of sympathy on the part of the sailors for their prey.

Particularly keen on entrapping one of the most active gays, Arnold sent one of his "best" sailors into the section of a park that the gay star was known to frequent, with instructions to obtain the usual incriminating evidence and, most important, to learn the boy's name.

The sailor presented himself to Arnold the next day and proudly announced his mission had been accomplished: the suspect was unmistakably an active homosexual. Pleased, Arnold asked for the name. The sailor had forgotten to get it. Sent out a second time, the sailor manfully did the deed but once again forgot to get the name. Totally exasperated, Arnold sent another sailor on the same mission, undoubtedly one with a better memory.

On May 1, 1919, the navy announced its findings. Sufficient evidence had been gathered to court-martial fifteen sailors, and more names were coming in at an alarming rate. The court dates for those arrested were not scheduled until autumn, so all of those charged had to sit in jail for four or five months. At the trials, some were released, others sentenced to jail terms of varying lengths.

According to Loughery, the matter might have ended there, since the navy had succeeded in keeping the entire matter secret. Having tasted blood, however, Arnold and his navy cohorts pushed on with their investigations. In their zeal, they made a serious misstep by arresting a popular and well-known Episcopal minister, Samuel Neal Kent; they claimed he was picking up sailors in the YMCA and paying them for sex.

The scandal surrounding such a well-respected figure as Kent brought the entire matter into the public eye as local newspapers covered the minister's downfall. The Reverent Kent had powerful friends who backed him in fighting the charges; in two separate trials, Kent was acquitted. But courtroom testimony brought out the sordid details of the navy's undercover homosexual sweep, all of which were covered in *The Providence Journal* and other papers. This produced a groundswell of shock and anger, not at the rampant gay activity the navy had uncovered in Newport, but at the sleazy, unlawful business of sending innocent sailors to entrap suspects by having sex with them. Rather than applauding the navy for cleaning up an outbreak of vice, newspapers focused on the outrageous misuse of servicemen. The underlying theme was, "This is not why American mothers and fathers send their sons into the military."

Outrage spread quickly as the story was picked up by the national press. When angry editorials appeared in *The New York Times* and elsewhere, the navy was forced to launch an investigation into the bizarre doings in Newport. No one was mollified by the navy's predictable whitewash, so an investigation was launched by the U.S. Senate. Franklin Roosevelt's acquiescence to the navy's methods was called "reprehensible," and *The Times* ran a headline: LAY NAVY SCANDAL TO F. D. ROOSEVELT.

Chief Machinist Mate Ervin Arnold and his sailor decoys were now a full-blown national scandal. Their unscrupulous zeal and ruthless methods came close to derailing the FDR juggernaut, which would have changed American history. But the disgrace and humiliation they suffered for so avidly pursuing homosexuals seems to have had no tempering effect on the virulence of Lawrence Lowell and his Secret Court, which swung into a similar antigay crusade less than a year later.

7

A Party in Perkins

———◆———

IN THE FALL of 1919, eight months before the formation of the Secret Court, sophomore Joseph Lumbard found himself with a new roommate in his Perkins Hall quarters, a nice-looking but delicate young man named Edward Say. Outwardly, the two appeared opposites. Lumbard was serious, studious, athletic, and quietly masculine. Say was lighthearted, eccentric, and nervously effeminate. But Lumbard recognized other qualities, qualities he felt they shared. He perceived in Say a sense of integrity and a forthright courageousness that belied the sissified trappings. The two became friends.

In the university records, Say's academic status is hazy. For some reason, he was not assigned to a particular Harvard class, which was unusual. In order to have been housed with sophomores, he had, in all likelihood, first attended college elsewhere. Both men came from middle-class families for whom it was a strain to finance a son's education at Harvard. In 1916 Say's father had started a grocery store with his brother in Waterbury, Connecticut, but the business apparently failed or was sold because in 1921 he is listed in town records as working for the Manville Machine Company. Lumbard's father was a reasonably successful anesthesiologist, but having undertaken the support of two unmarried sisters, he had his immediate family on a tight budget. In order to attend Harvard, Joseph had to win financial aid from the university, which he did.

When, in his second year at Harvard, Joe Lumbard was thrown together with Edward Say, he was put off by his roommate's light-footed manner. Like most college students, Lumbard was acutely aware of the dangers of dubious friends and associations. At the same time, he, like many of his classmates, felt that being at Harvard—rather than at Tufts or the University of Massachusetts—placed him above such superficial, frat-house concerns and enabled him to be guided by higher impulses.

Lumbard knew what a social liability Say's mannerisms could be and how many of his classmates, Harvard notwithstanding, viewed such unmanly types with disdain. But Lumbard had a highly developed sense of right and wrong, a strong component of which was an empathy for those negatively judged by false or superficial standards. Say became Lumbard's friend, to be sure, but he also became his cause. To what degree this noble stance was reinforced by Lumbard's own inner doubts and insecurities can only be guessed.

In the first days, when Lumbard was struggling with his aversion to Say's oddities, he interrupted a civil, impersonal conversation they were having to blurt a sharp question.

"I hope you don't mind my asking, Edward, but is that rouge you're wearing?"

Say looked at the floor and said, "Yes, it is."

"Aren't you afraid of what people might think?"

"I suppose I am. Is it so obvious?"

Lumbard felt that question had already been answered. "But why do you do it?"

"It's a long story. I was born with a spinal deformity. I spent the first eight years of my life in a cast, then another two years in a device like a straitjacket. Eventually the malformation was remedied, but I've always felt I did not appear healthy."

"You look fine. As for making you look healthier, believe me, that stuff is doing you far more harm than good."

Say took no offense at Lumbard's lecture, but he continued wearing makeup. Lumbard did not mention it again.

For all the disparities in their social appeal, Say seemed to have more friends and more of a social life than the studious Lumbard, who had few friends of his own. As a result, Lumbard became an oc-

casional tagalong to Say's social activities. On one occasion, Say jour-
neyed north to New Hampshire to visit some friends at Dartmouth.
Lumbard joined him for a few days. He later reported having had a
good time and said that Say's friends seemed to him to be "fine
chaps." Say became friendly with some Boston boys who were "somewhat odd," Lumbard later admitted. Occasionally Say would permit
the town boys to sleep over in their dormitory room. Lumbard con-
sented to this and once permitted a town boy to share his bed. He
would later insist that nothing improper occurred.

Having been assigned Edward Say as a roommate would later appear to have been a stroke of very bad luck for Joe Lumbard. An
equally unfortunate happenstance is that their room, 24 Perkins Hall,
was only a few doors from 28 Perkins Hall, the scene of Ernest
Roberts's notorious parties. This was the place that the Harvard authorities came to view as the epicenter of university gayness. Lumbard was aware, as was everyone in the dormitory, of the outlandish
parties that Roberts threw in his campus quarters.

Along with the students at Roberts's gatherings, the guest list invariably included an assortment of unsavory young men from Boston.
Lumbard had heard of one dormmate entering the communal lavatory
to find a town boy changing into women's clothes, then brazenly applying makeup in front of the very public mirror. According to Roberts,
his parties were celebrations of open-mindedness, mold breaking,
and freedom, but Lumbard felt certain that these qualities went in one
direction only: homosexuality.

Say had been to a few of these parties and always urged Lumbard
to come with him. When Lumbard expressed misgivings, Say admon-
ished him.

"Oh, Joe. Don't be such a prude. College is supposed to broaden
one's experiences. Besides, there is nothing to fear, really. Ernest's little gatherings are really quite respectable."

Eventually, Lumbard gave in and agreed to attend one.

As they approached the neighboring room on the evening of the
party, Say and Lumbard could hear loud music. The gramophone
was playing the day's big hit, Al Jolson's recording of "Swanee." Just

after they knocked, the door swung open to reveal Ernest Roberts. Lumbard noted that he was suavely handsome and correctly dressed in a tweed suit, white collar, and necktie. In fact, he looked altogether the proper and affluent Harvard undergraduate except that he had a large gold-loop earring affixed to one ear.

Throwing out his arms to embrace Say, he sang in mock Jolson imitation: "I've been away from you a long time." He turned to Lumbard. "Good evening, Mr. Lumbard. I am so happy you decided to join our little debauchery." Roberts had obviously asked Say to bring his roommate to the parties.

Lumbard had not previously been in the rooms, but he had heard others talk about the "gorgeous" decorations. Fringed damask curtains covered the windows; a few framed paintings featured mostly nude gods and goddesses; on a round table between two armchairs was an oriental vase converted into a reading lamp with a red silk shade, also fringed; and a tablecloth of dark green velvet showed off a collection of crystal paperweights. One corner of the sitting room was dominated by a black-lacquer folding screen, which had an inlaid oriental design in what appeared to be mother-of-pearl. The room's overall effect was not of a dormitory room, but of the Beacon Hill parlor of a wealthy bachelor with a refined aesthetic.

Lumbard addressed his host. "Your furnishings are quite impressive, Ernest."

"That's very sweet of you to say. I'm told I have a flair. I may end up doing decoration for a living. There's so little work for adagio dancers these days. And more and more people are hiring professional decorators to select their fabrics and gewgaws."

The room was well lit—a relief to Lumbard—and he could spot about fifteen guests. Since women were not permitted in the dormitories at night, there was nothing surprising about the all-male group. Still, Lumbard was shocked to see two sailors in uniform. They were young, perhaps a bit younger than the students present, rough-hewn working-class boys who seemed to relish the attentions of the well-dressed young men around them.

Lumbard either knew or recognized some of the students present, including Stanley Gilkey and Cyril Wilcox, who was rumored to be having an affair with a Boston man. Lumbard was surprised to see Kenneth Day, whom he knew only as a one of the sophomore class's most promising athletes. All of the students present seemed to be relaxed and enjoying themselves. Lumbard knew that Roberts's father had been a U.S. congressman and was still a political power in Massachusetts. It flashed through his mind that, for the other boys, an awareness of their host's rich and prominent father probably had an emboldening effect, making them less fearful of the party's risks.

Lumbard could tell instantly that some boys present were not Harvard students. They were clearly that other breed, so unsettling to students torn between egalitarianism and Harvard elitism: *town boys.* The three or four present tended to be more assertively gay and more nervously boisterous than the students. Rooming with Edward Say, Lumbard had become expert at detecting signs of "differences."

Lumbard was surprised that the party, which defied the most fundamental norms of behavior, seemed to have created its own social conventions, mutually understood rules that were observed by all present. Some of the party manners were merely imports from the straight world: newcomers were addressed as "Mr. Lumbard," or "Mr. Say," guests rose from their chairs to greet new arrivals and shook hands on introductions. But other niceties were specific to the situation. For instance, everyone voiced admiration for some feature of the room's furnishings. Everyone complimented the other guests on some aspect of their appearance—a sweater, necktie, or haircut. And it became apparent to Lumbard that everyone was expected to smile or laugh at the most shocking remarks and innuendos, most of which came from Roberts.

Roberts led the two newcomers around the room, introducing them to everyone, usually with a bawdy insult or gibe. When he came to the two sailors, Roberts waxed into formal eloquence: "I am happy to present our two most distinguished visitors, Rear Admiral McGillicutty and Rear Admiral Rossi."

Lumbard pretended not to notice the leering emphasis Roberts gave to "rear." Without smiling, the two boys half rose from the window seat where they were sitting and offered their hands with exaggerated tough-guy masculinity.

"Now, darlings," Roberts said to Lumbard and Say, "drinks are a wee bit complicated. I have suspended a quart of gin and a fifth of scotch out the window on these two cords—white for gin, black for scotch. When you want a drink, just pull up the bottle of your choice, pour your drink, then lower the bottle." To demonstrate, Roberts pulled up the scotch bottle.

"This byzantine arrangement," he said, "is a precaution against a sudden appearance of Congressman Volstead's Keystone Kops. Should they burst in, I merely back over to the window, like Tosca with her concealed dagger, and cut the cords. Voilà! They will find this to be an innocent, hoochless party."

As he gently lowered the bottle, he said, "If this should happen, wouldn't it be splendid if one of the bottles bonked our beloved President Lowell on the head as he passed below on his evening cruise of Harvard Yard?"

Roberts led them to a table with drinking glasses and setups—ice, soda, ginger ale. "Of course, some of my guests may have hip flasks, but that is at their own risk. I cannot be held responsible for that, can I?"

Pulling up the bottle of scotch, Lumbard and Say made drinks with ice and soda. Lumbard was impressed that the scotch was the real thing. Someone placed a new record on the phonograph. It was the popular song "I Wonder Who's Kissing Her Now." Several boys started to dance to the slow, sad waltz. Roberts sang along as he passed among his guests, offering canapés. "I wonder who's kissing me now . . . ."

In a voice all could hear, an arch young man said, "That could be most anyone in the room." Many laughed.

"I'm sure, Harold, you intended to wound," Roberts said with haughty indifference, "but I take your little gibe as a compliment."

Roberts called out to Lumbard and Say, who were chatting with some classmates. "Edward and Joseph, come over here for a minute and meet Harold Saxton. If you are wondering why he looks so much older than everyone else, he graduated ages ago but was unable to tear himself from the student *body,* so he now tutors the slower dears. To keep his hand in, so to speak."

As Roberts walked away, he said in a voice audible to all, "And to think they want to give people like *that* the vote."

The flurry of bitchery did nothing to lower the jolly mood. One of the more presentable town boys asked Lumbard if he would care to dance. Lumbard was at first stunned. Then, his head swirling in a confusion of protocol, propriety, and gender roles, he decided he had nothing to fear from any of this silliness and agreed.

Without comment, the boy let Joe take the lead position. Holding each other decorously, they began to dance to the sentimental song. As they made turns around the cleared space on the floor, Lumbard felt the sane world collapsing around him. He had never made love with a woman, not even the petting so common in his age group. In addition, he had believed the dire warnings and resolved to avoid masturbating. At the age of twenty, Joe Lumbard had somehow avoided the realization that he was a pulsating mass of sexual frustration.

With the attractive young man's face inches from his own—the boy seemed to be saying something—and his arm around Joe's waist, Lumbard felt a pleasurable stirring he had not anticipated. He didn't like it. The pleasure suddenly turned to alarm. The floor seemed to be giving away, and he thought his knees might buckle. The slow slide into he knew not what, which had begun on entering the room, came to an abrupt halt as Joe realized he was in serious danger. Telling the boy that he was not feeling well, that the drink had hit him, he left his partner standing alone in the dance area and returned to Edward Say, who was giggling with one of the sailors.

"Edward," Joe said, "I must leave right now."

Say looked surprised. "Are you all right?"

"It's nothing. You stay and have a good time. I'll see you back in the room."

GIVEN THE SECRET Court's perceived lack of importance in Harvard's history, an amazing amount of documentation has survived about its action and about the lives of its victims. Court testimony and letters, both personal and official, reveal even small details about the students' personalities, thoughts, and activities. Yet important aspects of the story are completely unknown and rise to the surface only as supposition. Often, however, evidence is so persuasive that even the most scrupulous chronicler would be remiss not to point out strong probabilities when they occur.

A prime example would be the likelihood that Lumbard and Say had sex together. The only evidence for this is that Lumbard maintained an attitude of loyalty and protectiveness toward a student whom most others considered an embarrassment. Also, Lumbard's willing participation in Say's clearly gay social life—even an overnight trek to Dartmouth—suggests that Lumbard's involvement in Say's world might have been more than that of a curious onlooker.

Whether or not something occurred between the roommates—and it is only relevant because of Lumbard's punishment and remarkable later life—he would soon realize that homosexuality was not for him. At the Court hearing, he admitted to attending a few more of Roberts's parties with Say, but he also stated that his closeness with Say diminished as Say became more and more involved with Roberts's circle. His own dabbling in this exotic world may have been motivated by curiosity, sexual frustration, or some sexual confusion of his own. Whatever prompted this brief phase in his life, it passed. Still, his flirtation with Ernest Roberts's version of "openness, mold breaking, and freedom" would land him in trouble as serious as any he would ever experience in an exemplary, highly distinguished, and action-filled life.

That Lumbard's trouble came from attending a few parties, not from sexual misconduct, says much about the Court's modus operandi. Had he merely made love with his roommate, there is no way the Court could have learned of it; Lumbard's college career would have proceeded smoothly. At Harvard in 1920, some students were severely punished not because they had sex with each other, but merely because they socialized with homosexuals.

8

The Court in Session

——◆——

HARVARD COULD BE overwhelming for students. Freshmen were cowed by the majestic university that had deigned to accept them—the centuries of tradition, the procession of great men, the best-of-breed faculty, the fusty grandeur of the buildings. The university itself was swathed in prideful superiority from all this, and a similar arrogance spread quickly to the students. As the new arrivals gradually discovered that they could handle the academic and social demands, their fears of inadequacy gave way to conceit about their glorious position. They came to realize that they were not only fortunate to share in Harvard's wondrous prestige, they were integral to it. They were the raw, top-grade material without which the school's massive endowment, its venerable buildings, its galleries of great men, and its intellectual legacy became dead emblems of past glories. Together with the faculty, they, the students, were now Harvard.

In his 1935 novel, *Of Time and the River,* Thomas Wolfe, folding in the usual raptures of youth, captured the exuberance of the Harvard undergraduate: "They knew that the most fortunate, good and happy life that any man had ever known was theirs, if they would take it: they knew that it impended instantly—the fortune, fame, and love for which their souls were panting: neither had yet turned the dark column, they knew that they were twenty and that they could never die." The country itself was still in an ebullient mood due to the end of World War I. In his epochal novel, *Three Soldiers,* John Dos Passos wrote that in 1919 "currents of energy seemed to be breaking out everywhere as young guys climbed out of their uniforms. . . ."

Adding to this euphoria in May 1920 was the thundering beauty of a New England spring. The lofty elms that arched over the green-carpeted Harvard Yard were in full leaf; flowering cherry trees, rhodo-dendron, and other well-tended, financially well-endowed plantings splashed color and softened the austerity of the dark-stone buildings. Whatever tests and trials students had endured were now behind them, and they faced only a summer free from being force-fed Western culture. They awaited a teenager's idyllic summer with the sweet knowledge that they would return in the fall to friends, studies, and the greater prestige of a higher Harvard class. As June approached, life for most Harvard undergraduates was an exhilarating blessing.

For some twenty-two of them, however, life on the Harvard campus in May 1920 had become an unimaginable nightmare. Each had received a curt note from the dean's office demanding his presence before the dean at a specific hour the next day. Given the speed with which news of the Court and its mission flew around the campus, all who received the summons knew with a sick, sobering dread the reason why they had been called in.

A few of these summons letters survive. While there are minor differences in wording, all have the same preemptory tone and all insist that the dean would accept no excuse for not arriving at the precise time stated, even if it meant missing an examination. In the university milieu, no words could bring home more resoundingly the gravity of the summons.

Arriving at the dean's office, each student was led into a darkened room where he found seated Deans Greenough, Gay, and Murdock, Dr. Lee, and Regent Luce. President Lowell appears to have attended the Court's proceedings only when the man being interviewed was a member of his faculty; mere students were left to the men of the Court. The notes, usually taken by Dean Greenough, were in a hasty scrawl that is sometimes indecipherable. At other times, his words are legible but their meaning is incomprehensible to an outsider.

Occasionally a leap in the notes' logical flow suggests a sizable omission—not a lost page but a section of the interrogation that was deliberately not recorded. These moments will be pointed out as they come up. In all the notes, the names of the students have been concealed with Wite-Out and replaced with code numbers, but this code was deciphered by *The Harvard Crimson* in all of the most important cases, and the real names were replaced. For all the many problems the notes present a researcher, they still provide an ample picture of the Secret Court's thinking, aims, and methods.

Each of those summoned was submitted to a barrage of questions that can be reconstructed, to a great extent, by the recorded responses: Did you know Cyril Wilcox? Were you surprised by his suicide? Did you know Ernest Roberts? How well? Did you drop by his room? How often? Did you attend his parties? Do you know about homosexuality? How did you first learn about it? What are your general thoughts about it? Have you read Freud? Havelock Ellis? Why did you read these writers? What was your impression of their ideas about homosexuality? Have you ever masturbated? When? How often? When was the last time? How do you feel about women? Have you had sexual relations with a woman? The last time? Has anyone ever tried to discuss homosexuality with you? Have you ever been approached by another man? When and how? Did you acquiesce? Have you ever had unnatural relations with any man? Since coming to Harvard? Have you been to a restaurant called the Green Shutters? The Lighted Lamp? The Golden Rooster? Do you know Edward Say? Eugene Cummings? Harold Saxton? Kenneth Day? How well? How often do you see these men? Did you suspect any of them were abnormal? If you did, why did you continue to associate with them? Can you tell us the names of anyone else at Harvard you suspect of being sexually abnormal?

A few of the interviews have a date scribbled at the head, but most are undated. There is reason to believe that the notes, while flowing from page to page in a logical way, are not necessarily in chronological order. They are presented here in the order in which they were recorded. The first students interviewed were asked only a few questions and quickly dismissed as "innocent." According to the notes, the next important "suspect" to be interrogated after Kenneth Day was not a student but Donald Clark, a twenty-four-year-old assistant professor of philosophy. Because he was the only faculty member under suspicion of being a homosexual, this session of the Court was attended by President Lowell. For some reason, the two assistant deans, Murdock and Gay, were absent.

Clark was a short, slight man who looked like a student but was highly educated and had an exotic background. He had been born in Rome and was fluent in Italian, French, and German. A Phi Beta Kappa graduate of Wesleyan, he had received a master's degree in philosophy from Harvard in 1918 and was working on his Ph.D. there. During World War I he had served as a special agent for the Department of Justice, probably using his language skills. Now this unprepossessing package of erudition and experience was led into a darkened room to face a dean, a regent, and President Lowell.

Most of those summoned before the Court had been named either by Harry Dreyfus, the anonymous letter, the proctor, or any combination of the three. Clark, however, had not been mentioned by any of these but had been directly accused by one of his own students, who claimed Clark had propositioned him and also claimed that Clark had made favorable statements about homosexuality in his psychology lectures.

When the Court confronted Clark about the student's accusations, he became agitated, began to stammer, yet vigorously denied having made advances toward any student. He also denied ever having discussed "homosexualism" in his lectures. The Court asked if he had ever quoted medical opinions on the subject or made it seem attractive in any way? He did not recall ever having alluded to it in his classes.

The line of questioning makes one wonder how Harvard restrained its classics professors when they lectured on the ancient Greeks. Did they station monitors in the lecture halls to make sure that, when discussing the man-boy tradition, the professors did not allow a note of approbation to creep into their voices? Did they register an appropriate note of disgust? With certain subjects, it was dangerously insufficient for Harvard to give students the facts; they also had to tell them what to think about them.

President Lowell and the Court clearly did not believe Clark's denials and pressured him mercilessly. Why would a student lie about such a thing? Many reports had come to them about his immoral lectures. They had other evidence. Why not be man enough to tell the truth?

Clark finally broke down and, sobbing, admitted he had been lying. Recovering himself, he said to the Court, "I have been engaged in homosexual practices for some time, but I have been trying to cure myself and thought I was succeeding."

President Lowell and the Court were unimpressed with Clark's rehabilitation effort. For them, that was akin to saying, "Yes, I have murdered a few people, but I am making progress in giving up the practice."

The Court was concerned only with his admission of guilt. With this in hand, President Lowell took charge of the proceedings. He skipped the formal niceties, such as "It is my sad duty to tell you . . ." or "I have no choice but to inform you. . . ." With barely controlled anger, Lowell told the shattered Clark that he would not be reappointed as an assistant professor and that he had to withdraw as a Ph.D. candidate.

As if making a major concession, Lowell went on to say that Clark would be permitted to grade examination papers, but "under no circumstances was he to speak before a class or speak directly to any student." Sometime later, President Lowell personally crossed Clark's name off all university records.

Later the same day, Lowell summoned Professor Langfeld to appear before the Court to discuss his classes in psychology to which Clark had alluded. Langfeld denied ever having lectured on homosexuality. He told the deans that Clark had confided in him about his sexuality problem. Langfeld did not hesitate to provide the Court with lurid sexual details from Clark's "confidences." The Court records then have a summary note: "Langfeld's idea on entire matter perfectly sound."

Given the extreme ideas Lowell and the Court were demonstrating on the "entire matter," their idea of sound judgment can only produce a chill.

THE COURT'S NOTES indicate that it succeeded in bringing Harry Dreyfus into the sinister interrogation room. It is hard to imagine that Dreyfus, knowing what the Court was about, would have had much enthusiasm for cooperating. In fact, it is hard to understand why he would consent to a barrage of personal questions of the most intrusive nature by a group of university dons. Having no connection with Harvard, Dreyfus was not under the authority of the Secret Court or President Lowell. Technically, Dreyfus was vulnerable to criminal charges, since sodomy laws were very much in effect in 1920. Also, since Dreyfus was the proprietor of a restaurant frequented by Harvard students, university officials were in a position to make threats that were far from idle. No record exists of how Dreyfus's cooperation was obtained, but it is not unreasonable to assume that considerable pressure was exerted on him.

It is hard to imagine a scene of greater mutual loathing. To Dreyfus, these university officials were emblematic of the most bigoted, moralistic community pillars. To them, he was an arch fiend of the entire sordid business in which they found themselves mired, an insidious agent of the corrupt external world that was infecting noble Harvard and spreading unspeakable sin and corruption. Looking at the men he faced, Dreyfus must surely have wondered how many fine young lives they would destroy with their sanctimonious crusade. Looking at him, the Court must have wondered how many fine young lives he had already destroyed with his evil appetites.

The record of the interview indicates that his appearance before the Court was a waste of time for all parties. Most of the notes are a reiteration of facts the Court already knew: that Dreyfus was Cyril Wilcox's lover, that he was the most notorious homosexual in Boston, and that he ran a bar called Café Dreyfus. The notes do not say that

Dreyfus agreed to any of these facts, just that the Court believed them to be true.

Only one note advances into new ground: Dreyfus denied responsibility for Cyril Wilcox's suicide. This is only mildly interesting in that the Court thought he might be. Since the judges knew Cyril had broken off with Dreyfus and not vice versa, they could not have been seeking a broken-heart motive. It appears they were trying to establish a broader panorama of guilt: Dreyfus had seduced the younger Wilcox into homosexual depravity, and this so disgusted the young man that he killed himself. Whatever the deans' hopes with this line of questioning, they quickly dropped it and ended the Dreyfus interview with the note "No action possible."

THE NEXT TO be interrogated was Keith Smerage. A junior in the class of 1921, Smerage was a year ahead of most of the students under investigation. As he sat down before his judges, they saw a neatly dressed young man, handsome in an F. Scott Fitzgerald way, with a soft, refined manner somewhere between high urbanity and outright femininity. Smerage had done a year at Tufts but had transferred to Harvard for the better dramatic club, into which he had been accepted a few days before being called in for questioning. The Court interviewed him at considerable length, energized by their evidence against him, but even more by his rashly cooperative testimony.

With everything going so well for him, especially his recent election to the dramatic club, Smerage desperately wanted to stay at Harvard, yet he naïvely believed that frank confessions and abject contrition would get him through the ordeal with some sort of disciplinary action. This is puzzling in that Day and Clark had already been expelled, and word of these harsh sentences had spread quickly. He may have erroneously believed that their crimes had been greater than his.

The Court began its interrogation by asking Smerage if he knew any homosexuals. Smerage launched his testimony with an obvious lie.

"I know of only one case, that of Cyril Wilcox."

"How did you meet Wilcox?"

"I used to visit a student in Standish Hall who lived on the floor above Wilcox. About a year ago, my friend introduced us."

"How did you hear of his death?"

"I was dining at the Green Shutters with a friend from the business school, and I heard about Cyril from a friend of mine I ran into there, Hazel Webster."

The deans looked at each other. Murdock spoke.

"Isn't Miss Webster a prostitute who frequents bohemian restaurants?"

"I do not believe that is true."

Greenough asked, "Have you had sexual relations with Hazel Webster?"

"Never."

"Do you know Harry Dreyfus?"

"I know him only as the owner of the Café Dreyfus and as the lover of Cyril Wilcox. You see, I play the piano and once spoke to Dreyfus about a job playing at his café."

Mr. Luce was shocked. "You knew he was the lover of another man and you went to him for a job?"

"I didn't know about Dreyfus's character when I applied for a job."

Dean Gay shifted directions. "Are you familiar with the jargon homosexuals use? Do you know what 'faggot' means?"

"Yes."

"How did you learn that?"

Smerage realized the interview was going badly. "One drifts about and hears these terms."

"Have you heard of Havelock Ellis?" Dr. Lee asked.

"Yes."

Greenough brought the questioning back to Harvard. "Do you know Ernest Roberts?"

"Yes, I know him quite well." Opting for candor rather than caution, Smerage added, "I used his room as my headquarters last year."

"When in Roberts's room, you never saw anything queer?"

"Not that I recall."

"You know no other homosexuals at Harvard beside Wilcox?"

"Roberts introduced me to Stanley Gilkey, who has the reputation of being homosexual."

Trying to maintain an even tone to his questions, Greenough realized he had on his hands a witness who was remarkably forthcoming.

"Mr. Smerage, have you ever been approached by a man?"

"Never in college," he said thoughtfully, as if he had been asked if he had ever heard a Bruckner symphony, "but once in Boston."

"Describe that, if you would."

"It happened at the Golden Rooster. My friends and I were sitting next to a party of three men. They kept bothering us. I could tell that one of them was particularly interested in me."

"Have you been approached other times?"

"Oh, yes," he replied as if remembering something of little importance. "Once by a man named Rogers—although I didn't know his name at the time. It happened on the street. A fellow student later told me his name."

Dr. Lee pushed for incrimination. "Are we to understand, Mr. Smerage, that you have had relations with men?"

With no idea what the words would cost him, Smerage replied, "I have fooled around with this homosexual business, but I haven't slept with a man, not in any unnatural sense, since coming to college."

"I regret to tell you, we have evidence to the contrary."

Smerage appeared confused. "Well, I guess since I've been at Harvard I have been indiscreet one or two times."

"Describe them, please," Dean Gay said in a pained voice.

"The first time was when I was first at college, just after I got out of the army. A fellow student introduced me to the practice."

"Who?" two of the panel said at once.

"I don't recall his name."

"And the next time since you were at Harvard?"

"It was quite recent, about Christmastime, but it had occurred outside of college."

"With whom?"

"It was Rogers."

"The man you met on the street?"

"Yes. He took me back to his apartment."

"Where?"

"Thirty Hemenway Street."

"What happened?"

"He took off all my clothes and we . . ." Smerage faltered.

"You what?"

"We masturbated each other."

"Have you had relations with other men?"

"Yes. I met a man once on the train to Buffalo."

"No other men at Harvard? Just the one you mentioned whose name you cannot recall?"

"I have had some narrow escapes. Usually when I have had to sleep with others. I have resisted attempts many times. Once was the night before the Yale game. A man named Goddard or something. He was a pal of Rogers."

"How did you first get into these homosexual practices?" Dr. Lee asked in his most scientific voice.

"It first happened with an older boy in my hometown. He started fooling around and I guess I got excited."

"Do you presently masturbate?"

"No, I have conquered that habit."

When did he last masturbate? "About nine months ago."

"Have you ever had sexual relations with a woman?"

"Yes, but not since last summer."

Feeling they had more than enough evidence against Smerage, the Court pressed him about other students on its list.

"Roberts once boasted of having had sex with Gilkey. And now that I think about it, Gilkey had gotten rather gay with me one time. He rubbed my knee, nuzzled up to me . . ."

"Is there anything else you would like to tell us, Mr. Smerage?"

"I think I have remembered everything."

Smerage knew he had talked himself into serious trouble. From what he said next, he may have felt his only hope of showing contrition and a desire to mend his ways was to cooperate with the Court and give it any information he could. As Dean Greenough was preparing to end the interview, Smerage said, "There was another undergraduate who approached me."

"Who was that?"

"It was a premed student from Buffalo, Nathaniel Wollf. He got me into his room one night. It was before the fall production of the Dramatic Club. We are both members."

"What happened in the room?"

"Wollf took off all my clothes. He wanted me to do mutual masturbation with him."

"Did you?"

"I would not masturbate Wollf."

"But you let him . . ." Dean Murdock couldn't say the words.

"Yes, I was a party to the affair."

At this point in the Court's notes there is a cryptic entry: "Is silly to have this stand as a final record." It is not clear whether the note is quoting a blunt criticism from Smerage of the Court's prurient prying or if the notetaker is commenting on Smerage's reckless confessions. It is unlikely that any member of the Court would use the word "silly" to describe any of their actions. Also, from Smerage's subsequent outspoken criticism of the Court, it was most likely a foretaste of his anger at his judges.

Called before the Court for a second time, Smerage had apparently reconciled himself to his failure to win the Court's sympathy and started off on a defiant note and refused to offer any more names. The notes become maddeningly illegible: "also thinks that [illegible] doing right in cleaning house."

If the word is "Court" or "Harvard" (it looks like neither), it would indicate Smerage's endorsement of the gay purge. Also, "cleaning house" is usually a phrase of approbation. On the other hand, if the word is "not," the sentence then becomes a bold criticism that would be more consistent with Smerage's increasing disapproval of the Court. It is probably the former, an attempt to soften his defiant stand by voicing approval of the university's attack on gays.

The Court then told Smerage that he could either help their investigation or not. He told them he could name fifty more students but he would not. They asked him specifically about several students and he remained noncommittal, saying things like "I have no idea" or "I do not know him."

Smerage was then told he was to be expelled from Harvard. The words hit him like a shovel to the back of his head. He expected harsh punishment, but not that harsh. He could not speak. He rose to his feet, then steadied himself before starting out of the room.

As he was leaving, Dean Gay, still rankled by Smerage's I-could-name-fifty testimony, made a remark that reveals his hostile vindictiveness. Greenough considered it worth repeating in his notes:

"It looks like your fifty has shrunk some, hasn't it?"

Expulsion was not enough for Dean Gay. He felt the situation also called for a good kick.

9

The Cunning and the Damned

————◆————

SOPHOMORE STANLEY GILKEY came from a middle-class New Hampshire family that was proud to have a son at Harvard. Good-looking with a sincere directness, he projected a matinee-idol suavity unusual for a boy of nineteen. He had not been named in any of the accusatory letters but had been summoned before the Court because Keith Smerage had accused Gilkey of having propositioned him and because the Court had heard Roberts boast of having had sex with Gilkey.

Even before arriving at Harvard, Gilkey knew he wanted to make a career in the theater. He liked acting but was not convinced he was good enough to succeed as a professional. Whether on the stage or behind the scenes, however, Gilkey had no doubt this was the world he wanted. So certain was he that he might well have skipped college altogether but for his father's determination that his son should have the solid credential of a Harvard diploma before braving the vagaries of the New York theater. While in college, he pursued this interest. After his freshman year, Gilkey got a summer job with the prestigious Hyannis stock company on Cape Cod and, at Harvard, he was a member of the Dramatic Club.

Many of his college friends were part of the gay group; he was a good friend of Ernest Roberts and a regular at his parties. Two students claimed Gilkey had made advances toward them. There is little doubt that Gilkey, who would lead a totally gay life after leaving Harvard, had been actively gay since coming to Harvard. The Court's interrogation of Gilkey and its conclusions about him are strong evidence of prosecutorial ineptitude and a myopic lack of fairness.

The judges started by asking the usual questions about Cyril Wilcox. Was Gilkey aware of his suicide? Although everyone at Harvard knew of it, the Court seemed to believe this was insider gossip of the gay circle and therefore incriminating information to possess.

With cool aplomb, Gilkey said, "I met Wilcox in Roberts's room but did not know him intimately. I'd heard he died but didn't know it had been suicide."

The Court made no comment about this unlikely half-knowledge.

"What were you doing in Roberts's room?"

"I had gone there to borrow Ernest's tuxedo coat."

"Have you been to any of Roberts's parties?"

"No, but I'd heard about them."

Asked if he had ever attended "such a party" anywhere, Gilkey said he had not.

"Have you ever been to a restaurant called the Green Shutters?

"I may have eaten one meal there but didn't much care for it. Both waiters there are queer."

His use of the vernacular term prompted Murdock to ask if he was knowledgeable about homosexuality.

"A bit. I have read some of Havelock Ellis and taken various psychology courses."

"Do you have a particular interest in the subject?"

"I am interested, yes," he replied, "but only insofar as I am interested in the broad subject of criminality."

Tired of this feckless sparring, Dean Gay asked Gilkey if he had ever been approached by a man.

"Yes, when I was fifteen, but I was able to get rid of the fellow."

"You seem to know the slang, Mr. Gilkey."

"It is not that esoteric. Everybody knows it."

Greenough shifted to a question that, from his arch delivery, he clearly felt could incriminate his witness. "Is it true, Mr. Gilkey, you once boasted of being able to spot queer people?"

"I never said such a thing," he said firmly. "I could not feel out a queer person, not for a certainty, unless the suspicion was backed up by hearsay."

The importance the deans gave to this question is indicative of their ignorance about the subject they were investigating. To boast of being able to spot a homosexual is hardly evidence of being one. If that were a test of sexual orientation, few heterosexual males, then or now, would pass it. If anything, the boast smacks of homophobia. One learns to spot them in order to protect oneself from them—that would be the thinking. Ill informed as the allegation was, it is an indication of the straws the Court was grasping to build its cases.

"Have you ever been to a restaurant called the Golden Rooster?"

"Yes. I was there once and ran into Roberts and Keith Smerage. I was ashamed because I was with a decent girl. Roberts was OK. I wouldn't mind introducing Roberts to anyone, but Smerage talked with a foolish accent and had a slovenly appearance. Also, there was something about his smile I didn't like."

The gratuitous slams at Smerage may be evidence that Gilkey knew of Smerage's accusations against him and volunteered these disparagements in retaliation.

After a few more questions about his associations, Gilkey burst out, "I am in no way part of that crowd. In fact, I find them all quite repulsive."

With no prompting from the Court, Gilkey said that when he had performed with the Hyannis stock company the previous summer, two classmates had played there as well, and they would vouch for his good conduct throughout the summer.

Mr. Luce broke in. "Mr. Gilkey, what is your opinion of Edward Say?"

Gilkey paused thoughtfully. "I am dubious about him. I mean, I certainly would not take him home to my family. Nor would I care to be seen on the street with him."

The Court told Gilkey that he had been seen at one of Roberts's parties.

"Well, yes, that was when I went by the room to return the tuxedo."

"We were told you stayed quite a while."

"Were you? Let me think. Oh, I remember. Roberts urged me to stay. He said that an actor from Boston was due to arrive and there would be a drag."

"So you knew it was to be a party, one in which people dressed up."

"Yes, I thoroughly understood it was to be a party. I only stayed because I was interested in acting and wanted to size up the actor."

"And what was the party like?"

"Some people came in, records were played, nothing queer was said or done."

Dean Greenough tried to gather together all Gilkey had been telling them. "With your interest in Havelock Ellis and Freud, your friendship with Roberts and his circle, your interest in discussing homosexuality, did you not think you might have a problem? Why did you not visit Dr. Lee to discuss the matter?"

"It never occurred to me."

Gilkey was working hard to convey that he did not think such curiosity or anything he had done constituted a problem. "As for discussing homosexuality," he went on, "I am sure that I never brought homosexual knowledge to anyone who was innocent." The Court looked puzzled, then took the offensive.

"But Mr. Gilkey," Dean Gay said with exasperation, "you knew what sort of man Roberts was, yet continued to see him."

"He was merely an acquaintance from whom I occasionally borrowed clothes."

Then from Dean Murdock: "You were heard discussing homosexuality in a restaurant."

Gilkey was beginning to have trouble believing the absurdity of the evidence that had placed him in such trouble. With a degree of defiance rare among the summoned students, he nobly tried to shift the discussion to a saner level. "I think it would be unjust for you to condemn me for discussing homosexuality, and I do not see why I should have stopped speaking to Roberts because I found out he was queer."

From the shocked look on their faces and their angry mutterings, Gilkey knew he had gone too far. However wrongheaded the Court's procedures, he knew these men could destroy him. His tone changed to one of pleading.

"You should ask my roommates about me. They know I am a good boy. I am always in bed while they are still playing cards."

While Gilkey may have defied the Court to an extent, his evasions and outright lies indicate that, unlike Day and Smerage, he sensed the high risk of honesty. It is sadly ironic that the most innocent boys, those with no sense of the Court's horror of homosexuality, were more honest and forthcoming, while a confirmed and active homosexual such as Gilkey knew the behaviors to deplore, the actions to deny, and the incriminating evidence to explain away. Far-fetched as some of his explanations were—throughout the questioning, his need to borrow dinner clothes grew absurdly—he succeeded in hoodwinking the Court and left the judges with no unequivocal admissions.

Had they asked their other witnesses if they had seen Gilkey at more than one of Roberts's parties, they would have learned he had attended not one, as he said, but many. For the Court, lying was almost as incriminating as admitting to having had sex with a man. Sadly, the Court's ineptitude did nothing to lessen its lethal power. Gilkey had figured out a successful strategy for dealing with it and had saved his neck.

IN THE NEXT few days the members of the Court interrogated a number of students who they determined were innocent of any behavior they considered actionable. By later events it turned out that the Court felt it was not necessary to have proof of homosexual activity; it was enough that a student had shown bad judgment in associating too freely with boys who were known to be actively gay. In subsequent letters to parents, however, the deans were careful to make this distinction and to say that they were leaving the door open to readmission at a later date. No such hope would be held out to those who confessed to homosexual acts.

Most of those testifying said they knew Roberts and his outrageous circle, but only slightly, or by their notoriety alone. All voiced their disgust and repugnance at the behavior of this group. Each was asked if he could offer any additional information about Roberts, Say, Cummings, or any other students the Court felt were guilty. Smerage, in thinly veiled contempt for such clumsy methods, would later say he was disinclined "to pass along gossip for Harvard College to act upon."

Given the gravity with which the inquiry was conducted, it was a rare student who, when facing the powerful panel in a darkened room, expressed disapproval of the Court's action and methods. Most often, the students were distressingly quick to condemn their classmates. Some of the guilty even voiced approval of the Court's attack on wickedness.

ALTHOUGH LUMBARD WAS not the only student who told the Court about Ernest Roberts's threat to make "publicity" if he were expelled, the corroboration of the threat did nothing to weaken its resolve to bring him down. Nor did the specter of Roberts's powerful father. Unanimously at the top of everyone's roster of gay infamy, Roberts was seen by the Court as the linchpin of Harvard's homosexual scourge. Had the Court shown him leniency, its harsh treatment of others would have been blatantly unfair.

But far more important, the judges had come to believe that Roberts was not just guilty of homosexual acts himself: he was a diligent proselytizer and had corrupted many students into the despicable practices. They saw him as an agent of evil on the Harvard campus, a spreader of insidious contagion. They had no choice but to deal severely and promptly with their primary adversary, a student who was working as hard to promote homosexuality as they were to eliminate it.

Given the homophobic context of the times, it is hard to understand Roberts's fearless attitude and flamboyant, in-your-face gayness. If he believed that the harsh Newport punishments had been meted out only to lowly sailors and working-class boys, he must have known that those persecutions would eventually reach the eminent

Episcopal clergyman. The scandal had been well covered in the newspapers; it was in fact the high-level arrests that had brought the navy's
antigay sting operation into public view.

In disregarding these clear warnings, Roberts may have felt invulnerable because of his powerful father. Or he may have been awarding
himself the aristocrat's indifference to propriety. Or he may have felt
his status as a Harvard student placed him above such bourgeois
moralistic qualms. Or he may just have been very stupid. For whatever
reason, Roberts seems to have had no fear of censure from his Harvard colleagues and superiors, and even less fear of an intervention
from the local authorities, who would have been within their legal
rights to arrest him.

The Court was aware that Roberts's strengths made him a greater
threat to the university's moral health. Since he was a popular student
with a wealthy, influential father, his strident behavior undoubtedly
emboldened less intrepid gay undergraduates to join the merry frolics
in Perkins 28. Both through personality and family connections,
Ernest Roberts was ideal for the role of alpha gay.

His father, Ernest William Roberts, had served for eighteen years
in the U.S. Congress from the Chelsea district outside Boston. A Republican, he was not renominated in 1918 but still retained substantial
political power in Massachusetts and had a lucrative law practice in
Washington, D.C. The family lived well in Washington, Boston, and
in a summer home on the Massachusetts coast, near Gloucester.

Congressman Roberts had not been born to wealth. He had attended public high schools, then earned a college equivalency degree
from Highland Military Academy and a law degree from Boston University. He married Sara Weeks, a descendant of George Weeks, who
arrived in Falmouth, Massachusetts, in 1630. Another forebear,
Richard Warren, arrived on the *Mayflower* ten years earlier. While her
husband served in Congress, Sara Roberts was active in philanthropic
work, serving as president of the National Library for the Blind, a
founder of the Consumers' League, and a member of the executive
committee of the National Homeopathic Hospital. Their son Ernest
Weeks Roberts was one of four children, three boys and a girl.

Even before the Court realized the key role Ernest Roberts played in Harvard's homosexual underworld, he was already in trouble with the deans. His problems, however, were academic, not personal. His goal was to enter Harvard's medical school and become a doctor, but his grades fell below the required levels. Having earned two Ds and an E on his midterm examinations, he was placed on probation by Dean Murdock in December 1919. When this warning prompted an alarmed letter from Roberts's father, Murdock hastily assured the former congressman that Ernest's grades had to improve only slightly for him to be back on track for medical school. As Ernest's letter to Wilcox indicates, he continued to do badly and was blithely unperturbed about it.

The Court had far more serious concerns about Roberts than his academic problems. By first interrogating others of the circle, the judges sought to build the strongest possible case against Roberts. Already possessing so much evidence, they may have also wanted to hone their interrogation techniques before taking on the principal target. On May 27, just hours after interviewing Ken Day, Dean Greenough sent Roberts a particularly curt note ordering him to appear before the Court. "I expect you, whatever your engagement may be, to appear at my office tomorrow, May 28th at 2:45 P.M."

The summons letter concluded, "If necessary you are directed to cut a final examination in order to keep this appointment." The deans knew that for this particular sophomore, final examinations were irrelevant.

For a group of academics who were revolted that any Harvard student would even be civil to a man known to be homosexual, it is not hard to imagine their opinion of a student who wore drag and vowed to get his fiancée's younger brother in bed for a lovemaking session that would "last for 2 days and 2 nights without taking it out."

When Roberts finally sat down before the Secret Court, he projected a cavalier nonchalance and a puzzling ease at discussing a sex life he must have known the deans abhorred. He understood the price he would have to pay for speaking frankly but was resigned to the hopelessness of his case and knew that the most energetic lying would not save him.

For their part, the men of the Court, who had not previously met Roberts, were surprised to see before them not a painted, mincing, eye-rolling horror, but a self-possessed, attractive, and impeccably groomed young man. Wearing a charcoal gray suit, starched white shirt, and crimson necktie, he appeared an exemplary undergraduate who might have been president of the Harvard debating society. His fine-featured face had an innocent openness about it, and he seemed almost cheerful as he recounted his youthful career of depravity. None of this softened the Court's loathing, which they did little to conceal.

For all Roberts's seeming indifference to the Court and its sin-purging objectives, he occasionally lied to them—not to present himself as straight, just a little less gay. These falsehoods may have been a reflex. Or they may have been the reactivation of long-dormant guilt. Whatever their origin, they were pointless efforts at mitigating testimony from many sources, all of it abundantly damning. If he did not plan to return to Harvard in the fall, as he told friends before the scandal broke, he probably cared little if he was expelled. Of course, there were his parents to consider, but they were already dismayed by his woeful academic performance, so even that area of potential disgrace did not worry him overmuch.

When Roberts arrived in the interrogation room, he sat down and crossed his legs casually, showing off highly polished English shoes that glistened in the dim light. As the five academics shuffled their notes and cleared their throats, an air of "main event" permeated the darkened room. As with the others interrogated, the questioning of Roberts began with Cyril Wilcox.

"Yes, we had been friends," Roberts replied evenly.

"Were you surprised by his suicide?"

"No, I wasn't," Roberts said, casually shooting a cuff to reveal a discreet cuff link of gold and black onyx. "Cyril had been despondent and had spoken often of taking his life." He said this as if reporting that Cyril had often spoken of visiting Cape Cod.

Showing his impatience with Roberts's suave self-assurance, Greenough said in a sharp, contradictory tone, "His family says he was never despondent."

Unperturbed, Roberts replied in a world-weary voice, "Families often know little of their children's lives."

Greenough was clearly displeased to be instructed on the family by Ernest Roberts. He switched to firmer ground.

"Were you aware, Mr. Roberts, of Wilcox's relationship with a Boston man named Harry Dreyfus?"

Roberts shifted his weight to make himself more comfortable in the chair. "Indeed I was. I was dining with Cyril in the Lighted Lamp—that's a Beacon Hill restaurant—the night he met Dreyfus. I knew the man slightly, so he came over to the table to greet me. This surprised me, as he had never been so friendly before. I figured out why when he started addressing all of his remarks to Cyril. The two hit it off instantly, so I asked him to join us. I sensed what was happening, so excused myself to speak to some other friends. When I returned, Cyril and Dreyfus were leaving together."

Roberts had no qualms as he warmed to his narrative. Cyril was dead and Dreyfus, whom Roberts disliked, was beyond Harvard's reach. Assuming he was doomed, Roberts relished flailing the Court with the routine banality of homosexuality and, in this case, strongly implying the commonplace nature of such quick pickups. When he paused in his tale of awakening love on Beacon Hill, Harvard's Secret Court sat in shocked silence. For a knockout punch, Roberts tossed out a final piece of information. "After that night, Cyril practically lived at Dreyfus's apartment."

The Court rallied and pushed to conclude this repugnant line of questioning. "How did this affair end?" Dean Gay asked glumly.

"Well you see, Cyril grew increasingly unhappy about it all. Dreyfus could be very difficult. Cyril finally gave him up. Dreyfus, so angry at his dismissal, threatened to expose Cyril to the college authorities. Not a nice man. He also threatened to expose me in the bargain. He knew how close Cyril and I were and was convinced I had encouraged Cyril to break it off."

Visibly uncomfortable with this detailed discussion of gay love affairs, the Court turned toward Roberts's parties. Were they large affairs or were there only two or three guests?

"Generally more than two or three, but never more than ten. At least not before Christmas."

"Is it true," Greenough asked, "that men attended your parties in women's clothes?"

"Yes," Roberts replied, "but they were rehearsing for a fraternity play. I asked them not to come dressed as women, but they did so anyway." To underscore the harmlessness of it all, he added, "I once played a woman in a fraternity play."

Having caught Roberts in a number of contradictions, the Court zeroed in on his sexual activities. He began with a bold understatement, saying he was familiar with homosexuality "to a certain extent in his experiences."

"I first became involved with this sort of activity a few years ago. When I was at high school, I had been taught by another student." Then wistfully: "I thought this was all behind me, but this year I was led astray by Cyril Wilcox."

Even for the Court with its sketchy information, the notion of Roberts being led astray by anyone was laughable.

The judges brought up Roberts's letter. "Who was this Bradlee fellow you intended to *seduce*?" asked Mr. Luce, spitting the last word with undisguised contempt.

"He is a boy in Brookline," Roberts replied casually, omitting that he was also his fiancée's brother.

The Court had had enough. Before forever ridding themselves—and Harvard—of this odious presence, the Court dutifully sought incriminating information about others. They asked for Roberts's opinion of each name on their list. Without hesitation, Roberts threw himself into the task. Saxton, Say, and two town boys mentioned were "guilty." Ken Day was "partly guilty." Several other students were "innocent." As for Lumbard, Roberts knew of nothing that would incriminate him.

He then volunteered that he had had "abnormal relations" with Eugene Cummings but added, "I haven't done anything of that sort with anyone for three months now."

This blatant falsehood in no way helped Roberts's case. For the

Court, there was no statute of limitations on homosexual guilt. Three months ago or three days, any sexuality with another man rendered Roberts totally, irredeemably guilty.

For all his bravado and indifference to the Court's power to bring ruin, Roberts showed less inclination than some other students to imply criticism of the Court's aims and methods. In a few instances, a particular student's refusal to answer questions or to name names came across as the strongest kind of censure in that all present knew such defiance carried considerable risk. But Roberts wanted to appear cooperative, offering some distortions and outright falsehoods but cheerfully volunteering information that would damage others, and providing more than enough truth about himself to end his Harvard career.

The Court's dismissal of Roberts was the only time in the entire session when they wielded the upper hand. Dean Greenough spoke the sentence. "Mr. Roberts, because of your appalling and immoral behavior, you are hereby expelled permanently from Harvard. You and your belongings must be gone from Cambridge in three days."

Later that afternoon, Dean Greenough had a blunt, fifteen-word note delivered to Roberts's room:

Tomorrow I shall write to your father. I advise you to write first.
                                        Sincerely yours,
                                        C. N. Greenough

10

Farce to Tragedy

———◄██►———

ON MAY 31, the fourth day of the Court's interrogations, Greenough received a third letter from Lester Wilcox telling of a visit he received from a friend of his brother's, Eugene Cummings. Although Cummings was three years older than Wilcox, it was inevitable that the two should be good friends. In addition to being Fall River neighbors, they were both at Harvard—Cummings in his fifth and last year at the School of Dentistry—and they were both gay.

The letter doesn't say why Cummings paid a visit to the home of his deceased friend's older brother. Since the conversation, as reported by Lester, dealt almost exclusively with the homosexual issue, it is safe to assume that Cummings heard about the inquisition then in progress and knew as well about Lester's role in it. Word of the letters summoning students to the dean's office had shot across the campus, and most students, especially those with something to fear, knew about the crackdown on homosexuals that was under way. In addition, Lester's visit to Dreyfus would have ensured that every member of the Roberts-Wilcox circle knew that the rampage of Cyril's hotheaded brother had propelled the university into action. It is most likely that, working on the assumption that he had been named and that Lester was central to the proceedings, Cummings was hoping to deflect, or at least soften, Lester's view of him.

It was a pleasant spring day and Wilcox suggested they take a walk so they could "talk in private." It turned out that he had another motive for not wanting Cummings inside his house. Leaving the Wilcox home, they strolled down High Street, which afforded sporadic views of the Taunton River below. They surely discussed Cyril, but Lester's letter makes no mention of this. In his Court testimony, Cummings said he had only known Cyril for about three months. This is hard to believe, as their lives ran such parallel courses, and, according to a later newspaper account, the two young men were "inseparable." But as with so much of the students' statements about themselves, this falsehood must be seen as Cummings's effort to distance himself from one whose homosexuality was clearly established.

Cummings told Lester that "he personally was all right," but that Ernest Roberts was "not a moral man" and "addicted to the same practices as Dreyfus." Dreyfus, he added, was one of the most notorious men in Boston and that he, Cummings, did not know him. Lester was in no mood to be bamboozled and told Cummings that Dreyfus claimed to know *him*: he had in fact named Cummings as a member of the active homosexual group on Harvard's campus. Cornered, Cummings made a strained attempt at dissembling. Relaying the reply in his letter, Lester wrote that Cummings said he "had been seen once at the Copley Plaza by a friend of Dreyfus's, which accounts for [Dreyfus] knowing him so well!!!" (The Copley lobby was then a popular cruising area for Boston homosexuals.)

As for the reason Dreyfus had placed Roberts at the top of the active-gay list, Cummings said he did it because he was envious of Roberts. In a man-to-man aside to Dean Greenough, Lester wrote, "Such people are jealous of each other, I am told." Cummings admitted to Lester that he had attended parties in Roberts's rooms.

"Did you see men in women's clothes?" Lester asked angrily.

"Yes," Cummings said slowly, then brightly added, "but they were rehearsing for a play."

"What play was that?" Making no effort to hide his disbelief, Lester had found his own route to the Court's third-degree techniques.

"I don't remember the title," Cummings said sadly.

In summing up his feelings about the notorious Roberts, Cummings told Lester he believed that Roberts, for all his immorality, would be much better left at Harvard.

"What are you talking about?" Lester said incredulously.

"I know he's evil, but if he is kept in school," Cummings said, "his influence would be more local."

When quoting this remark in his letter, Lester added three exclamation marks after "local." Cummings's extraordinary reasoning seems to have been that, if Roberts were permitted to stay at Harvard, he would merely cause the moral ruin of other Harvard boys; the rest of the world would remain safe.

If Cummings had the intelligence to get through dentistry school, he did not seem to be using it that afternoon. But he knew he was facing not only the disgrace of exposure as a homosexual, but the annihilation of five years at Harvard if he was expelled. Within two weeks, events would establish the crushing weight of these anxieties on Cummings at the time of his talk with Lester.

In a terse description of the walk's conclusion, Lester wrote, "The interview ended the same as the one I had with Dreyfus." This is Lester's subtle way of saying he gave Cummings a thorough thrashing, something he had planned to do as soon as he could obtain from him as much information as possible. The primary purpose of the pleasant spring stroll was to avoid breaking any of Mrs. Wilcox's porcelain figurines.

Lester finished the letter by reporting that Cummings had telephoned his house the next day. Lester was at work and Cummings would not leave his name, but Mrs. Wilcox recognized the voice. Later, when Lester was at home, Cummings called again. When asked if he had called earlier, Cummings denied it. This unnecessary deception can be seen as further evidence of the student's confused state of mind. Lester said Cummings had phoned to find out how much Lester knew about Cummings's "activities." To make such a call to a man who had just given him a beating reveals the terror that gripped Cummings. Lester finished his report to Greenough by saying, "Trust this may be of service to you. Yours truly, Lester Wilcox."

He added a P.S.: "Perhaps you can get it by setting Cummings and Roberts against each other. I told him that Roberts had told me the same thing about himself [that is, Cummings]."

Apparently, the "it" Greenough was to get was an admission from the students that they were engaged in homosexual acts. "The same thing" that Roberts had said about Cummings, according to Lester, must have been that he was an "immoral man." In this atmosphere of rising frenzy, "immoral" meant only one thing: male-to-male sex.

MEANWHILE, THE COURT proceeded on its implacable course. A number of students about whom the Court had only the flimsiest suspicions were interviewed and quickly judged innocent. Of these, several mentioned the décor in Roberts's room as being unusual for student quarters. Heavy window fabrics, Chinese screens, and fringed lamps were all considered signs of sexual deviance and became part of the Court's interrogation arsenal. They would ask, "Did you find anything unusual about the furnishings in Mr. Roberts's room?" Then, they would wait eagerly to hear whether the witness thought they were "a bit odd" or "gorgeous." The opinion would be carefully recorded in the notes.

Along with the students, a number of town boys were interviewed. It is noteworthy that the Court felt totally justified in "summoning" boys over whom it had no jurisdiction. Even more remarkable, the Court felt no hesitancy in subjecting these town boys to the same intrusive questions put to the students. The thinking seems to have been that if any person, regardless of affiliation, had dealings with Harvard students, he fell within the disciplinary reach of the university administration. North of the Charles River, Harvard was the law.

The interviews make clear that the university did not limit its pursuit of town boys to a mere search for information about its students. If one believes Harvard was within its rights to investigate its students' sex lives, then this would be a legitimate line of inquiry. But the Court went a good bit further. After the interrogation of Ned Courtney, one of the most frequently named local boys, the Court notes state that he worked as a waiter at Dreyfus's café and that "Dr. Parmenter will see to it that he is not reemployed."

Courtney's crime was that he had had sex with several Harvard students, as had a number of other Boston boys, according to evidence brought before the Court. Although Courtney had no direct link to the university, the deans still took it upon themselves to destroy his livelihood. This is the only recorded example of the Court seeking to punish implicated town boys, but there is no reason to believe that Courtney was the only one of them to feel the sting of the Court's wrath.

The offhand remark about ending Courtney's waiter job is a rare glimpse of the scope of the Court's horror at homosexuality and does damage to a major defense of the Court's vendetta. The argument runs that, while these worldly deans surely knew that homosexuality was commonplace in the rest of the world, it could not be permitted to exist at *Harvard*. The purge was not aimed at homosexuals per se, but at protecting the idealized Harvard man that the university was dedicated to creating. The attack on Courtney's waiter job shows that the Court felt homosexuality was so wicked that it had to be ferreted out and punished wherever it was encountered.

AT TWENTY-FIVE, Harold Saxton was five years older than most of the students under investigation. He had graduated from Harvard in the class of 1919. In one source he is listed as an assistant professor of philosophy, but if this was ever true, it was not the case when he was called before the Court. In the spring of 1920, he made his living entirely by tutoring undergraduates and lived with his parents on Hancock Street in Cambridge. Since the Court had in its possession the incriminating letter he had written to "Salome's child," Saxton had little hope when he sat down to face the questioning. He had also been named in the anonymous letter. While it is a subject for speculation what powers the Court actually had over Saxton, neither he nor they had any doubt that they could end his livelihood if they chose.

He told the deans that he knew Mr. Wilcox but was surprised by his suicide. When showed his letter, he admitted to having known Wilcox very well but insisted the letter had been a joke and was in no way to be taken seriously. He had been to Roberts's room only once, having been taken there by Wilcox. He had met Mr. Cummings. Apparently the Court tripped up Saxton on one statement, as the notes have the words "contradiction," and later "inconsistency admitted." Finally, the notes contain the damning words "admits one act." In a summation of his testimony, the notes state, "When pressed, he practically confessed to an act, but later retracted." The notes give no indication in what way Saxton was "pressed."

Not surprisingly, the Court found Saxton guilty. Because he had already graduated, however, they were unable to punish him further, and their notes suggest frustration: "No further action possible beyond warning appointment office." This meant that, should Saxton wish to mention to future employers that he was a Harvard graduate, they would also learn that he had been found guilty in a homosexual scandal. In effect, his Harvard degree was rendered worthless.

In a final stab at vindictiveness, President Lowell ordered Saxton's name to be expunged from all university records. He was not a former student, a graduate who was later disgraced. With the stroke of the pen, Lowell transformed Saxton into a man who had never been associated with Harvard in any way. This technique was later used in Stalin's purge trials. All records of the condemned men were destroyed. In Russia's eyes, they had never existed.

FOR AN APPEARANCE before Harvard's Secret Court, the homosexual bona fides of Edward Say was strong: a place on the proctor's short list of frequenters of Roberts's room and mention in the anonymous letter. In interviews, he had also been dubbed "guilty" by Ernest Roberts and Ken Day. In spite of this barrage of accusations and in spite of an obvious effeminate manner—although he had skipped the rouge for this meeting—Say vigorously denied to the Court that he was homosexual.

Clearly eager to get the interrogation finished as quickly as possible, the Court peppered Say with rapid-fire questions. In answer to their first questions, he told the judges that he had not known Wilcox well and was surprised to hear of his death.

"Do you know what a faggoty party is, Mr. Say?" Dean Murdock asked.

"I can only guess," Say replied forlornly.

"How well did you know Ernest Roberts?"

"Rather well. His room was close by mine. I once played bridge with him. He never bothered me to any extent."

"Didn't you once go to the theater with him?"

"No."

"Did he ever make advances toward you?"

"No, he never approached me in any indecent sense."

"But you attended the parties in Roberts's room, did you not?"

"I went to one," Say lied.

"Didn't you know the parties were for homosexuals?"

"I suppose I had an idea that the room and the parties were linked to homosexuality. My room was so close, it was unavoidable that I not know what was going on."

"But you went anyway? Weren't you disgusted by what you saw and heard?"

"I heard nothing terribly unusual. The conversation was typical of a college room."

"So you stayed at the party?"

Say realized he was admitting more than he intended. "No, after a short time I grew disgusted and left."

Greenough sighed with exasperation, then said, "You saw nothing unusual and yet you became disgusted and left? Did you go to subsequent parties there?"

"I was always invited but did not go. In fact, I cut all possible relations with the men involved."

Greenough leaned across the table. "I feel you are not being honest with us, Mr. Say. You see, several students have testified that you were at many of Roberts's parties. We also know that you knew Cyril Wilcox well. Several students have told us so, and the Fall River newspaper wrote that you and he were 'inseparable.' "

Say started to break down. "Yes, that is true. Cyril and I became close in the last year."

"Then you knew all about his affair with Dreyfus and that he was depressed?"

Holding back his tears, Say hung his head and said quietly, "Yes."

With no further doubt they had on their hands a liar and a pervert, Dr. Lee said sternly, "How often do you masturbate, Mr. Say?"

"About once a week."

The five Court members exchanged glances. Greenough spoke. "Mr. Say, I am afraid you have done yourself no good with your contradictory and dishonest replies to our questions. It is our decision that you are expelled and should leave the university at once."

For the last fifteen minutes of his interrogation, Say knew the Court believed nothing he said and would expel him. He only wondered how they would do it. Still, when the words were spoken, he was stunned. Saying nothing, he rose and left the room as the five Court members stared at him in silence.

THE NEXT DAY, Edward Say asked to speak with the Court again. When he was seated before the men who had just condemned him, he began, "I first want to say that I am very much surprised the Court should ask me to leave college. I feel that this unjust decision was based more than anything on some mannerisms I have that can be misinterpreted." Clearly uncomfortable, the deans remained silent.

Say continued, "You see, as a child I spent my first eight years in a plaster cast, then a straitjacket. I could never take part in athletics. So you see, I am naturally effeminate to some degree."

"But Mr Say." Greenough's voice was firm. "I assure you that we based our decision not on your mannerisms, but on your contradictions and evasions. More than that, we based it on the testimony of many witnesses."

Say leaned forward in his chair. "Anyone who says I am homosexual is lying. I am quite ready to face anyone who would make such slanderous accusations against me."

The Court was not accustomed to such boldness, and the use of the legal term "slanderous" provoked an uneasy stir among the five judges. Dean Greenough broke the silence. "That would serve little purpose, Mr. Say. You see we have the testimony of—"

Say interrupted, "Of whom? Ernest Roberts? Last night I confronted Roberts and asked if he had mentioned me in his letter to Cyril. He denied that he had. He said it must have been someone else."

"What he said about the letter is true," Greenough said slowly. "He did not mention you in his letter." He spoke the last words carefully.

"But he did mention me then? If he did, he is lying. I will say so to his face."

Dean Murdock spoke. "There is little point in naming your accusers. There were many."

Greenough added, "And in our interrogation yesterday, you contradicted yourself repeatedly."

"I do not recall doing so."

"For instance, you first told us you had attended only one of Roberts's parties. Later you admitted to having been to several."

"I was nervous," Say said sullenly.

Greenough would later say to a colleague, "We gave Edward Say every opportunity to make explanations, but his efforts along these lines were ludicrously inadequate."

Now, with Say before him with his head lowered, Greenough closed his notebook to indicate the interview was over. "I'm afraid our decision to expel you from Harvard must stand," he said as he removed his black-rimmed glasses. "We feel strongly that you have been tailoring your replies to get out of trouble." Two members of the Court rose to leave.

Still sitting in his chair before the Court, Say said quietly but firmly, "I have nothing to get out of."

WHEN THE COURT was asking one student about other students under suspicion, the name of Joseph Lumbard was mentioned, along with several others. Usually the students were quick to implicate others, but in this case the student being interrogated insisted Lumbard was not like Roberts, Say, and Cummings. He was, the student said, "a person of a far higher order." However admirable Lumbard might appear to his classmates, he had been named as having questionable friends and had been seen at Roberts's parties. In the eyes of the Court, Mr. Lumbard had much explaining to do.

While every student called before the deans was fearful to varying degrees, especially as word got out about expulsions, Joe Lumbard had an additional worry. He was at Harvard on a university scholarship and so was more vulnerable than the other students. More important, Lumbard had a strong sense of probity. He was deeply humiliated by the summons and was furious at himself for allowing himself to be accused of any sort of wrongdoing.

He appeared calm as he sat down before the Court. Although nattily dressed in a dark brown tweed suit, a starched white collar, and rust-colored necktie, he still look more a boy than a man. For all his appearance of youthful innocence, Lumbard still projected a greater self-assurance and adult seriousness than the other students. It would later emerge that Lumbard felt the Court was overreacting to a minor problem and was highly injudicious in many of its actions. Now, sitting before its members, he was aware of their power to wreck his life, but he felt little respect for them.

The interrogation started with the usual questions about Cyril Wilcox, the degree to which Lumbard knew Wilcox, and his awareness of his suicide. He said he had known him slightly and had heard about the suicide.

"Did you know Mr. Wilcox's reputation?"

"I knew he was dissipated," Lumbard replied, "and that he liked wild parties."

"Did you know about his sexual relationship with a Boston man named Harry Dreyfus?"

"Yes, I had heard about it."

"How did you come to know Ernest Roberts?"

Lumbard explained that he had met him through his roommate,

Edward Say, and had gotten to know Roberts and his group "pretty well." Then the judges asked if he had heard allegations of sexual impropriety against Cummings, Day, and Smerage? Lumbard tried to appear cooperative, but the worst he said about any of them was that he "had heard rumors."

"Mr. Lumbard," Dean Greenough said, "have you ever been to any of Roberts's parties?

"Yes. Edward, my roommate, took me to several. The first was in December."

"What were these parties like?"

Lumbard struck a mild blow for liberality. "Broad-minded people would not have objected to anything that happened there."

With growing exasperation, Greenough said, "Were there any men present dressed as women?"

"A few."

"Were there town boys?"

As the tone of the questions grew more strident, Lumbard grew more reckless. In one answer, he used a slang term the Court believed was known only to those deeply involved in homosexuality. "Yes, there were a few Boston faggots at the party."

Dean Murdock cleared his throat. "Did you see any erotic interplay between men?"

Still with the same even nonchalance, Lumbard replied, "There was some kissing."

"Why did you stop attending the parties?"

"I wasn't invited to any more of them." He then added, "I had no reason to go because I do not drink."

"But why did you go in the first place?"

"I had heard about the parties and merely looked in on a few because I was interested. But I stayed only a few minutes."

"You are quite close with Edward Say, are you not?"

"He's my roommate."

"Yes, yes, Mr. Lumbard, we are aware of that," Dean Greenough said testily, "but roommates can be civil to each other without becoming good friends. Don't you find Mr. Say rather effeminate?"

"I suppose I do."

"Does he wear rouge?"

"Sometimes, but he explained to me he wears it because of bad health."

"What is your opinion of Ernest Roberts?"

"I do not like him. And I suspect he doesn't like me."

"Why is that?"

"Not long ago he invited me to go into Boston with him and some of his crowd, but I refused to go. I think that made them angry."

The Court asked Lumbard a number of questions about his having taken messages for members of this group from the communal telephone in Perkins Hall. Because this was the way town gay boys communicated with Harvard friends, the Court often asked targeted students about message taking, seeing it as a highly suspect form of cooperation. In a subsequent letter to Lumbard's father, Greenough wrote, "[Your son] is seriously at fault in serving as a kind of intermediary by answering telephone calls and communicating them, making him a kind of link in the chain." Since others might see relaying messages as an elementary courtesy, the Court's straining for signs of homosexual collusion indicates ineptitude coupled with an overreaching zeal in its dogged quest for incriminating evidence.

Not believing that message taking was proof of sexual malfeasance, Lumbard admitted that, living in the same entryway, he had performed this service for Roberts and his group. He said to the Court, "If a caller asked me to tell a student to call him, I would do so. I don't see anything wrong in this."

"Mr. Lumbard," Dr. Lee said somberly, "do you masturbate?"

Unabashed, Lumbard responded, "I had done it up until six years ago, but then stopped. I haven't done it since."

"Have you ever had sexual relations with a woman?"

"No."

Dean Murdock took up a line of questioning he clearly felt would be more fruitful than phone messages. "Is it true, Mr. Lumbard, that you have permitted various young men from Boston to sleep in your room?" He made "young men from Boston" sound as unsavory as panhandlers and thieves.

"Yes, friends of my roommate's. They slept over three or four times, maybe four or five times. One boy, Pat, slept there maybe seven or eight times."

"Did you ever share a bed with any of them?"

Lumbard knew this was highly dangerous ground, but he also knew how unlikely it would be not to share one of the suite's two beds if there had been more than one guest.

"Yes, I once allowed a town boy named Bill Toomey to sleep in my bed. But I can assure you absolutely nothing improper took place."

Lumbard's tone was so firm it almost made the Court ashamed to have raised the question. The deans indicated they were finished with their interrogation. As an afterthought, Lumbard said, "You know that Roberts has threatened to make publicity if he is expelled."

The Court had indeed heard this but did not respond. Greenough said stiffly, "Thank you, Mr. Lumbard. We will be contacting you shortly."

Joe Lumbard had succeeded in convincing the Court he was innocent of sexual misconduct. He had not seemed intent on making himself appear totally uninvolved with Harvard's gay world, as Edward Say so ludicrously had. Even more important, Lumbard did not seem to the uninformed men of the Court to be "the type" to engage in homosexual activity. He had impressed them with his directness and his manly demeanor. While his case would not be dismissed lightly—he had, after all, admitted to intimacy with boys the Court knew to be guilty—the judges were willing to grant Lumbard a degree of naïveté they granted few others. Still, he was told to leave Harvard.

CROSSING HARVARD YARD one day, Nathaniel Wollf encountered Dean Greenough. He stopped the dean and told him he knew certain things concerning the suicide of Cyril Wilcox that might be valuable to the dean's investigation. Greenough immediately asked Wollf to appear before the Court. When Keith Smerage told the Court of his mutual masturbation session with Wollf, the deans were considerably more eager to speak with him. From the notes, it appears Wollf first had a one-to-one meeting with Dr. Lee, perhaps to relay his information about Wilcox's death. But in the course of that discussion, Wollf had told Dr. Lee "everything." Lee may very well have confronted Wollf with Smerage's accusation.

When, shortly afterward, Wollf was brought before the entire Court, they started out by asking him about his college career, then segued into his associations. He had already taken some courses at the medical school and worked for two months in the dental lab, where he had met Eugene Cummings. He did not see Cummings again until this year. The previous Monday, the two met in Holt (where Wollf had gone to see Cyril Wilcox). Cummings dropped by Wilcox's room while he was there. The conversation turned toward the need for wider sex education. Wilcox told the entire story of his relationship with Dreyfus, adding that he had had no relations with Harvard undergraduates. It was apparently this knowledge that made Wollf think he had special information that might be helpful to the Court's understanding of Wilcox's suicide.

The Court asked if Wollf knew there was a homosexual group among the undergraduates. Yes, he did, but had no idea who they were. Did he believe Mr. Cummings was part of the group? No, he didn't think so. Had Cummings mentioned Ernest Roberts to him? No. Before this year he had heard of only one other case in which two students were said to have had sex. He had heard Keith Smerage's name mentioned in this regard. Wollf's implication of Smerage, whom he had only a month earlier courted and seduced, would appear gratuitous, if not vindictive, except that Wollf knew the Court was aware of his encounters with Smerage. He would get credit for being cooperative without doing Smerage further harm.

Wollf was called back for a second interview. Dr. Lee began by outlining what Smerage had told them about his sexual activity with Wollf. The deans asked if he could elaborate or offer any explanations. He said he had told Dr. Lee everything the night of their first meeting. When pressed for more background information, Wollf said that, from age twelve to sixteen, he had gone to a boys' boarding school that was permeated with homosexuality and considerable mutual masturbation. He was "attacked twice." He had only committed two homosexual acts in his first two years at Harvard, then he "set a check on himself." That is, until he met Smerage. They had supper together. From the sexual allusions Smerage made, Wollf knew he was homosexual. Smerage went back with him to Wollf's room and stayed a couple of hours. They took off all their clothes. Mutual masturbation took place.

The Court asked Wollf about earlier sexual experiences. He had had two heterosexual encounters with prostitutes. He then admitted to one more encounter with Smerage. He was walking in the Yard one evening and dropped by Smerage's room. They went back to Wollf's room. Same occurrence. Wollf added that he thought this experience had "broken him with homosexuality."

Perhaps Wollf did not realize how damning his confessions were in the eyes of the Court. Even if he did, his final comment takes on a pathetic note. He told the Court that if anyone said anything more about his homosexual activities, "it is slander."

BY THE TIME Eugene Cummings was called before the Court in early June, he was in a state of near collapse. Aside from the usual anxieties of final exams, he knew he was in serious trouble with the gay-purging Court that had become the talk of the campus. He had been living an active, poorly concealed gay life for several years and had gone regularly to Roberts's parties. He either was friends with or well acquainted with everyone the Court had summoned. His summons to testify came as no surprise. He would soon learn that he had been named as a core member of Harvard's homosexual circle by several sources: Dreyfus's list, the anonymous letter, and the proctor's list. His one attempt to mitigate the case against him, his visit to Lester Wilcox, had ended with a beating.

Cummings had been at Harvard for five years, which was a financial strain on his father, who taught school in Fall River. He had entered the freshman class in the fall of 1915, then after a year transferred to the School of Dentistry. He should have received his degree three years later, but, as Dr. Lee nastily would later point out to the press, Cummings took four years to complete the dentistry courses. But complete them he had, and he was within a few days of finally receiving his degree, only to see it all about to come crashing down. Unlike some who testified before the Court, Cummings knew the university regarded homosexuality among its students as criminality of the highest order. Ernest Roberts was not happy at Harvard and did not care what the Court did with him. Cummings cared desperately.

As with the others, the Court started its interrogation of Cummings with questions about Cyril Wilcox. He said he didn't feel there was any great mystery about Wilcox's suicide, nor was he surprised at Wilcox's self-loathing. He had known Wilcox only a short time, but in that time had become Wilcox's confidant. As such, he had heard a good many facts about Wilcox's life. He then added he had known Wilcox for approximately three months.

Cummings denied knowing "the group Wilcox played into." He met Roberts about the same time he met Wilcox but knew him even less than he had known Wilcox. Cummings said he had been to Roberts's room several times. Yes, he had met both Ken Day and Edward Say. He was not suspicious of the Roberts group at first. His suspicions were later aroused by their conversation while he was with them. No, he did not take part in those conversations. Had any member of Roberts's group approached Cummings in an improper way? No. If Cummings felt the conversation had been unnatural, why didn't he stop going to the room? Cummings replied that he didn't "know he was being dragged into it." He probably did not think that merely tolerating such talk in his presence would later incriminate him as an active homosexual.

The Court asked Cummings if anything abnormal had happened while he was in Roberts's room. No, nothing but conversation. On further prompting, he recalled there had once been some men in women's clothes. Were they masquerading? No, they were taking pictures. The deans asked him about the more notorious town boys; he admitted to having met them. After a brief discussion of Ned Courtney, the notes then state: "We do not consider Courtney as a Galahad." Shown Dreyfus's photograph, Cummings said that he knew him and had spent one night in his apartment, but Dreyfus had not been present. Did he know the proctor of Perkins, Windsor Hosmer? Cummings said that he knew him.

The Court felt it had caught Cummings in an outright lie when he said he knew Cyril Wilcox "only slightly" and that he had gone to Roberts's room only a few times. The judges also felt they had enough evidence against him with the numerous accusations. If the Court asked Cummings about his visit with Lester Wilcox, there is no mention of this in the interrogation notes. This is odd, as many might see Cummings's visit to Cyril's older brother as an indication of guilt, an attempt to temper the judgment of the gay purge's instigator. Since Lester Wilcox related this entire meeting in a letter to Dean Greenough dated May 31, all the men of the Court knew of the encounter. On other occasions, they had seized on less incriminating information in their possession.

Even before learning he was expelled, Cummings could tell by the Court's hostility toward him and its dismissal of his denials that he was finished at Harvard. His five years of classes, studying, lab work, exams were all to be wiped out. His family's sacrifices were for nothing. The Court's angry questions left no doubt about their abhorrence of homosexuality. None of the students considered guilty by the Court got through the proceedings without being made to feel like a contemptible wretch, a disgrace both to his family and to Harvard. Cummings was no exception.

Perhaps tired of the pointless fencing, Dean Gay asked him directly: had he ever had homosexual relations? Cummings vehemently denied this. Without responding to the denial, Greenough told Cummings, with icy finality, that the interrogation was over. He was expelled from Harvard.

Cummings left the room in a daze. Five years of Harvard wiped out with one sentence. His fought-for dental degree only days away, and now he had nothing. He had ruined a promising career; an assured berth of economic security, perhaps wealth; the degree for which he had worked so hard and for which his family had sacrificed much. He was branded a sexual pervert, a miserable degenerate who had sacrificed an auspicious future for his twisted lusts. As he arrived back in his room, he collapsed and was taken to the infirmary. While there, he received an official note from the dean of the School of Dentistry reiterating that he was expelled and that he should leave Cambridge immediately.

Greenough's notes of Cummings's interview end abruptly with the following entry, which is astonishing for its cold-bloodedness: "Proved guilty" (underlined by Greenough). Immediately after this pronouncement, Greenough wrote, "But took ether and corrosive sublimate upon receiving news from Dean Smith. Died on the morning of June 11, 1920."

With his medical training, Cummings knew which drugs he needed and where in the infirmary to find them. Dr. Lee would later say that Cummings was suffering from nervous exhaustion brought on by the pressure of final examinations. He did not mention that Cummings knew, at the time of his suicide, that he would not be permitted to take the exams. Six years earlier, in his high-school yearbook, Cummings had stated his motto: "Never Say Die."

That the Court had driven a student to suicide was not considered worth any further comment in the notes. No shock, dismay, sympathy—and certainly no contrition. The Court had done its job, fulfilled its moral obligations. There was no reason to feel the slightest culpability. And from the notes of the Court's proceedings, it is clear that their verdict of *guilt*—not the suicide—was for them the more important development in the case of Eugene Cummings. In the event that this priority was lost on anyone, the bleak recording of his suicide was written in normal script, but the guilty verdict, Cummings's death sentence, was underlined.

11

Enduring Wrath

BY THE TIME the Court had wrapped up its proceedings, it had declared guilty fourteen of the more than thirty men it had interviewed. Of these, five were not affiliated with Harvard: Harry Dreyfus and four others. Of those linked to the university, there was alumnus Harold Saxton, Assistant Professor Donald Clark, and seven undergraduates. Four of the latter—Roberts, Day, Cummings, and Say— were considered prime offenders, confirmed homosexuals, and were offered no hope of readmission. The last three—Gilkey, Lumbard, and Wollf—were deemed guilty more of carelessness in their associations than outright homosexuality. They had a chance, they were told, of being welcomed back to Harvard after six months or so—time to think over their indiscretions.

From the interrogation notes, it is not always clear how the Court reached its conclusions. Of those shown leniency, one of them— Gilkey—was accused of as much homosexual activity as some who were permanently condemned. As the future lives of all the students are examined, it becomes clear that there is no connection between a student's sexual orientation and the Court's punishments. Several of the most harshly punished boys were predominantly straight and went on to lead enthusiastically heterosexual lives. At least one who was clearly gay—judging from his activities as a student and from his later life—was eventually readmitted and allowed to graduate.

Donald Clark was fired as an assistant professor and forced out of the Ph.D. program. With Harold Saxton, who had already graduated, the Court had to content itself with undermining his future and expunging him from Harvard's rolls, which in effect stripped him of his Harvard degree. As for the four town boys, there is no record of action taken against them. Judging by the one line in the notes about Courtney, however—that Dr. Parmenter would see to it he was not reemployed at his restaurant job—there is every likelihood the Court sought retribution against the others as well.

WHAT HAD THE Court accomplished with its reign of terror? It had certainly driven every campus manifestation of homosexuality deeply underground. There would be no more bitch parties with sailors and drag queens in dormitory rooms. Students would only don women's clothes when required by the Hasty Pudding or Dramatic Club to round out Harvard's vision of manhood. No students would ever wear the slightest hint of rouge or nail polish. Homosexual predators, whether at Harvard or in the neighborhood, would hesitate before approaching attractive students. The Boston bars and restaurants with "bohemian" reputations would lose their Harvard clientele. And every homosexual would be extremely careful about what he wrote in letters to friends.

All of these victories for the Court succeeded in suppressing what were essentially surface expressions of gayness. The more serious business of homosexuality—male-to-male sex—may have been reduced somewhat, but it would be fatuous to think it had been eliminated. The sexually ambiguous students, like Day and Lumbard, or the merely curious undoubtedly cut from their lives this area of experimentation, but those who acknowledged and accepted their orientation, recognizing kindred spirits and feeling attraction, would proceed as they always had—and always would. Even a wrathful Harvard could not turn off the surge of sexual energy of nineteen-year-olds.

One could reasonably conjecture that perhaps all the Court sought was the elimination of the most blatant displays of gay activity, that the deans never deluded themselves into thinking they had eliminated the problem in all its forms. But given their shock and disgust that such activities should occur at Harvard, it is doubtful that the Court would have closed down its investigation after three weeks had they thought they had succeeded in expelling only a few of the more outrageous gays and alerted the rest to be more discreet.

Indeed, the notes indicate that the Court was highly suspicious of some against whom they were unable to build a case. Much of the testimony from this group would appear to the most innocent observer to come from committed gays. With such witnesses, however, the Court was only able to establish suspect friendships, plus familiarity with the haunts and the jargon, but not the proof it sought of gay sex. After the notes of these interviews is written, "Not Proven."

The Court's records give no indication of how the deans viewed their results. The notes speak of "summaries" of the investigation and charts of who was expelled and who exonerated. There are no chest beatings about the triumph of good over evil, no cries of victory or even self-congratulations for a job well done. There is, however, a sense of work completed, of few loose ends. Granting the time and diligence given to the problem—it is hard to believe the five members of the Court had time for any other activity—and the alarm with which they viewed the blight, they seem to have decided they had found most of the cancer and removed it. Whoever they had missed would, with luck, wither and die of shame.

ONE OF THE oddities of the Secret Court is the view of homosexuality that informed its judgments and punishments. Since the judges made no outright declaration of guiding principles and did not even define what, for them, constituted homosexuality, their views must be gleaned by inference. One of the most singular assumptions that emerges is that any male who has sexual relations with another male is ipso facto a homosexual, or at least indelibly contaminated.

In the U.S. military, up to the present, it is not unusual for straight soldiers—that is, soldiers whose heterosexual credentials arc in order—either to rape an obvious gay among them or to force the gay to perform fellatio on them. When such cases are made public or brought to trial, the straight soldiers might be punished for violence, indecency, or a number of other misdemeanors, but they are never considered homosexuals or tried as such. Regardless of what sexual acts they instigated, even forced, they continue to be viewed by the gay-phobic military as staunch heterosexuals.

Court records stretching far back into U.S. history show a similar pattern: the authorities have consistently made this distinction, seeing confirmed homosexuals as an altogether separate species from heterosexuals who were merely availing themselves of perverts' services. More to the point, they also see the confirmed gays as social outcasts who must be condemned, while the switch-hitting straights are just good old boys taking release where they can find it. The gays receive opprobrium and harsh punishments, the crossover straights receive a shrug.

For better or for worse, Harvard in 1920 was unwilling or unable to make any such distinction. If one of its students had sex with another male, he was as homosexual and as guilty as the most painted transvestite in a Beacon Hill bar. It mattered little to the administration if the guilty preferred sex with women or if, as Ken Day claimed, they had gotten drunk one night and allowed a gay friend to service them. Guilt was determined by the action itself, just as in ancient Greece, where sin (not including homosexuality) was seen more as a disease than an optional pastime. You either have it or you don't. With this view of homosexuality, a given boy's dedication to the pursuit of male-male sex was irrelevant. It was the deed that counted, not the underlying motive or zeal. The sentences imposed by the Court suggest the deans weren't so much interested in ridding Harvard of homosexuals per se, but in punishing any male who had had sex with another male.

Such thinking would be consistent with an attitude of the Court that emerges in other contexts: the concept of homosexuality's contagious nature. The deans viewed anyone capable of enjoying sex with another male as a dangerous "carrier" of the depravity virus. There is even some evidence, most particularly in the case of Ken Day, which will be examined in some detail later, that the Court was more vindictive when dealing with the masculine, borderline cases than it was with the obvious homosexuals. One reason for this might have been the belief that the borderline converts like Day represented not only, in themselves, a spread of the disease but a potential proselytizer to other potential experimenters like themselves.

Whatever the exact thinking, the Secret Court condemned all who had had sex with another male—the totally gay, to be sure, but also the camp followers, the switch-hitters, the purely opportunistic, or the hapless students, bursting with all the urges of nineteen-year-olds, who found themselves housed with a homosexual roommate two doors from Roberts's ongoing gay carnival.

WHEN VIEWING HARVARD'S 1920 purge of gays in the context of the broad sweep of American homosexual history, it is not immediately obvious what sets this particular witch-hunt apart from all the others that have occurred throughout the years—and that still occur in the United States, primarily in the military. The most obvious difference is that this purge occurred at *Harvard,* an institution from which the world has come to expect the kind of enlightenment and compassion that would forbid the intemperate, intolerant, destructive, moralistic responses embodied by the Secret Court.

A second sizable difference between the Court and other gay inquisitions is the university's decades-long pursuit of the expelled students. Not content to terminate their Harvard education, with all the devastation this act alone would inflict on young lives, the Court went to pains to ensure that those found guilty would be punished throughout their lives. This was done by aggressively stigmatizing the offending former students by means of the university's Appointments Office, the agency to which all future employers and other colleges went for recommendations.

Most young men trying to get ahead in the world would mention their time at Harvard, even if they were only there for a year or two. Or if they left college in disgrace and prudently dropped Harvard from their résumés, the information would probably emerge in any case. Missing years had to be accounted for, grade transcripts had to be produced, and so on. After the Court's verdicts, if any of the expelled students applied for a job or admission to a different school, the sought-after organization invariably wrote to Harvard for information. The Appointments Office routinely wrote back a damning letter. The wording was blunt: "We cannot recommend this person for any position of responsibility." Or, "Harvard cannot show any confidence in this individual." As if such statements might not be sufficiently lethal, they were followed by an invitation to contact the dean's office if further details were desired. Such invitations were usually accepted, if for no other reason than perverse curiosity.

Astonishingly, this went on for many years. The files contain a memo of one such condemnation that was written in 1953, thirty-three years after the Court disbanded. Even before the age of computers, Harvard's bar-sinister record keeping was infallible, its damnation reflex unstoppable.

This determination to destroy the lifetime career chances of the condemned students places Harvard in a class by itself for gay persecution. Most institutions, especially those as far above the world's nastiness as Harvard, would be content merely to rid themselves of offenders and stifle chances of another outbreak. Not so Harvard in 1920. The Court's judges felt a moral obligation to ensure that other organizations, academic or otherwise, did not fall victim to the carriers of vice they had apprehended in Cambridge.

The thinking behind the ongoing vendetta ruled out the possibility that the disgraced students might alter their conduct or renounce homosexuality. Nor would Harvard allow for future lives of extreme discretion in which the men acted on their natures only in total privacy and only with partners who were of like mind. To Lowell and his Court, those tainted to any degree must not be permitted to go into the world with the word "Harvard" in their curricula vitae. They had proven themselves men of insufficient moral character to withstand homosexual temptations and would always be a threat to decent people. Their depravity was permanent, and it disqualified them from the desirable situations that resulted from Harvard credentials.

On June 13, 1920, Dean Greenough wrote a letter to the Appointments Office. He was surely aware of the lifelong condemnation the letter would carry. The letter was written specifically about the two nonstudents affiliated with Harvard, Donald Clark and Harold Saxton, but very shortly letters with the same career-destroying power were issued about every student the Court had judged guilty. The mechanisms of bureaucracy being what they are, the Appointments Office continued to mail out these poison-pen letters long after President Lowell and the men of his Court had disappeared from the scene.

Greenough's letter to the director of the Appointments Office, a Miss Nork, "strongly suggests" she and her staff issue no statement that implies Harvard "has confidence" in Harold Saxton or Donald Clark until they have first consulted with the dean.

The most remarkable aspect of this model of aggressive vindictiveness was that the letter was dated just two days after Eugene Cummings committed suicide. Having caused the death of one student, the men of the Court wasted no time inflicting as much damage as they could on the futures of those who hoped to go on with their lives. Two days after the first letter, June 15, Greenough wrote another letter to the Appointments Office that is even more explicit in inflicting the same lifelong condemnation on all of the expelled students. The letter says that before indicating any confidence in Roberts, Day, Smerage, Gilkey, Wollf, Lumbard, and Clark, they should consult "someone" in the dean's office (indicating Greenough had alerted his staff). To prevent any slipups in the ongoing vendetta, he adds, "If they do not know what is meant, tell them to look in the disciplinary file in an envelope marked Roberts, E. W., and others."

When this letter was written, Cummings had been dead for four days. Pity and sentiment could not be permitted to weaken the resolve of those entrusted with ridding Harvard of the terrible homosexual scourge and seeing to it that the guilty could never so much as mention their years at Harvard without harsh reprisal. There is no greater indication of the Court's deep-seated abhorrence of homosexuality and its dread of the threat homosexuals posed to decent people than this harsh action. It is also doubtful if other vendettas against gay men in the nineteenth and twentieth centuries put into motion such self-perpetuating and lifelong punishments.

ON JUNE 19, over a week after Cummings's suicide, *The Boston American* ran an unsigned lead story with the headline TWO HARVARD MEN DIE SUDDENLY, followed by the subhead "One a Suicide and the Other Accidentally Killed by Gas." Both men were from Fall River and were, according to the article, "inseparable." No doubt is left about the cause of Cummings's death, as the story reports he died from a deliberate ingestion of corrosive sublimate tablets. Cyril Wilcox's death, however, is still referred to as an accident, even though more than a month had passed and most people, including the Wilcox family and the Harvard deans, referred to it as suicide. Linking the two deaths in a headline indicates that the newspaper believed there might be a connection between them and suspected something strange was going on at Harvard.

The article makes an indirect allusion to the Secret Court:

> According to friends of the two in Fall River, Cummings, who was *said to be unbalanced* [emphasis added], told a story of an alleged inquisition which he claimed was held in the college following Wilcox's death. He said that he was taken into the office, which was shrouded in gloom with but one light dimly burning, and there questioned exhaustively. The story, which was denied by the authorities, was said to have "sprung from his disordered mind."

The article does not mention whether Cummings had told his friends the focus of the "alleged inquisition." It seems unlikely, however, that friends close enough to have been told details about his humiliating interrogation would not also have been told the reason for it. By the time Cummings was questioned, most everyone on the Harvard campus was aware of the homosexual purge then in progress. Although the reporter surely asked why Cummings was being interrogated, it's possible his friends decided not to stigmatize their deceased friend. Even if the reporter knew homosexuality was the matter under investigation, which is far more likely, it is possible that the newspaper shied away from openly discussing anything so shameful in connection with Harvard. Still, the omission from the article is very odd.

The most significant aspect of the news story is the authorities' denial of an inquisition. They knew that everything Cummings had told his friends about his brutal interrogation was absolutely true, yet they told the newspaper it was the imaginings of a disordered mind. Equally false was the statement of Dr. Lee, the one medical man who sat on the Court. According to the article, "Dr. Roger I. Lee, professor of hygiene, said Cummings, who had been acting in a queer manner, ingested the tablets during the dental school examination period." Then, for a gratuitous slight, Lee added that Cummings had been in his fourth year at the dental school in a course that ordinarily would have taken three years.

The Court's dishonest public posture over Cummings's death provides a rare glimpse of its attitude toward the crusade its members had launched. Not only did they deny Cummings had been subjected to questioning—an outright lie—they went on to slander the dead student's sanity by saying his interrogation story was pure delusion. To substantiate this claim, they added that lately Cummings had been acting in an odd way. In a final thrust to throw the Boston newspaper off the track, they said that Cummings had had difficulty getting through his dental courses, that the pressures of final examinations had pushed him over the edge.

While it is somewhat understandable that the Court feared Cummings's death could erupt into a major scandal, it had options other than defamatory lies about a student it had just destroyed. The Court might have said Cummings was being investigated on a disciplinary matter that must remain confidential. Or it might have gone further with the truth to say that he had just been expelled for reasons that would be pointless to reveal now that he was dead.

But for these men to go to such dishonorable lengths to keep hidden their campaign to rid Harvard of homosexuals suggests something more was at play than mere avoidance of scandal. Seven undergraduates expelled from the entire university would hardly make Harvard appear a cesspool of perversion. If the judges truly believed they were battling wickedness, upholding morality, doing God's work, why would they so fear exposure that they would outright lie about it? Even the Salem witch trials were conducted in public.

The obsession with secrecy suggests that the Court saw the gay problem as something specific to their beloved university, a blight highly damaging to Harvard's august reputation. They may also have sensed the conflict between the enlightened tolerance expected of great seats of learning and Harvard's vicious purge of a despised minority. Their determination to keep the Court's actions secret is a rare hint that they knew they were not battling global evil so much as they were battling Harvard's dreaded queer reputation.

While this may have been a propelling motive, acknowledged just enough to inspire secrecy, the members of the Court had clearly convinced themselves that their purge was first and foremost a moral crusade. Whatever the explanation, the secrecy reveals the welter of conflicting attitudes that drove the Court.

The Court's dishonesty tells us more. Cummings's suicide laid before the deans unavoidable proof that their campaign was lethal, that it was inflicting devastating blows on young men who might not be resilient enough to survive them. To cause anyone's death over what was, at worst, moral malfeasance is horrifying. But to doggedly maintain secrecy—at the cost of honesty and honor—indicates that the men of the Court lacked sufficient confidence in the rightness of their course to believe the world at large would consider the problem as dire as they did, let alone condone their methods in combating it.

All of these possibilities raise a third reason why the *Boston American* reporter, so clearly suspicious that something major was happening at Harvard, did not follow up on his or her suspicions. It would have been a simple matter for the journalist to learn if the interrogation Cummings reported had indeed taken place and what it had been about. Almost any student in Harvard Yard could have offered the information and would have had no reason to refuse it. Credulity is strained to think that a reporter, having made the impressive journalistic leap that Cummings's death was a clue to a far bigger story, failed to ask the routine questions that would have confirmed his suspicions and filled out the bizarre tale's missing pieces. When the entire episode is viewed in the light of journalistic imperatives, it becomes increasingly probable that Harvard put massive pressure on *The Boston American* to kill the story.

It is obvious that Harvard had the muscle to do this. Then, too, in that time it is doubtful that any newspaper would pit its own integrity against the integrity of Harvard. It is also obvious that this was a matter of the utmost importance to Lawrence Lowell and his colleagues. To be sure, they did not want their beloved university to appear in a bad light. Subsequent actions, however, suggest they were motivated by an even more immediate reason. If word of the Court had gotten out and the public had condemned their crusade, it might have mitigated, even terminated, the Court's proceedings. For the men of the Court, this would have been an even greater calamity than a momentary newspaper scandal.

Such was their conviction of the rightness of their cause, and the greater good for Harvard that would result from their proceedings: they could not allow a publicity flap to stand in their way. Such, too, was their belief in the horrendous nature of the crimes they confronted. The Court clearly did not feel that one student's death, while unfortunate, was sufficiently tragic to prompt a rethinking of its crusade to rid Harvard of homosexuals. Cummings's suicide, so clearly a direct result of the Secret Court's actions, did not slow them down in the slightest.

This one news story in a Boston paper was as close as Harvard's homosexual purge came to emerging into public view. This is quite remarkable given the large numbers of people, mostly students and faculty, who knew about the Court, and given the sensational nature of the scandal. The less noteworthy homosexual scandal a year earlier in Newport had created newspaper headlines across the country. And that had involved the navy, a well-known sanctuary for perversion and low behavior. But this exorcism of sinful corruption concerned Harvard, the nation's—if not the world's—most distinguished institute of higher learning. What a story! Despite a series of expulsions, two suicides, and a questioning newspaper article, Harvard somehow succeeded in keeping the entire matter buried for eighty-two years.

ON JUNE 22, the father of Eugene Cummings wrote the following letter to Dean Greenough:

> *My dear sir,*
> *If convenient, I should like to see you Friday afternoon or*
> *Saturday of this week. Last week, I had a talk with Dean Smith*
> *of the Medical School, which I thought at the time, sufficient.*
> *Information which has come to me since, plus an article in* The
> Boston American, *make it imperative I see you this week.*
> *I trust you will find it convenient to make an appointment.*
> *Respectfully yours,*
> *[father of Cummings]*

In the Court records, there is a note from Greenough to one of his Court colleagues, perhaps to President Lowell himself. It reads:

> *On June 25th I had a rather long interview with the father of*
> *Cummings who [illegible] to feel satisfied with the activities of*
> *the Court and manner in which the case had been conducted. He*
> *particularly appreciated the kindness of Dean Smith of the*
> *Dental School.*
> *C. N. Greenough*

In spite of the unintelligible word, it is clear that Greenough felt Cummings's father was mollified by their meeting. The father's "particular" appreciation of Dean Smith's kindness implies he also appreciated the Court's just behavior in handling his son's case. If so, it is all but impossible to understand. The father's letter to Greenough stated that he was at first satisfied by Dean Smith of the School of Dentistry—who surely put out the official line about odd behavior, extreme nervousness, and so on. But new information from the *Boston American* article and other sources—probably friends of his son—impelled the father to seek more answers from Greenough. In other words, the father had read in the newspaper of his son's interrogation in a darkened room by Harvard deans. More was clearly afoot, and Mr. Cummings wanted to know what undergraduate misbehavior was sufficiently egregious to drive his son to his death.

According to Greenough's note, after hearing the dean's side of things—that is, the charges against his son—Mr. Cummings came to believe the Court had acted properly. If true, this is astounding. It is conceivable that the senior Cummings viewed homosexuality with the same horror and disgust as the Court. Even in the present day, there are parents who would rather see their children dead than gay, and such an extreme attitude was probably more common eighty years ago. The father's letter, however, strongly suggests he had learned about the Court and its reasons for hounding his son. If he was so homophobic, he would have approved the Court's actions and felt his son got what he deserved. What would there have been to discuss with the dean?

The picture that emerges from the scraps of information that have survived is an aggrieved father angrily demanding to question the dean about the official persecution that resulted in his son's death. Somehow, Greenough converted this understandable parental fury into a meek endorsement of the Court's brutal justice. Since the men of the Court showed a willingness to lie to *The Boston American,* it is possible that they fabricated a dossier of rampant depravity for Eugene Cummings so repugnant that his father, like Herod aghast at his lascivious stepdaughter, Salome, felt the harshest punishment was appropriate, even if it meant his child's death.

It is more likely that Greenough, facing Cummings's father, hammered away about the damage being done to venerable Harvard by homosexual wickedness to the point that the distraught father agreed that the Court had simply done what had to be done. In any case, it would have been most interesting to have heard the conversation between the dean and Cummings's father and the arguments justifying the fatal persecution of the troubled Cummings.

Had Greenough taken the tack that homosexuality had gotten out of hand on the Harvard campus and measures had to be taken, few would have disagreed with him. That the judges had to pronounce their summary sentences and let the ax fall where it would—even on a sickly, high-strung boy just days from graduation—shows the terrible momentum of the Court's vindictive juggernaut. Having dealt with the unpleasant business of a dead student's father, Greenough immediately resumed his notes to the Appointments Office, stigmatizing for all time any of the Court's guilty students who attempted to obtain documentation of their years at Harvard.

Cyril Wilcox's suicide on May 13, 1920, brought to light the homosexual group among Harvard undergraduates and triggered the inquisition. *(Courtesy of Harvard University Archives, HUD 322.01)*

The Wilcox house on High Street in Fall River, where Cyril's body was found. *(William Wright)*

The tragedy plagued Wilcox family: a young Cyril; his formidable mother, Mary; his older brother, Lester; and his father, George. *(Courtesy of Richard Wilcox, from his personal collection)*

Lester Wilcox, Cyril's older brother, in shock and grief over his death, blamed Harvard for his brother's homosexuality and suicide. *(Courtesy of Richard Wilcox, from his personal collection)*

Harry Dreyfus, Cyril's lover, received a stormy visit from Lester Wilcox. *(Courtesy of Harvard University Archives, UA III 5.33, Box 601)*

A. Lawrence Lowell, Harvard's president from 1909 to 1933, was the primary force behind the harsh actions of the Secret Court. John Singer Sargent's portrait captures Lowell's divine-right imperiousness. *(Courtesy of Harvard University Portrait Collection, H357)*

Ernest Weeks Roberts, the leader of the undergraduate gay group and, in Harvard's eyes, enemy number one. *(Courtesy of Harvard University Archives, HUD 322.25)*

Perkins Hall today, where eighty-five years earlier Ernest Roberts held his scandalous parties. *(William Wright)*

A group of relatives pooled resources to send Kenneth Day through Harvard, where he excelled at both academics and sports. *(Courtesy of Harvard University Archives, HUD 322.25)*

Joseph Lumbard was an excellent student and popular with both faculty and undergraduates. *(Courtesy of Harvard University Archives, HUD 322.25)*

Keith Smerage's mother ran an inn in Topsfield, Massachusetts, and struggled to finance her son's education. *(Courtesy of Harvard University Archives, HUD 321.25)*

From a wealthy Buffalo family, Nathaniel Wolff was headed for Harvard Medical School. *(Courtesy of Harvard University Archives, HUD 319.01)*

Unlike most of the Court's victims,
Harold Saxton had graduated from
Harvard (in 1919) and supported himself
tutoring undergraduates. *(Courtesy of
Harvard University Archives, HUD 319.01)*

CUMMINGS, EUGENE RAPHAEL. Age: 17. Gore C 21
Home Address: 631 Middle St., Fall River, Mass.
College Address 1915–16: Fairfax 29–30
Preparatory School: B. M. C. Durfee High School

Just days before completing his five-year dentistry course, Eugene Cummings killed himself on learning he was expelled. *(Courtesy of Harvard
University Archives, HUD 318.01)*

ON SHOULD RANK THI[...]

STS

U. S. TO COLLECT UNPAID TAXES

Thousands Due Uncle Sam From Delinquent Boston Firms in Luxury Class

The Internal Revenue Department will receive thousands of dollars additional revenue from luxury taxes omitted by the taxpayers in their original returns, Collector Mitchell announces, as the result of a collection drive being conducted in Boston by Assistant Supervisor H. L. Cather of Washington.

One candy firm alone, the collector said, will pay $20,000 in overlooked taxes and $8,000 in penalties. Another candy maker will pay $5,000 and penalties. Several places will be forced to pay about $1,000 additional taxes.

Although the taxpayers will be compelled to pay the fixed penalties, they were absolved of any intent to defraud the government. Every case of underpaid taxes was said to be due to a misunderstanding. The penalties are 5 per cent. additional if not paid when due, and 1 per cent. for every month allowed to lapse.

All of the taxpayers found delinquent had made a return and paid taxes. Heads of several business houses, in the luxury class voluntarily called at Internal Revenue headquarters to discuss the tax return liabilities with Federal agents.

Massachusetts drinks the most soda water, is the best patron of theatres, and her corporations have the greatest amount of capital stock of any State in the Union, according to facts revealed in records forwarded to John J. Mitchell, collector for Massachusetts. The records covered the various luxury and excise taxes collected by the government.

In transportation taxes Massachusetts is second; in the amount of excise taxes paid by manufacturers, third; in jewelry, fifth; and in wearing apparel, thirty-fourth.

BRIDGE AT WELLINGTON CLOSED TO SHIPPING

The Boston & Maine Railroad bridge over the Mystic River between East Somerville and the Wellington stations on the Western Division, will be closed to shipping for one month beginning June 25. Trains will be operated over the bridge but it will not be opened for vessels to pass through. The railroad will install steel trusses in place of the wooden ones at present in use. Orders for the work have been issued by the Department of Public Works, division of waterways and public lands of the Commonwealth of Massachusetts.

Weds Another While Wooer Is Away

MRS. GILBERT W. L. SORTERUP.

"Congratulations upon your marriage to Mr. ———."

"To Mr. Gilbert Sorterup," chimed in the charming young lady addressed, who, until recently, was Miss Ruth Matilda Anderson.

"Mr. Sorterup?" they queried.

"Why, I thought it was going to be ———."

"Never mind what you thought. I'm Mrs. Sorterup, and I'm leaving on my honeymoon." And the erstwhile Miss Anderson hastened

2 HARVARD [...] DIE SUDDEN[...]

One a Suicide and the O[...] Accidentally Killed by Gas

The sudden deaths of two Har[...] men, both residents of Fall [...] and inseparable companions, and [...] an admitted suicide, are being [...] vestigated.

The deaths occurred within a [...] days of each other, one at the [...] man Infirmary at Cambridge and [...] other at the home of one of the [...]

The last to succumb was Eu[...] Raphael Cummings, aged tw[...] three, of No. 631 Middle street, [...] River, a student at the Harva[...] Dental School.

He died at the Infirmary after [...] ing corrosive sublimate tablets w[...] suicidal intent, according to [...] David Dow, medical examiner [...] Middlesex County.

Cummings' suicide, the news of [...] was not made public, followed the [...] of his friend, Cyril B. Wilcox, age[...] of No. 637 High street, Fall Rive[...] student in the academic course at [...] vard. Young Wilcox' body was fo[...] in a gas-filled room at his home, [...] according to the medical examine[...] has death was accidental.

According to friends of the two in [...] River, Cummings, who was said to h[...] been mentally unbalanced, told a s[...] of an alleged inquisition which [...] claimed was held in the college o[...] following Wilcox' death.

He said that he was taken into [...] office, which was shrouded in gloo[...] with but one light dimly burning, [...] there questioned exhaustively. [...] story, which was denied by the co[...] authorities, was said to have spr[...] from his disordered mind.

Dr. Roger I. Lee, professor [...] hygiene, said Cummings, who h[...] been acting in a queer manner, h[...] the poison tablets during the [...] school examination period. He [...] that the man had been a student [...] years, taking a course that ordin[...] could have been finished in thre[...] left a mother, sister and brot[...] Wilcox was the son of Mr. and M[...] George B. Wilcox.

WAR VETERAN MARRIES MELROSE "FARMERETTE"

Miss Mazie Isabel Howard, daug[...] ter of ex-Alderman and Mrs. Jam[...] V. Howard, No. 45 Vinton street, Me[...] rose, and Victor L. Klefbeck, a Bosto[...] newspaper man, were married toda[...]

---

ved in ding e

twenty wrence nforce- Carthy, its are

ts will al ar-

f Mc- an in- in this is be- he men ief Mc- Director fer the

reveal er sus- ntimate to say, pects is liquor

om the Michael Essex d. Mr. ue offi- ty when known o Law

TE 97,131

all, wife 48 Com- tate ap- personal. t $965,- 99 and 15. Lib- war in- $161,000 ry: pic- : furni- -a-brac, s $3,565; 610.30.

O PLACE

am has the Re- gress in h Con- t, now he had nination

A sole article in *The Boston American*, which sensed a mystery, was the only time the operations of the Secret Court came close to being revealed to the public. *(Courtesy of Boston Public Library)*

The ever-optimistic Keith Smerage in his family's inn, The Homestead, after leaving Harvard. *(Courtesy of Topsfield Historical Society)*

A building, now out of use, at the Taunton State Hospital for the Insane. *(William Wright)*

Part Two

SURVIVING

HARVARD

12

Settling Dust

———◆———

IN THE DAYS following the conclusion of the Secret Court's formal proceedings, Lawrence Lowell resumed his principal task: presiding over the administration of Harvard, planning for its future, and pondering the direction of Western civilization. Foremost among these outside interests was his eagerness to defeat the Democratic candidate for president, James M. Cox, a cause that succeeded the following November with the election of Republican Warren G. Harding.

Six years later Lowell would emerge briefly into the national political spotlight when he accepted an appointment by the Massachusetts governor to head a three-man commission to review the robbery-murder convictions of anarchists Nicola Sacco and Bartolomeo Vanzetti, one of the most politically charged prosecutions in American history. When the two men were convicted in 1921, the liberal-minded throughout America and Europe—long convinced the case was an anti-radical, anti-foreigner, anti-poor lynching—erupted with protests and demonstrations.

Appeals dragged on for years, with many of the day's most prominent artists and intellectuals making public appeals on behalf of the two men. When Lowell and his commission had carefully reviewed the testimony, they concluded that Sacco was definitely guilty and that Vanzetti was complicit. That this has also become the verdict of history, primarily due to death-bed confessions by two people closely involved and by more modern forensic evidence, does not lessen the fact that at the time Lowell, in his decision, was going up against a tidal wave of the most "enlightened" thought. What little standing he had with the educated and liberal elite after instituting racial and ethnic quotas for students in 1922 was destroyed by his refusal to intercede on behalf of Sacco and Vanzetti.

The deans and Dr. Lee went back to their administrative duties and their chosen intellectual fields. Regent Luce could now concentrate on his business interests, with occasional deliberations about Harvard's long-range decisions. The expelled boys and their families set out to reconstruct their shattered lives.

If the men of the Court congratulated themselves about nothing else, they surely rejoiced about their expulsion of Ernest Weeks Roberts, whom they had come to see as the vibrant wellspring of all their problems. For them, Roberts with his den of depravity in Perkins Hall was the Pied Piper of gay sex, merrily leading innocent Harvard boys to their doom. With Roberts gone, at least half their problems were solved. As it turned out, getting him off the campus proved more difficult than anticipated.

Although Greenough in his note of June 4 had forcefully asked Roberts to tell his father the full story behind his expulsion, he had little confidence that Roberts would do so. To back up this request, Greenough sent Congressman Roberts a letter on June 7 that came quite close to spelling out his son's transgression, but the fastidious dean could not bring himself to enunciate the crime clearly. In fact, the letter, which concerns a matter of the utmost importance, is remarkable for its Victorian coyness.

My Dear Mr. Roberts,

I am greatly distressed and embarrassed to have to tell you that your son, Ernest, has involved himself in difficulties so extraordinarily grave that the President has instructed me to advise your son to leave the University at once. I have communicated these instructions to your son, and he is leaving. He has promised to tell you all about the matter, and I hope he will tell you the whole truth. His offense has nothing to do with low scholarship; it is not gambling, or drink or ordinary sexual intercourse. If he does not confess to something worse than these things, he will not have told you the whole story. In that case, I can of course tell you all about it, if you will come to Cambridge.

 The investigation, which was precipitated by the suicide of another student involved in this matter, has been conducted with great care; the evidence is absolutely conclusive, and, in point of fact, your son has confessed his guilt. The matter is altogether the most distressing that has occurred since I have been in office.

Yours very truly,
C. N. Greenough

Greenough's twenty-questions approach to naming the crime approaches the comic. The love that dare not speak its name had become the love that must be guessed by clues and hints: worse than adultery but less grave than patricide; in the nature of sexual activity, but not natural. The underlining of the adjective "ordinary" in reference to intercourse says that when considering sexuality, the questioner is getting warm. While "not ordinary" narrows the range, it still leaves open so many nasty possibilities—bestiality, child abuse, necrophilia. Congressman Roberts, even if as homophobic as Greenough, must have been relieved to learn his son was merely homosexual.

In a note to Ernest Roberts the same day, Greenough wrote:

The letter that I am sending to your father this morning, although it does not tell him everything, necessitates your telling him everything. I beg you on every ground not to attempt to evade this disagreeable task.

Your truly, C. N. Greenough

The fervor in Greenough's tone suggests that he was intent not so much on giving the father a clear picture of his son's wickedness, but rather on having him understand why Harvard had no choice but to expel his son. On June 8, Congressman Roberts wrote Greenough that he had received his letter and also one from his son that *gives the substance of your letter of the 7th, without going into details which he promises to give when he gets home.*

If you are a parent, you will understand how this dreadful news has upset me, far more on the boy's account than on my own. He writes that the practices were discontinued about last Christmas time. Will you please inform me if your investigations bear out this statement.

In the margin next to this request Greenough wrote, "Afraid this is not true." Congressman Roberts also asked to be informed if the practices originated in his son's fraternity and, if so, who in particular was to blame. In the margin, Greenough wrote that the practices did not start at the fraternity but were instigated by "a man in Boston." The father also asked if this "deplorable affair" was to be made public. Next to this question in the typed letter, Greenough wrote in large letters, "NO!" On June 10, Greenough wrote a letter based on his marginal notes, to which he added that Ernest appeared to have taken up these "atrocious habits" in school. Harvard, in other words, was not to blame.

On June 12, Greenough wrote another note to Roberts's father, this one abrupt, with no salutation or closing cordiality or words of commiseration:

Mr. Roberts,
Your son, Ernest Roberts, is still in Cambridge, in spite of our instructions. Strongly urge that you send for him or come for him yourself at once. He has been ordered to leave Cambridge today. Consequences of disobedience of this order would be most serious.

C. N. Greenough

Anyone unaccustomed to the might and majesty of Harvard might be struck by the dean's demand that Roberts immediately leave not just Harvard, but Cambridge. In all probability, had Roberts quit classes but rented a room off Harvard Square, that would have been totally unacceptable to the Court, but it is hard to see how they had the authority to make this demand. Cambridge was still part of the continental United States and Roberts was still a citizen. When dealing with Harvard, however, geographical boundaries meant little; a higher sovereignty—uncodified and ineffable—magically spread for a radius of at least three miles.

Letters concerning the removal of Ernest Roberts from Cambridge were now crossing each other in the mail. Congressman Roberts wrote an apologetic note saying neither he nor his son understood that young Roberts would not be given time to clear his possessions from his room. A truck had been arranged for, but the items had to be prepared for moving, etc. If Ernest was not allowed to organize his things and meet the truck at the room, the father said he would have to do it himself. Greenough wrote back that when Ernest was dismissed from Harvard by President Lowell, he was told to leave "at once." Then Greenough, clearly out of patience, added. "Apparently these last two words did not sink in." But he quickly changed tone: "I would not for anything force you to come on to attend to closing up his room." Greenough's fury at Roberts was at war with his fear of the powerful politician.

Roberts was permitted to return to the notorious room number 28 in Perkins Hall but was allowed to speak only with the building's janitor—no one else. His florid furnishings and art, the cause of student gossip, were boxed and crated and trucked off to the Roberts family summer cottage in Rockport, just north of Boston.

THERE WERE MANY unusual elements that came together to bring about Harvard's Secret Court of 1920 and its attempt to purge the university of homosexuality: the suicide of Cyril Wilcox, the revelations in the letters to him, and the hotheaded reaction of his brother, Lester. There was the puritanical horror of homosexuality of President Lawrence Lowell, not unusual for the day (but not incvitable either, as evidenced by the casual response of Amherst's president to accusations of homosexuality against one of his faculty), but surely exacerbated in Lowell's case by the embarrassment caused by his out-rageously gay sister, Amy.

For all the gay activity on the Harvard campus, even allowing for the small percentage uncovered by the Court, there is no evidence that Harvard had any more gays than many other universities. Thus it is unlikely that numbers were a major factor in the crackdown. However, the outrageousness of the group's behavior may well have been an im-portant facet of the problem, which brings the discussion back to Ernest Weeks Roberts.

It is doubtful if any university or college administrators ever had to deal with a homosexual as blithely indifferent to student and faculty reaction to his enthusiastic flaunting of the most minimal standards of propriety. No newcomer to the homosexual game, Roberts knew how sailors and transvestites would appear to the most innocent observer, but he did not care. He merrily used the Harvard dormitory as his personal homosexual high-camp, cross-dressing, straight-seducing playground.

Part of this recklessness might have been an arrogance he assumed by being at Harvard—above the crowd, embraced by an elite, not cowed by the strictures of the bourgeoisie, and so on. And part of it might have been his indifference to remaining in school. Few would argue that he asked for his fate in a big way, and it is doubtful Harvard, or any university, will see his like again. And while the Court was probably correct in assuming that, with Roberts gone, a large part of its problem was solved, when his truck arrived for the Chinese fans, silk hangings, and Greek figurines, there was something sad about America's preeminent university losing what surely must have been one of the country's preeminent queens.

But, then, maybe not. Within a year of his expulsion, Roberts mar-ried his cherished Brookline girlfriend. They settled in Wellesley, where they had one child, and he had a successful career as a decora-tor. From all evidence, it was a solid and happy marriage. Rather than an obscene gesture at the Court, his marriage might be seen as a pleas-ant gesture at their obscenity.

For some reason, the compilers of the anniversary reports of all

Harvard alumni permitted even expelled students to join their class-mates with short summaries of their post-Harvard lives. In his twenty-fifth anniversary book, Roberts expresses guilt about having been so unsociable with his former classmates over the years. He excuses him-self by saying that he and his wife have such a wonderful marriage, the family is so content with each other, they forget to keep up with old friends. After saying that his life will "be totally dwarfed by the ac-complishments of others," he writes:

> Each life falls into its own pattern, and mine, while uneventful, has been blessed with the happiest of marriages. In fact, we have been so self sufficient that we have neglected outside inter-ests and led a more or less anti-social life, a thing that one or the other may live to regret. I think we have centered out lives on our son, interesting ourselves in him and his friends through all his stages.

It is at the very least a sizable irony that Roberts, who led so many students astray, perhaps permanently, was able to step out of his ram-pant gayness like a no-longer-needed bit of Hasty Pudding drag and find happiness in the straight world of marriage and children. Perhaps he hadn't been gay at all but merely liked damask curtains.

BY EARLY JULY the upheaval caused by the Secret Court had sub-sided and life at Harvard returned to normal. All of the expelled stu-dents had left Cambridge as ordered, and had done so just ahead of the normal summer exodus, making their disgrace apparent to every-one in the vicinity. With students scattered across the nation for the summer holidays, gossip about the gay purge diminished, and the deans could congratulate themselves on a nasty job done as tidily as possible.

Their self-approval suffered a blow when a second letter was re-ceived from " '21," the anonymous letter writer who had written on the very first day of the Secret Court's interrogations. The writer, so approving of the Court's mission and so keen on seeing homosexuals driven from Harvard, was not at all pleased by the Court's performance. Once again his letter is typed and addressed to Dean Greenough.

The letter starts off with a reference to his earlier letter on the "Day-Smerage-Say-Cummings matter" in which he assumed an investigation would expose "most, if not all" of the guilty students. The writer is distressed that this did not happen, and that the deans overlooked many of those involved. He blames this failure on the manner in which their investigation was conducted.

He then backs up to explain to the deans the impact their first interview with Roberts had had on the many students ("about 22") who were deeply involved. The news traveled quickly and precipitated "a hasty, and most excitable conference, both in person and by phone." The result was an agreement among those expecting to be summoned before the Court that they would all confess and provide information in exchange for being permitted to resign rather than endure "the disgrace expulsion would cause their parents."

The letter writer condescendingly tells the deans that, had they thought of this, they would have realized how unnecessary it was to have conducted their hearings in "the manner that Cummings described before his death."

He states that at least fifty were guilty but only half of them were regulars at Roberts's parties. The others, although equally homosexual, did not like Roberts or his group and formed "little cliques of their own, and continued their practices within the student body and spreading it."

The writer's implication is clear: by concentrating on the Roberts circle, the Court had missed many just as guilty. This oversight could have been avoided had they only conducted their investigation in the way he felt had been self-evident. He sounds an ominous warning: the students who escaped the deans' wrath would be returning in the fall and would "no doubt continue in this mis-conduct [sic] and will continue to spread the practice until it may get, [sic] beyond you."

Clearly irritated by the Court's ineptitude, the writer hammers repeatedly at his rebuke. Had they first obtained confessions, they could then have offered a lighter punishment than expulsion ("probation, etc.") if the students would name others and "by this method, you no doubt would have accomplished great good" putting an end to this widespread practice.

While many then and now thought the Court's actions were excessive, the anonymous letter writer feels they were halfhearted and the Court insufficiently outraged. He tells the deans: "This is a very serious state of affairs, and one which you would be greatly alarmed if you fully realized the extent to which it has progressed. Remaining very truly yours, '21"

It is odd that the writer had such strong ideas about the way the Court should conduct its prosecution, yet offered no such advice in his first letter. His tone suggests that he assumed the deans would go about matters as he envisioned, and he was exasperated when they did not. So well informed about some aspects of the investigation, he was quite wrong about their failure to induce boys to name others. Almost all of them did.

But many questions remain. How did he know the deans had not conducted their investigation as he wished? How did he know that deals were not offered for information? How did he know the Court considered its work finished? It might have been the first wave of several interrogations. How did he know that all the students under suspicion had been contacted? Many more might be on the summons list.

The second letter raises two new possibilities. The most obvious would be that the letter writer was a roommate of one of the guilty students and had heard many details of the Secret Court proceedings both from the roommate's firsthand accounts and from reports of other students undergoing interrogation. But this would not explain the writer's confidence about his knowledge of the Court's most private deliberations. Even students who had been subjected to lengthy questioning or called back for a second time would not know the Court's assessments of the other witnesses or its future plans, and so on. Although it sounds far-fetched, the letter writer might have been a student who worked in the dean's office and had access to extensive information about both the students and the Court's deliberations.

And, of course, he would also have to have been one with a particularly keen interest in this proceeding.

The identity of the anonymous letter writer was never learned. Of all the curiosities and puzzles set into motion by Harvard's Secret Court of 1920, the anonymous letter writer is one of the most intriguing mysteries. He was not in any way pivotal to the sad tale's progress. He only relayed information already in the Court's possession—suspects' names and the flagrant activities in Perkins Hall. But in his righteous indignation and moral anger he became an invisible Greek chorus, fervently endorsing the Court's mission while criticizing their performance with sharp candor. He lies somewhere between an *éminence grise* in the innermost chambers of Versailles and a Deep Throat in a Washington garage—watching and judging everything, occasionally attempting to manipulate events, and always as determined as the men of the Court, perhaps more so, to see Harvard purified of all traces of homosexuality.

13

The Kenneth Day Story

————◆————

WITH THE COURT'S interrogations completed, the deans set about the painful chore of dealing with the distraught families. But even before opening that floodgate of anguish and dismay, they had the practical matter of inducing the guilty students to leave college with dispatch. Fired employees might have a few boxes of personal possessions to remove and could be gone from an office in an hour or so. Students, who had to deal with clothes and furnishings, needed time to pack and organize transport. The Court was not patient. The expelled boys were told to clear out immediately.

The Court also worried that the students would not tell their families the real reason for their dismissal. On the day of Kenneth Day's appearance before the Court, Dean Greenough wrote him a note saying that if Day was considering appealing the Court's decision to expel him to President Lowell, he should do so immediately, because as soon as the matter was "really settled," Day's family would have to know about it. And "it would be better for them to hear it from you than from me."

In subsequent letters to students, Greenough strengthened this stern line. If the boys' families felt the reason for expulsion was insufficient, he warned, "we will have no choice but to tell them everything." Greenough was confident that as soon as the families knew the charge was homosexuality, they would immediately concur with the expulsion verdict. In this, sadly, he was mostly correct.

Since Ken Day's parents were both dead, he informed Greenough that his family would be represented by his first cousin, Homer Day. About ten years older than Ken, Homer had finished college and was doing well in a junior management position in the New York offices of a railroad, the Atlantic Coast Line. Despite the difference in their ages, the cousins were both raised by their grandmother, so were like brothers. When Ken found himself in serious trouble at Harvard, then expelled, Homer assumed the parental role. Never questioning the gravity of what Harvard considered Ken's crime, Homer took responsibly for his kinsman's "rehabilitation."

On June 5, Greenough wrote his first communication to Homer Day saying that, since Kenneth's parents were both dead, his grades and other progress reports would ordinarily be sent to his grandmother. But he was writing to Homer instead, since "the present difficulties are not of a sort I could possibly communicate to her." He informed Homer that Kenneth had been asked to leave Harvard over a disciplinary matter.

Homer responded to Greenough's letter before he knew the reason Ken had been expelled. He had heard from Ken about the matter, but the cause of his expulsion, Ken "had found impossible to write in a letter." He assured Greenough that Ken felt "your actions have been eminently fair," but then proceeded to undermine this assertion by quoting from Ken's letter to him:

> *I have been asked to leave for what I consider an unjust cause. I could not tell the whole story to the Board. The only thing I can say is I am the least involved of any, and the Board seems to realize that. This sounds as if I were trying to shield myself, but it is the absolute truth.*

In his letter, Homer wrote of Ken's orphan status and the joint contributions of relatives to put him through Harvard. Ken was reluctant to accept this aid, he said, wanting to "stand on his own feet." It was only through the urging of Homer that Ken agreed to accept the financial assistance. Homer's reason for going into all this was his fear that, if Ken stayed away from college too long, "it will be impossible for me to prevail upon him to again resume his studies, which will be a matter of very deep regret to me."

If Homer's aim was to soften Greenough's heart, it did not succeed. On June 12 Homer received an angry telegram:

Kenneth Day is still in Cambridge in spite of our instructions. Strongly urge that you send for him or come for him yourself at once. He has been ordered to leave Cambridge today. Consequences of disobedience of this order would be most serious.

Without delay, Homer went to Cambridge to help Kenneth move, and, while there, arranged a private meeting with Greenough. After their meeting Greenough reported having told Homer that "if Kenneth were to come back in a year or two with evidence sufficient to remove the impression which his recent conduct has made, I, for one, would gladly vote for his readmission." The cousins agreed that Ken would come live with Homer in Manhattan, and Homer immediately set about finding a job for Ken.

Once the cousins had discussed the matter thoroughly and Homer knew the full extent of Ken's crimes, he wrote Greenough a long letter stating that, while he and Ken agreed that his two sexual encounters with Roberts were unpardonable, much of the fault lay with Harvard in placing Ken in a room with such a disreputable character as Cyril Wilcox. When Homer visited Ken during his freshman year, he was so repulsed by both Wilcox and his friends, including Roberts, that he and Ken had thought seriously about having him transferred from the room. The only reason they did not was a reluctance to injure Wilcox on mere suspicions. Homer implied that Harvard was at fault for admitting someone like Wilcox in the first place.

Greenough responded by saying that, before accepting a student, Harvard required a statement of his good character from the principal of his preparatory school. Each student was given a physical examination upon arrival. Greenough could not think of anything else the university could do "without causing serious offense." As for the assigned room, he said that students were free to request a change of roommate at any time and were not required to give a reason. He then slyly and not illogically added that, while it was unfortunate Ken felt he was forced to room with Wilcox, Greenough would have thought that this bad experience in his freshman year would have put him more on guard his sophomore year.

With unwavering grace and civility, Homer launched a lengthy correspondence with Greenough, offering reports on Ken's exemplary behavior in New York and always pleading for his eventual readmission. His importuning letters rival those of Grace Smerage's for persistence and tenacity. Even more than Grace, Homer appeared consumed by the idea that the life of a truly worthwhile, even outstanding, young man was being destroyed. At many times during Homer's campaign, Ken felt his cause was hopeless, that Harvard would never relent, but Homer never gave up. Of all the parents and others who battled for the disgraced students, Homer Day emerged as one of the most fiercely determined champions.

In early September, both Ken and Homer wrote letters to Greenough pleading for reconsideration and readmission to the college for the fall term. Ken wrote, "More than anything in my life I want to go back to college and show it, and my cousin and myself that I am not the cur that I might have turned out to be." He insisted nothing of this sort would ever occur again. Homer's letter is more in the nature of a testimonial to the solid citizen Ken had become:

> *[My cousin] has been with me continuously since the time he left Cambridge, occupying the same room with me and all his leisure hours have been spent with me and I know that he has no habits fastened on him which would justify his exclusion from Harvard University.*

In his response, Greenough told Homer that Dean Yeomans had returned to resume his duties as dean and that he would respond to

Homer's letter as soon as he was settled. Greenough wrote, "While I profoundly sympathize with your cousin and you in this matter, I am confident there is no chance of Kenneth's being readmitted to Harvard College at present. [This] does not preclude the possibility of a conference between us." He suggested that if Homer wished to write further about the case, he write to him directly, not Yeomans, and provided his new address.

While Greenough was invariably cordial and sympathetic in his letters to all the expelled students and their families, he clearly took an interest in Ken Day's case that he showed none of the others. He may simply have liked Ken, he may have been touched by the cousins' warm relationship, and he may have agreed inwardly with Homer that Ken was not like the other expelled boys and was being unjustly pilloried. Whatever the reason, something about Ken Day or his situation finally brought out the humanity of Chester Greenough.

On September 17, the same day Greenough wrote the above letter to Homer, he wrote to his friend and successor as dean of Harvard, Henry Yeomans. He discussed the letter to Homer, which had been retyped:

I particularly want your approval of it, because I do not concur with Mr. Lowell in the attitude the letter represents. I am confident that, unless all those men, including Joseph Lumbard are to be permanently separated from Harvard, we ought to consider the readmission sooner or later of Lumbard, Day, Gilkey and Wollf. I think that before taking an attitude in this matter from which we cannot retreat, it might be well for Mr. Lowell to get the opinion of Dr. Lee and Mr. Luce, who, I think, would agree with me in what I have here said.

Miss Weeks [his secretary] will show you certain letters I wrote to Day and his cousin last spring. In them, as you will see, some hope is held out of readmission later. The attitude reflected in these letters was that of other members of the committee of inquiry, and my impression is that Mr. Lowell did not dissent, but of this I cannot be sure.

When the fall term passed, with no readmission, the letters dropped off, only to pick up again in the summer of 1921, when Homer wrote with renewed energy and enthusiasm about Ken's unassailable behavior: he had been working for a private banking house, Lawrence Turnure & Company, at 64 Wall Street and had taken business courses at New York University three nights a week the previous winter and spring. After work almost every day "Ken would spend an hour or more at the West Side Y.M.C.A where he boxes and does other physical exercise." Homer added that he had "made it a point to join him whenever possible at unexpected times."

To soften the clear implication of snooping on his cousin, Homer wrote, "My close observation of him in the last year has not been from any distrust but that I must absolutely know that I was not endangering others or himself in sending him back to college." Homer said that if Ken was readmitted, he would personally pay his tuition as a loan, which Ken had promised to repay. He was therefore doubly convinced Ken would feel "the responsibility that rests upon him to make the most of his opportunities, and you need have no fear that any future act of his will endanger the good name of Harvard University."

Three days later Greenough wrote back from a hotel in Scarborough, Maine, expressing his pleasure at Ken's exemplary behavior and overall progress. He promised to bring up the subject (most favorable for Ken, he hinted) at the Administrative Board meeting in September. The board, which wanted no part of the investigation and expulsions, had apparently become involved in decisions on student readmissions. Greenough suggested that Homer and Ken call on him in Cambridge sometime before the meeting. He asked Ken to bring letters from his employer, from New York University, and from "any other responsible people who have worked with him this last year."

He mentioned having received a letter from Ken ("a very good one"), then continued in the confidential tone to Homer:

> *I agree with you that your cousin's case is not like that of the other man whose name you mentioned [Roberts]. At the same*

time, this was a horrible affair and we cannot be too careful in
considering how to balance the welfare of the individual with
that of the college in such a way as to mitigate the chances of
another outbreak. All this we will talk about at greater length
when I see you.

Greenough wrote a similar letter to Ken and thanked him for his "excellent letter." In the first week of September, Ken and Homer diligently assembled a number of letters to support Ken's readmission. From his employers, Lawrence Turnure & Company, he received glowing praise from Lawrence Turnure himself: "We have the highest estimation of his character and ability." Then later, "If he resigns his place with us to return to college, he will have our best wishes for every success, and we are absolutely sure that he will succeed."

On the stationery of the R. & J. Dick Company, industrial belt manufacturers, there is a letter from one J. A. Pandel, who wrote: "Mr. Day and myself are living at the same house in New York City, and I have occasion to see him practically every evening of the past year. He is seldom out of his room after dinner, and spends his time reading and studying." Homer also sent Greenough a transcript of Ken's night-school grades, two of which were good and the rest adequate.

On September 15, Greenough wrote Ken that he had all the papers assembled and that Ken's part of assembling the case was complete. He added that he spoke to President Lowell about "the way your case should be taken up," and Mr. Lowell thought it should come before the board, which "as I told you does not meet until September 23."

Since that was only one week away, it sounded as if Greenough was attempting to obtain from Lowell an immediate approval for readmission. Lowell's demurral was ominous. On September 28, a full five days after the meeting of the Administrative Board, Kenneth Day received the following letter from Dean Greenough:

Dear Mr. Day,
I am very sorry to have to tell you that we do not see how you can
return to Harvard. The matter has been very thoroughly gone

into and taken up with the President, whose position in this matter is embodied in this ruling.

I know that you are deeply disappointed, and I have no expectation of being able to write a letter that will be of any comfort to you. Two points, however, I beg you to bear in mind. First, the chief thing in this world is to do right and be of service, whether at Harvard or outside. I know that you will keep on trying wherever you are. Secondly, please remember that if there is ever anything I can personally do to help you, I shall be glad to know it and to do it.

Very truly yours,
C. N. Greenough

There is no doubt that Chester Greenough was very unhappy about the decision, which seems to have been exclusively that of President Lowell. The rest of the board was either halfheartedly in favor of reinstating Day or easily swayed against doing so by the president's strong opinion. The board might be members of a parliamentary committee, but Lowell was the pre–Magna Carta king. Greenough appears to have been the only one who felt strongly that an injustice was being committed, but Greenough was the only one who knew the details of the case, and the rest of the Court usually went along with his judgments. Lowell's obduracy might have been caused by Day's admission of having had sex with another student. Lumbard and Gilkey steadfastly refused to admit this, although the evidence against them both was strong. But if admissions of guilt were the threshold for permanent expulsion, why would Greenough have had difficulty understanding Lowell's adamant stand? In a later letter to a colleague he said that he found Lowell's unmovable opposition to Ken Day "inexplicable."

If Lowell ever explained his stance, he would most likely have done so to Day's champion on the Court, Greenough. But he did not, so one can only conjecture. A possibility might have been that Lowell fell into a Billy Budd syndrome and was especially antagonistic toward this particular student because of his masculine demeanor, his good looks, his proficiency at boxing and track—as if Day had sullied in an unforgivable way his manly assets. But Lumbard also fell into the category of robust masculinity, and Lowell did not object to his readmission. On the other hand, Lumbard had not, like Day, admitted to any homosexual activity, just close association with boys proven guilty.

There is a slight chance that Ken, at the time he was expelled, obtained the private audience with Lowell he had requested. While the records of the Court are extensive, there is almost no record of Lowell's involvement, although he was clearly closely involved. If Kenneth Day was granted his meeting with Lowell, he might have blurted something in anger that Lowell found unforgivable, and so maintained a personal vendetta against Day. This would have been inconsistent with Day's gentlemanly deportment at all other times (although his daughter would later say he had a temper). Still, it was certainly a moment of supreme stress, and Day might have exploded at the august president who was destroying his life. Unlikely as that is, some reason must exist for Lowell's rigidity regarding Day, but none has been found.

IN APRIL 1926, Ken married Gertrude Carter of Douglaston, Long Island. The couple moved to Hastings-on-Hudson, New York, a suburban town where Ken found a job as a bank teller. The couple had two daughters, Nancy and Barbara. As the girls grew up, the Days never had a house, as most middle-class suburban families did, instead living in an apartment on the edge of town.

Ken Day's younger daughter, Nancy, married and moved to Texas. She was forty when her mother died and remembers her parents as having had a particularly strong marriage. "They were both extremely good-looking," she said. "People stopped and turned around when they passed." In speaking of her father's working life, she said, "He was always just a teller at the bank." Her husband corrected her: "He was *head* teller."

Nancy Day reminisced about her childhood. "My parents ran with a rich crowd. We lived very simply but never wanted for anything, so we didn't think about not having as much as the others. Both my sister and I were sent to boarding school. My father belonged to the Ardsley Country Club, where he loved to play golf. He was very good at golf. He seemed to be a very happy man. I heard my father had a temper, but I never saw it. He was extremely friendly to everyone, young or old. He had excellent manners—exceptional. He always rose when a woman entered the room. He was almost courtly."

Kenneth Day's wife died when he was seventy-one, but he would marry two more times. He had no interest in facing life without an intimate relationship with a woman. Day had no more children by his later wives, both of whom died before he did. From his two daughters by Gertrude, he had four grandchildren.

When *The Harvard Crimson* approached Nancy Day in 2002 and told her that her father had been involved in a homosexual scandal while a Harvard undergraduate in 1920, her response was incredulity. She implied that her father had been a bit of a skirt chaser. He had been fascinated by women, she told the reporter, in a way she did not think homosexuals generally were. She later toned down the skirt-chaser allegation, perhaps out of respect for her mother, but she left no doubt she felt he did not have a shred of homosexuality in him. And there are many who would agree that, his two sessions with Ernest Roberts notwithstanding, there was nothing in Kenneth Day's record, at Harvard or after, to suggest that he did.

It cannot be said that Kenneth Day's post-expulsion life was as bleak as that of some of the others who had been found guilty, but it was not the life he would have had as a Harvard graduate or for that matter a graduate of any college. By nature of his intellect, his charm, his looks, his family background, and his drive he was clearly cut out for a higher rung on the accomplishment ladder, but he spent his life in a teller's cage, somehow managing to eke out the upper-middle-class existence that was rightfully his.

Day and his cousin were convinced that only readmission could expunge his Harvard disgrace, but the two years that he and Homer wasted fighting for readmission were a draining, humiliating, and ultimately futile effort. Lawrence Lowell had his victory, and Kenneth

Day never fulfilled his promise. Although it is doubtful if he ever thought much about his Cambridge adversaries, the life he managed to salvage from the Secret Court wreckage was far happier than that of the childless, unhappily married Lawrence Lowell.

14

The Joe Lumbard Story

————— ◆◈◆ —————

JOE LUMBARD'S STORY did not end as unhappily as those of most of the other expelled students. In fact, his life was a triumph. Although Harvard had worked assiduously to undermine his future, he had a long and happy marriage, complete with children and grandchildren, and a brilliant, highly honorable career of public service in the nation's power elite. It was the kind of life for which Harvard worked so fervently to groom its students. As a lawyer, Lumbard spent most of his career in public service, but he was in private practice long enough to amass considerable wealth. More than any of the other students who ran afoul of the Secret Court, Lumbard, with his significant contributions to the nation and its institutions, illustrates the potential for great damage of the Court's misguided righteousness.

Although the deans could not prove that Lumbard had engaged in homosexual acts, they at first punished him as severely as students who admitted to them. In his freshman year, finding himself the roommate of Edward Say, one of the more obvious and active gay undergraduates, Lumbard committed the reckless act of becoming friends with Say and with some of Say's blatantly homosexual student pals. To put it succinctly, he was expelled for accepting as friends boys Harvard had accepted as students.

On June 15, 1920, five days after Lumbard had been told to leave school, Greenough wrote a letter to his father, then practicing anesthesiology in Manhattan. With the usual expressions of regret, Greenough said that his son had been asked to leave Harvard and would explain the reasons when he arrived home. Then Greenough went on to offer his own explanation:

> *His difficulties are, in brief, as follows. A certain group of Harvard students, in connection with a group of older men in Boston, have been guilty of homosexual practices, and one of the men deeply involved is your son's roommate. Your son, though we believe him to be innocent of any homosexual act, is in the following ways, too closely connected with those who are guilty of those acts.*

Greenough then listed Lumbard's crimes: he attended a party in Roberts's room, the nature of which he knew in advance, and stayed two hours. (Greenough spared the father the detail that Lumbard admitted to dancing with another boy at the party.) Second, he was "seriously at fault" for serving as an intermediary by taking phone messages for the most active boys. Finally, he was guilty of having permitted certain "grossly immoral men" to enjoy the hospitality of his room. (Once again Greenough spared the father, this time by omitting that Joe permitted one of the grossly immoral to share his bed.)

Repeating that the Court did not believe Joseph had committed any sexual act, it felt he had allowed his curiosity to draw him "far into this thing" and was highly negligent for not having withdrawn, "forcibly if necessary, from all contact with this group." The letter does not clarify the alarming notion of using force to end association with a group. Greenough concluded by saying Joseph had "had a terrible shock, and I hope that after the lesson sinks in he will ask me for readmission, and, that if readmitted, the rest of his career may be such as to make you forget this."

In an exchange of letters with Greenough, Joe Lumbard challenged the dean's assertion that, should he seek to enter another college, Harvard would "neither help nor hinder" that effort. With the rock-hard logic that distinguished his legal career, Lumbard told Greenough he felt such a position was "impossible," that withholding comment was in itself a condemnation.

It quickly became apparent that Harvard had no intention of exercising even this level of neutrality. The dean's office told any inquiring college that Lumbard had been "requested" to leave Harvard. If the colleges wished to know why, they had only to write to the dean. Not surprisingly, all the schools to which Lumbard applied did write to the dean, and all were told he was asked to leave Harvard because he was too friendly with a group of homosexuals.

In a very cozy letter to Greenough, the dean of Brown University, Otis Randall, expresses his thanks for

> *just the information we needed and it goes without saying we will inform Mr. Lumbard that we do not care to consider his application for admission to Brown. I feel your action in the matter was wise and just and that you deserve the support of the colleges to which young Lumbard may make application. How frequently we uncover messes of this sort, and how disagreeable it is to deal with such matters!*

To Lumbard, Greenough's letter to other colleges was indeed "hindering," and he asked for an explanation. Greenough wrote that Harvard had a duty to tell others the reason for Lumbard's expulsion, then added a final kick: "I am afraid there are not too many colleges that will take a man who has left Harvard under the circumstances that led to your leaving." As if to prove Greenough's point, Assistant Dean Kenneth Murdock wrote equally damning letters about Lumbard to the University of Virginia and Amherst, saying that Lumbard "was not entitled to an honorable discharge from Harvard College."

In spite of this relentless hounding, Greenough proved himself sincere in suggesting to Lumbard that he apply for readmission to Harvard after letting "the lesson sink in" for a year. In fact, Greenough seems to have abetted his character-rehabilitation plan by making sure Lumbard's year away from Harvard was as difficult as possible. Still, merciless—vindictive, some might feel—as Greenough was about Lumbard's efforts to gain admission to other colleges, his letters grew increasingly amenable to the possibility of Lumbard's return to Harvard in the fall of 1921. For some reason, Greenough seemed confident that his tough-love games would not break Lumbard's spirit or, worse, bring about another suicide.

In the spring of 1921, Lumbard's campaign for readmission was in high gear, and he had arranged a meeting with Greenough to plead his case. In the correspondence relating to this meeting, Lumbard asked if, while in Cambridge, he might visit friends in the dormitories or eat at Memorial Hall or at his club, the K.G.X. Greenough told him he should avoid doing any of these things.

In Lumbard's readmission campaign, he produced glowing tributes from employers and colleagues, but Greenough did not require as much along these lines as he did from some others, and Lumbard was readmitted in the fall of 1921, as he had hoped. While this seems to have been Greenough's plan all along, the year of bitter rejections he put Lumbard through suggests a strong punitive motive. Surely expulsion alone would have sufficed to let "the lesson sink in." It was as though Greenough was intent on demonstrating Harvard's power over the entire future of expelled students.

Because Lumbard had originally planned to finish his undergraduate work in three years, he had crammed as many courses as possible into his freshman and sophomore schedules. As a result, he was able to graduate with his class, the class of 1922, in spite of his year away from college. He then entered the Harvard Law School and graduated in 1925. With his life now back on track, he fell in love with an American girl, Polly Poindexter, who was studying architecture at the Château de Fontainebleau. Joe followed her there and, in 1929, they were married by the mayor of Fontainebleau ("diminutive and in an official sash and sneakers," he later wrote). They had an exceptionally happy marriage and two children.

OF ALL THE Harvard students who were pilloried by Harvard's Secret Court, none had as distinguished a career as Joe Lumbard. When he died in 1999 at the age of ninety-seven, *The New York Times* ran an obituary that filled half a page, saying, "His career as a lawyer, prosecutor and jurist spanned eight decades." In the 1930s Lumbard won glory as a federal prosecutor. For a brief period he sat on the New York Supreme Court. He was cofounder of the OSS (later the CIA) and concluded his long career as senior judge on the U.S. Court of Appeals. In 1967 Lumbard was about to be appointed to sit on the U.S. Supreme Court but lost out when Lyndon Johnson suddenly selected instead another lawyer from Lumbard's firm, Thurgood Marshall. Along with many honors and high-level posts, the most ironic surely was Lumbard's election to the Board of Overseers of Harvard from 1959 to 1969.

A few years out of law school, Lumbard got a job in the U.S. Attorney's office in Manhattan. When Governor Al Smith appointed a team to investigate sewage-construction kickbacks in Queens, a key member of the team was John Harlan, and Lumbard was named his assistant. The two men would become lifelong friends, Connecticut neighbors, and tennis partners. Harlan would eventually win historic distinction as a U.S. Supreme Court justice.

As a result of his outstanding contribution to the sewers probe, Lumbard was named chief of the criminal division of the U.S. Attorney's office in New York under Thomas Dewey, later governor of New York and presidential candidate. One of Dewey's most lauded prosecutions was against the corrupt O'Connell machine in Albany. When Dewey received accolades for his excellent work there, he said that his "most valuable asset was Joe Lumbard."

In 1933 Lumbard went into private practice, forming a law firm— Donovan, Leisure, Newton and Lumbard—with offices at 2 Wall Street. His cases ran the gamut from murder to corporate law. Discussing this period later, Lumbard said, the firm's practice has "taken us over the face of the earth wherever mankind traffics and fights, on matters public, private and top secret."

While Lumbard made considerable money in his years as a lawyer, he also did frequent pro bono work. In one of his most notable cases, he won acquittal for ten Mexicans charged with murdering a New Mexico sheriff. From the earliest days of his career, he tried to push through reforms in the court system, often changing procedures with the aim of

speeding up the judicial process. He worked hard, although not successfully, to make the staff of the D.A.'s office more representative of
the population demographics of New York—with more Jews, blacks,
and women.

Although politically conservative, Lumbard frequently came down
against conservative positions. For instance, he fought in court an effort by religious groups to ban *The Scarlet Letter,* a moral crusade he
found "ridiculous." He felt the legal system was in place to help people resolve conflicts, but not to impose anything on anyone. Years
later, when *Roe v. Wade* was being hotly debated, Lumbard went on
record saying it was not a decision for the courts; it was a woman's
own choice. The government had no business getting involved.

The Donovan in Lumbard's firm was William Donovan, who, in
spite of his nickname, "Wild Bill," was asked by President Roosevelt
in the early days of World War II to form the Office of Strategic Services, or OSS, the intelligence operation that would become the CIA.
As Donovan set about the momentous task of assembling the nation's
intelligence-gathering agency, one of the first people he persuaded to
assist in the project was Joe Lumbard.

With the OSS up and running, Lumbard returned to private practice but soon reentered public service when New York governor Herbert
Lehman asked him to be part of a prosecutorial team to investigate the
killing of a Brooklyn garage worker. Although the evidence against
the three killers was powerful, it appeared to be a mob hit, and a
frightened grand jury was unwilling to indict. When Lumbard and his
colleagues reopened the case, they won convictions of second-degree
murder.

In similar cases, Lumbard strengthened his already formidable
reputation as a highly effective crime fighter. He was named special assistant attorney general in charge of an election frauds bureau formed
in 1943. Four years later, at the age of forty-five, he accepted a temporary appointment to the New York Supreme Court.

After several more years in private practice, Lumbard became the
United States Attorney in Manhattan, and in 1955 he was named as a
judge on the U.S. Court of Appeals. He became chief judge in 1959

and, in 1971, was named senior judge. In 1974 the Supreme Court's chief justice, Warren Burger, named Lumbard to the Special Court of Appeals, his main duty being the appointment of special counsels. When the Watergate scandal came down to a series of criminal trials in 1973, Joe Lumbard was asked to be the judge. He turned down the job that John Sirica then accepted and that resulted in the convictions of H. R. Haldeman, John Ehrlichman, and former attorney general John Mitchell and that led to the resignation of Richard Nixon.

During his years on the bench, Lumbard made many important improvements to the antiquated court system. From 1964 to 1968 he was chairman of the American Bar Association's Committee to Develop Minimum Standards of Criminal Justice. In 1968 he was awarded the Bar Association's Gold Medal for his contributions to justice administration. Another U.S. Attorney, Robert Fiske, who had interned in Lumbard's office, said of him, "He was an inspirational mentor to many of the most outstanding judges and lawyers in the city."

REMARKABLY, LUMBARD'S AUSPICIOUS legal career left Harvard's Appointments Office unmoved. When, in 1931, he was being considered by the U.S. Attorney's Office in Manhattan, U.S. Attorney Haven Parker wrote to the university to learn the reason for Lumbard's suspension. Although Harvard was quick to provide the story, his transgression was apparently not as horrific to the law-enforcement branch of the U.S. government as it was to Harvard, and Lumbard got the job.

At the time of this early effort to block Lumbard's professional career, he was young and untested—except, of course, for having done well at Harvard Law School. It is remarkable, if not astounding, that Harvard made another attempt to derail Lumbard's career *thirty-three years later,* long after he had thoroughly distinguished himself as a lawyer, a prosecutor, and a judge.

When President-elect Eisenhower was considering Lumbard for a judgeship on the U.S. Court of Appeals, an FBI agent contacted the Harvard registrar, Sargent Kennedy, on January 8, 1953, to ask why

Lumbard had been suspended from Harvard in 1920. Kennedy wrote
the following memo about the exchange, apparently to the dean:

1/8/53

LUMBARD, JOSEPH EDWARD, JR
F.B.I agent Quinn re. Reasons for L's required withdrawal.
Gave him the facts in the case clearing L entirely of any
question. Required to withdraw solely because of association
with group spacially. L's roommate, Ernest Weeks ROBERTS
one of active members of the group.

sk

Quinn says this information will be buried.

Another agent might have wondered why Harvard felt it necessary
to dismiss Lumbard from Harvard if his only crime was association
with the gay group "spacially." While the tone of the memo suggests
that the 1953 Harvard officials felt they were exonerating Lumbard,
the memo still says that the former student's role in the gay scandal
was sufficient for his suspension from Harvard. Registrar Kennedy,
who incorrectly states that Roberts was Lumbard's roommate, might
have said that the whole thing had been a mistake and Lumbard
was guiltless, but in his zeal to render Harvard guiltless, he perpetu-
ated Lumbard's too-deep involvement with a group of sexually active
homosexuals. The response had the potential of being highly
damaging.

Of all the actions of the Secret Court, this clear evidence of the decades-long vindictiveness is the aspect that most sets this persecution
apart from other gay persecutions that have always gone on and go on
to this day. So great was the university's fear of any former student it
considered immoral using the name of Harvard to get ahead in the
world that the administrators remained resolute over the years in their
decision to impugn anyone touched by the homosexual scandal of
1920. And this in spite of having permitted students like Lumbard to
return and earn degrees after a year of atonement in the vast beyond-
Harvard wastes. One year of atonement could win readmission to

Harvard, but it could not totally expunge from Lumbard's permanent record his involvement in a gay scandal. Even the nation's criminal-justice system has mechanisms for removing crimes from the records of individuals who have, in one way or another, satisfied the state that the crime has been reappraised or sufficiently atoned for.

It is understandable that Harvard would have seen it as its duty to pass along character-relevant information about its students to anyone who asked. But this was done in a merciless, automatic way. There was no weighing of Lumbard's crime against the potential devastation of his ongoing punishment. Although the registrar took pains to point out to the FBI a difference between Lumbard's crime and those of the students proven guilty of gay sex, the fundamental character assassination remained. After thoroughly reviewing his case, Harvard came to the somber conclusion that Lumbard must remain stigmatized thirty years later. It is difficult not to wonder how many hundreds, perhaps thousands, of Harvard students and faculty led active and untroubled homosexual lives on the campus throughout the three decades since the university expelled Joe Lumbard and seven others.

Lumbard's career strongly suggests the necessity of a more tempered response. Free societies can be measured to a considerable degree by the quality of their judiciary and criminal-justice systems. In the United States, for every corrupt judge or dishonest prosecutor, there are countless men and women who strive to maintain the highest standards of integrity in the prosecution of criminals and in the level of justice achieved by the courts. No one familiar with Joe Lumbard's seven-decade legal career—as lawyer, prosecutor, and judge—would question that he was a standout among such crusaders, one who made major and lasting contributions to the legal system. The entire country benefited from his work.

Yet Harvard, the molder of the nation's leaders, its finest citizens, its best and brightest, worked hard to see that Lumbard's career never happened. Had Greenough not relented in his campaign to blackball Lumbard with other schools and with future employers, this talented man could have spent his working life in a string of third-rate jobs, as did Day, Clark, Saxton, and Smerage. Had the government agencies investigating Lumbard reacted as had the deans of Amherst, Brown, and the University of Virginia, his enormous contributions to society would have been sacrificed, as were those of the other students, to a pointless cause, a cause based in moral zeal, self-righteousness, and ignorance. When nineteen years old, Lumbard had danced with another boy at a campus party, so he must pay the price for the rest of his career.

It is quite ironic that a man who spent his life enhancing the integrity of his country's justice system was himself the victim of a gross injustice by one of the nation's most venerable institutions. The pillorying that Harvard put Lumbard through in 1920 and 1921 surely had a profound effect on him, but it did not serve to develop a horror of homosexuality, as Harvard had hoped. Rather, the excesses of the Secret Court must surely have demonstrated for him the misuse of judicial power and left him with a strong distaste for it.

Lumbard's grandson, also named Joseph Lumbard, said his grandfather was "the most fair-minded person" he had ever met. On the subject of gayness, the elder Lumbard felt that two people getting together and doing whatever they wanted was no one else's business and never should be in question. His grandson quoted him: "No people should fear to do what they want as long as it doesn't hurt anybody."

There is some evidence of a bureaucratic breakdown in Harvard's thirty-year effort to cripple Lumbard's career long after he had demonstrated many times over his value as a jurist, a citizen, and, for those who might require it, a heterosexual. While one side of Harvard was sending out letters to other schools and prospective employers throwing into question Lumbard's moral character, another side was honoring him with the position of university overseer. But when sending out their damning letters in 1931 and 1953, the university's Appointments Office was well aware that Joseph Lumbard had been readmitted to Harvard and had graduated from both the college and the law school. Yet they still felt obliged to send out the letters with no reference to the individual's accomplishments or, in Lumbard's case, the high regard in which he was held by society at large.

Although Harvard composed a letter that was specific to Lumbard, one that made clear his guilt was by association and not by sexual acts, this proves the administrators did not mistakenly send a form letter, that they gave his case some thought. Remarkably, that thought included a belief that friendliness with proven homosexuals was information Harvard could not in conscience withhold from anyone looking into Lumbard's character. Those inquiring might well have decided that, sex acts or no, Harvard considered Lumbard's actions serious enough for expulsion, and thus bar him from consideration. Fortunately for Lumbard, the damning letters were received by people of greater tolerance and understanding.

Harvard's current president, Lawrence H. Summers, now speaks of the Secret Court as an "abhorrent" mistake carried out under misguided attitudes of another day. The letters sent over decades by the university are convincing proof that, as of 1953, it did not feel a mistake had been made. Lumbard had been "too friendly" with a group of known homosexuals and therefore merited lifelong condemnation.

What was Lumbard's undergraduate fascination with the gay group all about? It could have been nothing more than simple curiosity triggered by his flamboyant roommate who became his good friend. Or he may have been going through a male-oriented phase of a bisexual nature. Or it may have been a combination of sexual confusion and sexual starvation. At nineteen, he had never been with a woman, he told the Court, and he had not masturbated in six years. Under those circumstances, no sexual activity short of a rape/murder should have condemned him for life.

In his twenty-fifth anniversary class book, Lumbard wrote a two-and-a-half-page account of his life, which is breezy and free of self-importance, yet depicts a life that was both meaningful and fulfilling. He concluded on a philosophical note: "If twenty-five years have taught the world and Mr. Lowell's cloistered young men of '22 anything, it is the oneness of all things, the world and everything in it." Although he doesn't mention homosexuals, his sweeping summation of wisdom would seem to include them.

When Lumbard's grandson was attending graduate school at Yale, he moved in with his grandfather, then a widower living alone with a housekeeper within commuting distance from Yale. Most evenings the two men dined together and enjoyed wide-ranging discussions. One night the senior Lumbard referred to a job he had had in 1920. Surprised, his grandson said he thought his grandfather had been at Harvard in 1920. There was a long pause.

"I was ahead of my class," Judge Lumbard finally said, "so I decided to take a year off so I could graduate with them."

The distinguished judge had drawn a curtain across an episode in his life he wished to bury. More significant, Harvard had succeeded in forcing one of its outstanding graduates and one of the country's most honorable and honest men to do something highly out of character: to lie.

15

The Keith Smerage Story

———◆———

AFTER HIS EXPULSION, Keith Smerage wrote many importuning letters to Dean Greenough. He wrote at greater length—one missive is thirty handwritten pages—and more frequently than any of the other expelled or suspended students. His fulminations reveal a philosophical streak, and his self-analyses do not shrink from criticisms. A curiosity of his writing style is his habit of pausing frequently to examine from different perspectives even his most commonplace observations.

Most admirably, his eloquent letters reveal a fierce determination to "get it right"; not only to speak the truth, but phrase it so meticulously that his meaning would be nailed to one interpretation only. He spared himself nothing, but neither did he spare Harvard. In fact, throughout the correspondence, Smerage came closer than any of those involved to telling his Harvard persecutors that their antihomosexual crusade was unfair and profoundly wrong.

Smerage was one of those who never recovered from the disaster of his expulsion. His future life grew increasingly sad and ended tragically. Throughout those years, however, even when writing from the pit of his despair, he maintained a dogged optimism, a quick humor, and a truly remarkable ability to see matters from his adversaries' point of view. He is a haunting figure.

In the first week of June 1920, Grace Smerage was unnerved to receive a letter on official Harvard stationery. It was addressed to Keith, who was still in Cambridge. Grace later explained that she opened it only because, knowing her son would be home soon, she wanted to find out if the letter had to be forwarded or if it could await his return.

As she stood in the lobby of the family's inn, called the Homestead, and read the letter, she felt the room begin to revolve. Her knees weakened and she steadied herself on the front desk. The letter was from Dean Gay and, without specifics, made clear that her beloved son had gotten into serious trouble and was being expelled from Harvard. Grace first envisioned the destruction of Keith's life. Then she saw twenty years of her own life, years of struggle and thankless sacrifice, negated and discarded with one letter. She felt that she would be sick. That night as she lay in bed, a thousand possibilities of the cause ran repeatedly through her mind. A few of them were correct.

Although Grace did not expect Keith for four more days, he arrived the next day. Trying not to show how devastated she was, she pleaded with him to tell her the cause of his expulsion. He told her he could not. Her pleas led to tears, first on her part, then on his.

Still not knowing the nature of Keith's crime, and with her son shut off in his room, Grace Smerage sat down and scribbled a seven-page letter to Dean Gay. She told the dean that she was emboldened to write because of the offer in his letter to Keith to help the boy in any way he could. This first letter from Grace Smerage to Harvard began a prolonged exchange that ranks high in the annals of mothers fighting for their sons. The yearlong correspondence is also a landmark, to-the-death, but always courteous battle in the ongoing war between homophobes in authority and the heterosexual middle class whose lives are devastated by their zealotry.

Grace started off by proclaiming Keith to have been a model son in every way: she could not imagine what trouble was so terrible that he could not even tell his own mother its nature. Repeatedly she mentioned her perplexity at the suddenness of the crisis, the speed with which Keith went from model son and student to disgraced outcast. Since his return she "never saw a boy look so sad." In spite of her ignorance of the problem, her letter veered close to a defense of her son's "difference," blaming herself for having oversheltered him. But there were occasional *cris de coeur*: "I have seen the goodness in him, the tenderness, etc. and *he must not be lost.* I put aside myself and the terrible disappointment it would be to me after the years of toil were he to be thrown out of college. And I think the disgrace would kill me."

In a postscript she said that she had talked with her son at last. Her more specific defense of abnormality indicated that she now knew for a certainty the crime she only suspected at the start of the letter. She focused on Keith's poor relationship with his father, "a good man, leading a good, quiet life, but [who] never talked anything over with his son. I have tried to be a father, mother, brother and sister to [Keith], and evidently have failed."

It is not hard to imagine how difficult the following week was in the Smerage household. Keith would later speak about the importance of the support given him by his parents. Had he not received this, he wrote in a letter, he probably would have taken the course of Wilcox and Cummings.

Grace did not accept Keith's fate with the same, forlorn resignation. In a six-page letter to Greenough on June 15 she wrote, "It is needless to tell you that this is indeed a stricken home. No home where even death has entered can compare with a case like this." She appealed to Greenough's sense of fairness before going into what she felt were exonerating facts.

First, she cited Keith's acute attack of rheumatism at age twelve, when "he had been always with me, never with men." She spoke of his having been assigned for a freshman roommate Ernest Roberts, of whose notoriety she had apparently learned. She listed Keith's youth and inexperience, which made him vulnerable to flattery and "being made much of"—all making him "an easy prey." She then added, "His very innocence was his undoing, I suppose."

Rising above her obvious mortification, Grace launched into a discussion of Keith's history of homosexual acts, which he confessed to the members of the Court and which, on her insistence, they told her about in full. One involved an incident with a playmate when he was five. (The image is worth dwelling on: three Harvard deans, one Harvard regent, and the director of Harvard's Department of Hygiene gravely sitting in a darkened room in earnest discussion about erotic play between two five-year-old boys.) Grace did not shy from Keith's encounter, as an adult, with a strange man on the train to Buffalo but attempted to mitigate the event by pointing out that Keith was alone, away from home and parents.

She writes that Keith had told her repeatedly of one of the men "on the Board" who appeared to be kind. She asks whether it might have given some hope to a devastated boy if one of the men had given him "one good kindly talk" before expelling him. While this letter was only the second of many, it attains a high point in her prolonged cry for mercy. "I feel now that you men could have done much good had you perhaps had a little less sense of justice and a little more of the spirit of Jesus in your hearts . . ."

Apparently resigned to the impossibility of reinstatement, Grace pathetically has lowered her pleas from exoneration to a kindly pre-banishment talk. She does not seem to realize—and the Court did not make clear to her, no doubt out of consideration for her feelings—the horror with which they viewed her son's crimes.

On the same day, Keith wrote a long letter to Greenough. He seems particularly intent on amending his testimony before the Court on June 3, which he admits was full of lies.

> *I would drive one way then tack back. It was a frantic effort to save my skin, and while I was sure that it was useless, I continued. Had I been as hardened and vile at heart, as I admit I was in deed, I should not have been such easy prey in the hands of my inquisitors, I admit I had no idea an investigation was in progress, I surely thought I was being called in for cuts, and the suddenness of the questioning caught me up. If, as you told my father, the only evidence in your hands previous to my confession, was the papers of a dead man, you surely led me along under a false impression.*

He also accused the judges of tricking him into confessions by dishonestly claiming they had more evidence against him than they actually had.

Smerage then corrected details of the train incident. He denied he was well acquainted with homosexuality before coming to Harvard. The childhood experience that he related to Dr. Lee "opened my eyes only a very little." During his freshman year at Tufts, he never heard of such things, "nor could have conceived or suspected the things I saw my first few weeks at Harvard." The snide innuendo about the university must surely have sent paroxysms of alarm through the deans. It was mere warm-up for Smerage's broadside:

> *Mother said she was warned never to send me to Harvard, but no specific reason was given. Now we know! Harvard has a reputation for this sort of thing that is nation wide. I have heard a most uncomplimentary song Princeton sings of Harvard along this theme. Through Roberts I met the leader of a similar set at Dartmouth. When I asked an acquaintance of mine there if he knew the lad, he said yes, and added "he and his gang should have gone to Harvard."*

The letter refers to Dean Gay's gratuitously cruel remark when Smerage left the interrogation room after being expelled: "Your fifty has shrunk some, hasn't it?" (That comment was in retaliation for Smerage blurting that he could name fifty equally guilty students *not* summoned before the Court.) He then asked that another member of the Court whose name he did not know (it was Robert Luce, the regent) be thanked for saying to him, "Don't lie to your governor, boy, as you have lied to us. Make a clean sweep to *him*. Tell him everything." Although the remark seems to carry more censure than sympathy, it must have been spoken in a kindly fashion because Smerage referred to it as "a pat in a shower of kicks."

He told Greenough that he very much regretted giving the Court even a few names. "To tell would expel them; while a word of warning, a helping hand, without the 'jolt' of ruining their life and careers, would help them out." Smerage proved himself adept at folding into his refusals to assist the Court subtle chastisements of their ham-fisted methods. In a final thrust he lifted the veil of respectful disagreement and stated forthrightly his opinion of the Court. Returning to naming names, he wrote:

> *I cannot bring this upon others. For Harvard's sake you asked*
> *for names. For Harvard's sake I gave them. But Harvard's*
> *representatives and administrators are Harvard. You all*
> *admitted the task was unpleasant. But unpleasantness, I do not*
> *think, warrants obliteration of humanity.*

It is interesting to speculate if any members of the Court, on reading this letter (and it is safe to assume Greenough circulated the letters to his colleagues), had an inkling, however faint, that they might be dealing with a better man than they were.

WHEN GREENOUGH ANSWERED Keith's letter a few days later, he told the former student that he saw little to be gained by another interview. If he wished, Keith could send a detailed report of his connection with "this deplorable affair." Greenough's response to the charge of Harvard's gay reputation is interesting: he did not deny it. "You charge that Harvard is rotten with this infectious disease, and yet you are willing to take the responsibility for allowing a large number of the victims to remain."

Also interesting is Greenough's reference to the campus homosexuals as "victims," then, in the same sentence, his insistence on the necessity of the harshest punishment: expulsion. His response on this point may carry a tacit acknowledgment of Keith's charge. Greenough may have been saying, "We know Harvard has a gay rep. Why do you think we're doing all this?" Even if Greenough's reply implied a public-relations motive in the proceedings, there is little doubt that he considered Keith's crimes exceedingly grave, as did his colleagues on the Court. On this score, at least, there was no hint of admiration, only disgust.

The same day, Greenough wrote a far different letter to Grace Smerage, offering sympathy and "deep sorrow for the boy." He made

clear that any emendations Keith made to his testimony would not alter the decision "to send him away or the possibility of his return."
Greenough defended Harvard's efforts to screen boys before they
were admitted, and he addressed the need for permanent expulsion,
which reflects a fundamental tenet of the Court's thinking: "I do not
see how you could ask us to risk the futures of clean boys who may
come in contact with the unfortunates who have been infected." Here
again is the alarming notion that, with homosexuals around, no one is
safe.

When Greenough suggested that Keith write a letter to fill out his
testimony rather than come in for another interview, he could not have
predicted the result: a thirty-page handwritten reiteration of each of
Smerage's homosexual encounters. The ex-student also told of the
Harvard influences that activated this side of his nature (primarily
finding himself Roberts's roommate his first year, but that appears to
have been a roll of the dice that would probably have turned Dean
Greenough gay). He gave a detailed guide to the bars and cruising areas
favored by gay students.

He bluntly criticized the Court for having permitted one student to
graduate (S11 in the code, but never identified) about whom he and others gave abundant evidence. Not only was this student clearly guilty, he
was, Smerage felt, particularly wicked in that he ruthlessly preyed upon
fellow students. Keith boasted that, of his twelve or so encounters while
an undergraduate, only one was with another student, Wollf, who "was
my senior and I am sure did not learn anything from me."

His letter makes the fullest venting to date of his agony over
whether or not to give the Court more names. This leads him into the
many causes of homosexual encounters, which are "as old and varied
as the centuries" and which, he insisted, could not be stopped by ruining the lives of a few students. He took exception to an inference—
from Dr. Lee's questions about his finances—that he was a male
prostitute. With a surprising absence of indignation he said that he
managed on his weekly allowance of four dollars, from which he had
to pay his carfare to Topsfield each weekend, and that he had never
accepted gifts of any sort from any of his liaisons.

He wrote at length about the innocence of most students and the many predators who took advantage of that. He spoke of the ongoing hostility to him from Dean Gay and said that if the dean always suspected him of being gay, he should have pulled him aside and counseled him, or at least given him a warning. For this, Smerage said, he would always consider Dean Gay an enemy.

ON JULY 10, Grace wrote Greenough another long letter that echoes many of the points made by her son. It was prompted by the published list of men who had just graduated. As with most of her letters, however, the pretext for writing quickly gave way to laments about their shattered lives, Keith's exemplary qualities, and the university's dereliction in enabling other students to corrupt her son.

Some of the boys who graduated were similarly accused, she asserted. One, according to her son, was as notorious as Roberts. How could they allow him to graduate? Was it money and position? In recounting Keith's goodness, she told of his having volunteered as a nurse during the terrible influenza epidemic of 1918 in spite of her pleas for him not to take such a risk. She spoke of his many letters of support, written by friends after his expulsion. Every letter, she said, stressed the Court's unfairness. The disgrace of it all would force the family to move from Topsfield, where Keith was much loved. In addressing the need to protect Harvard, Grace reached a high point of eloquence and sounded a prophetic note about the damage Harvard might be doing to itself.

> *Of course one has to think of Harvard, but don't make it an idol*
> *as I have done or it will break you. And there is always a way to*
> *touch everybody. While Harvard is wonderful, yet at its greatest,*
> *it is not worth the sacrifice of one of those dismissed. One can*
> *harm the name of Harvard as much as another, can they not?*

The phrase in the second sentence, "a way to touch everybody," seems a non sequitor, but whatever its function in this paragraph, it appears to be the basic motivation for Grace's dogged letter-writing campaign. Although she claimed to have given up on Keith's readmission, her letters are permeated with the hope that one line or one word would unlock reservoirs of compassion in Greenough, who would then take back her son. Even while importuning, however, she could not resist criticizing the Court and its methods. At one point she wrote, "If you judge too harshly, it will come back to haunt you one day."

In her last sentence Grace Smerage hints boldly that the deans, in their draconian efforts to protect Harvard's good name, might be doing as much damage to the school's reputation as the expelled students had. When viewed through the prism of the current day's tolerance and understanding, this pointed observation seems obvious. Viewed in the context of 1920, when homophobia was still rampant in America, it is remarkably prescient and wise.

GREENOUGH RESPONDED TO Grace's letter from his summer home in New Hampshire, where he was "resting after a very hard year." He summed up his own pain: "The most distressing thing I have ever had to do was the investigation of the matter about which you write." He denied that money and influence had any bearing on the students' fates, then addressed the Court's overall fairness:

> *I am sorry if you feel that your son was treated unfairly. But please remember that he was guilty of a most dreadful act, and that boys are dropped from Harvard for things ever so much less serious.*
>
> *We certainly cannot be held responsible for not acting on evidence we did not possess, especially when we have asked all the boys whom we have summoned if they had anything further to tell us. If boys choose to shield those who are guilty they must accept the incomplete results of a Board acting upon information which is inadequate because the boys themselves have chosen to let it be inadequate.*
>
> *All this, I realize, is poor comfort for you. I can only say once*

*more that we are all distressed beyond measure at having to
inflict this heavy blow to you. We should not have done it if we
could have found any other way of safeguarding the College. I
am confident that your son will rally and make good. I hope so,
with all my heart.*

*With deep sympathy for you and your husband, and with all
friendliness and encouragement to your son, I am*

Very truly yours,
C. N. Greenough

The next letter from Keith concerned his Harvard records, which
he hoped to obtain in order to get credit for work completed if he succeeded in entering another college. Rutgers was his choice. He
stressed the importance of course credit, as he was not in a financial
position to redo years he had completed at Harvard. Greenough wrote
darkly that if Harvard sent his grades, it would also have to say why he
left school. Perhaps blinded by his habitual optimism, Keith didn't
seem to understand this. He saw his grades as something quite apart
from the acts for which he was expelled. Finally, the whole matter was
turned over to the returning dean, Henry Yeomans, who had been involved with war work in Paris and was resuming the post that Greenough held in his absence.

Any hope that Yeomans would bring a fresh, unprejudiced eye to
the entire affair was quickly dashed by his first letter to Smerage. The
dean had not yet received any letter from Rutgers, he said, but "if it
comes, and I am asked for a statement in regard to your work and life
at Harvard, I shall have to send a reply that cannot be misunderstood.
I must make a plain statement of the facts."

This was clearly Harvard's agreed-on policy for dealing with future inquiries about the expelled students. The boys had a choice of
lying about where they had been for two years and thereby losing both
credit for courses passed and any mention of Harvard or explaining
away damning letters from Harvard that "cannot be misunderstood."
Yeomans had picked up the procedure quickly and unquestioningly.
Having dashed all of Smerage's future hopes, he closed his letter by

saying, "Whether or no you secure admission to Rutgers College, you can play a man's part from now on. To hear you have done so would be a satisfaction to me."

Smerage wrote Yeomans a stiff, formal letter on October 11, saying not to worry any longer about what to say about him when requests for information came in. With grim stoicism he wrote, "There will come no communication from Rutgers. I am sorry. In fact there will be no similar action by any college this year."

Keith had finally come to realize the reach and permanency of Harvard's wrath against him and had given up hope of entering any other school. He added that he was about "to quit this part of the world." Where he went and how he paid for a journey is not known, but if anyone had earned a respite from Harvard's pillorying, it was Smerage.

ON HIS RETURN, Keith got a job as assistant manager of a tearoom in Sudbury, Massachusetts, but he returned to Topsfield in May 1923 to become assistant manager at his mother's inn, the Homestead. Before long, he found an opportunity to pursue a lifelong dream, performing on the stage. He got jobs acting and singing with stock companies in Boston, Salem, and—ironically enough—Lawrence and Lowell. Between theater jobs, he would return to Topsfield, where he sang solos in the Congregational church and was a dedicated gardener, making the gardens around the Homestead the pride of Topsfield.

In the theater, there used to be a joke about the lowliest job of all, performing in a road company of *Blossom Time,* the Sigmund Romberg operetta based on melodies of Franz Schubert. The sweet, melodic show was a reliable crowd pleaser, a moneymaking staple for Broadway's Shubert Brothers, who sent increasingly threadbare productions throughout the major cities of the United States. The denigrating joke could have been taken one notch further down the scale of show-business prestige. The truly lowliest job in the theater was chorus boy in a road company of *Blossom Time,* and that appears to have been the spot that gave Keith Smerage, now Richard Keith, his only brush with the big time.

The Topsfield Historical Society has a considerable collection of Keith's papers and scrapbooks. Among the correspondence is a telegram from Lee Shubert offering him a second shot at *Blossom Time* if he can get to Chicago immediately and "at the same terms." It is possible the offer was for a small part, but doubtful; his later obituaries in local papers, straining for accomplishments to list, said only that he was with the company of *Blossom Time.*

The pinnacle of Keith's theatrical glory came in the mid-1920s, when he showed up as the lead in a stock-company musical, *Tangerine,* which played in a theater close to Topsfield. An interview with him in the local paper starts out by calling him "Topsfield's favorite son" and goes on to treat him like a star, with fawning questions about his early love of the theater (never without a puppet stage) and his thoughts about the current state of the American theater. When *Tangerine* opened, Keith's reviews were very favorable.

His one stock-company success did not lead to other parts and, after a few years, Keith abandoned his theatrical ambitions. In 1930, as the Depression was taking a deadly hold on the nation, Keith, then thirty-one years old, was living at 35 Grove Street in Greenwich Village and working as the assistant manager of a Savarin Restaurant, a somewhat upscale chain owned by the Pennsylvania Railroad. He shared an apartment with a friend named Phil, who was probably his lover. Because Phil worked days and Keith worked nights, the roommates saw little of each other, except on Thursday evenings, Keith's night off. While Phil was at work, Keith entertained friends in the apartment during the day, but Phil would later say he did not know most of them. In spite of the diverse schedules, there is no doubt the two men were close. Keith had taken Phil on visits to his family in Topsfield, and Phil signed a letter to the elder Smerages, "love to you both."

On September 5, 1930, Keith wrote a letter to his mother mainly about his difficulty in crating and sending off his Victrola. "It took up valuable space here. It is a darn good machine, but we have a portable one and a radio, so you better have it." The description of his problems with the Victrola ("What a mess!") and a description of the city heat and the difficulty he had sleeping ("I sleep very little anyway") are all related with his usual good humor.

He then passed along a rumor he heard that Wall Street was about to surge upward with another boom. (It didn't for another ten years.) Even when writing of a directive from the Pennsylvania Railroad imposing on all employees four to eight days off without pay each month, he ended with an effort at lightheartedness: "So it doesn't look like a cozy winter anywhere."

A letter written the next day to a friend is an even better example of Keith's dogged optimism. In speaking of his determination to break into advertising or publicity, he said that while none of those he approached had any openings, this nonetheless enabled him and hoped-for employers "to correspond and converse with all the beneficial results of leisurely consideration." Few people would be so quick to see a positive side to "no openings."

The same optimistic reflex surmounts the brick wall of rejection he met in his long-range goal of becoming a writer. ("I am neither poet, novelist or playwright, as yet.") Although no publication had bought anything he had written, he was highly encouraged when *The Tribune* frequently printed his letters to the editor. "I find that any practice stimulates every phrase—vocabulary, style, fluency, and point of attack and analysis of questions. Every printed letter regardless of subject matter or the opinion of the contents does represent my style and is valuable—to me—as 'sample copy.' So I persist."

After three typed pages, he concluded the letter with a gibe at his typing; even here he found encouraging progress. "I'll call this a letter and let 'er go. Maybe you don't think so, but I do, that my typing is improving. I don't do quite so badly, but it sometimes hurts to try to reread my letters."

The letter contains some uncharacteristic gossip: he hinted at the possible gayness of one of his friends, an actress named Viola Roach. "I hear that she and the new Mrs. Bevins are boon companions and that Mr. and Mrs. present Bevins and Viola are much together on the beach at Beechurst." Keith indulged his philosophical streak when he added, "Life is queer, and its human factors are queerer—or more so."

Two days later, on September 8, 1930, Keith Smerage's ever more wobbly scaffolding of hope and confidence collapsed. The might-have-been Harvard graduate, tearoom assistant manager, *Blossom Time* chorus boy killed himself by turning on the gas and going to bed.

BOTH THE CITY medical examiner and the Travelers Insurance investigator concluded there was no doubt that the death was self-inflicted. In a poignant letter from the roommate to Smerage's parents, Phil apologized if he had said to the insurance agent anything that might have rendered the suicide verdict unarguable. But this conversation took place after Phil felt the cause of death was firmly established. He told the Smerages that no one involved had any doubt, "and was so stated on the medical examiner's report after a thorough investigation here." Phil did not go into detail about his lack of doubt about suicide but wrote, "Things had to be left as they were found until [the medical examiner's] arrival—and could you have known as I did—well, I'm certain. Most awfully sorry, but still certain."

In her answer to Phil, Grace asked if there had been women in Keith's life. He discreetly replied that because of their work schedules, he rarely saw any of Keith's friends; he mentioned the few he knew; only two women, who shared an apartment nearby, were mentioned by name. Surely Phil was aware that Grace was asking, however delicately, if he was seeing any woman in particular, and the unspoken answer was no. Phil concluded this paragraph by saying, "No one was really close to him." Then next to that typed sentence is the handwritten insertion "—except myself—I must add." If Phil was Keith's lover, this last-minute addition to the letter could be a demonstration of a poignant dilemma: whether to portray the deceased to his parents as a friendless loner or as one whose only intimate companion was another male.

The Smerages in their earlier letter to Phil had raised the possibility of foul play. He responded, "Please don't think about it. It's hard enough all around and could not possibly have happened. Let's just go on knowing that it was a momentary mental lapse."

Grace Smerage, who had dedicated her life to her son and who had suffered greatly because of Harvard's vendetta and her son's predilections, was still hoping, even after his death, that her precious boy had straightened himself out, that perhaps he had found the girl he had said, a few days prior to his summons by the Secret Court, he hoped to find. But ten years later, the obviously bright and perhaps talented Keith, overwhelmed by the hopeless of it all and unable to get a career going, with a pathetic bag of accomplishments and one monumental failure, had decided to call it a day.

Of course the suicide of Keith Smerage cannot be blamed directly on Harvard's Secret Court. But if the glory of a Harvard degree is held against the disgrace of a Harvard expulsion, it is hard to avoid the conclusion that his college disaster contributed strongly to his woefully unsuccessful life. Had his interest in the theater been combined with the luster of a Harvard education, he might have slid easily into producing, directing, or managing—as did Stanley Gilkey. But the devastation brought to him and his family by his expulsion surely stigmatized him as a failure, if not to all the world, surely to himself. It was not the sort of disaster that is easily forgotten. If Keith was in any danger of forgetting, he had the constant spectacle of his shattered parents and their "stricken" home.

Compared to many in 1930, Keith Smerage was not so badly off. He had a job, an apartment, friends, and an adoring family. He even had a few slim prospects for improving his vocation. That he took his life at that moment suggests that the weight of guilt he had carried with him for ten years, coupled with his inability to lift himself above his Harvard defeat, finally became too much to bear. His comment on hearing of Cyril Wilcox's suicide resonates achingly, "Oh what a lesson!—better unlearned I should say."

16

Survival Struggles

———◆———

EIGHT WEEKS BEFORE Smerage's suicide, another gay student expelled in 1920 died suddenly. Edward Say, who asked the Court to be permitted to face down his accusers, was killed in a puzzling car crash late on a Sunday evening, July 13, 1930, outside his hometown of Waterbury, Connecticut. He was twenty-nine. Say's death was the third among the boys connected with the Harvard homosexual scandals of 1920, and because Wilcox and Cummings had taken their own lives, it was unavoidable to suspect that Say, too, had killed himself.

The crash did not involve another car and was never fully explained. Say's car was going too fast down a steep hill, went out of control, crashed through a fence, and dropped down a ten-foot embankment. It turned out, however, that Say had not been driving. He was just one of four young men in the car—one of them seventeen, another nineteen. The car's driver, a longtime close friend of Say's, was arrested and held on charges of reckless driving while under the influence of alcohol. No one posted the five-thousand-dollar bond, and the young man was still in jail twenty-four hours later.

To Harvard, Say had always insisted on his innocence. In the months following his expulsion, he strongly complained of the Court's treatment of him. He insisted he had never had homosexual relations—although several testified that he had—and believed he was being expelled for actions the Court forgave in others.

Say's father, who ran a grocery business in Waterbury, wrote to Greenough, asking to see proof of his son's guilt. Greenough wrote back citing "the great mass of evidence" he would have to send through the mail and "the extreme awkwardness" of putting such things on paper. This was disingenuous, as the "great mass" of evidence, at least those bits that hanged Say, amounted to a handful of sentences. Greenough suggested that Mr. Say visit him in person if he wanted the details. Say's father replied that coming to Boston was not possible for him at the moment and again requested the evidence by mail.

No further action seems to have been taken, but Say's mother wrote Greenough a letter that approached Grace Smerage's eloquence in its agonized pleading. The letters from Edward Say's parents both stress what a good son Edward had always been. According to his mother, "Edward is not a bad boy, never has been. He is liked by everyone and has always had the best of reputation. You could write to anyone here and no one would say a thing against him." The letters of both parents leave no doubt of the devastation and pain the family was suffering.

In one letter, Mrs. Say pointed out that her son's classmate, Joseph Lumbard, was readmitted to Harvard for crimes as bad as her son's and added, "My son's father is not a doctor, but he is a good, honest working father."

If Say's mother believed that her son's social status explained the harsher treatment he had received, Say himself thought it was his effeminacy. In this, he might have been right. The men of the Court were clearly disgusted by this prim, delicate young man who was given to wearing rouge. While they thought of themselves as even-handed, they denied him the benefit of every doubt in weighing equivocal evidence or hearsay. First Greenough, then Yeomans, was emphatic in refusing to consider Say's appeals for readmission.

Little record remains of Say's life after leaving college. He did not attend another school, whether from rejections or his own sense of futility in applying. He landed on his feet, however, as a securities salesman for a respected firm, Hincks Brothers & Company, and did well with the firm. He was an active and popular member of his community, on the vestry of his church and a member of the choir. Circum-

stances at the time of his death suggest Say was actively homosexual—
unmarried at twenty-nine, carousing with far younger men on a weekend night. In other ways he appears to have conformed to society's
rules. The newspaper photograph, a formal coat-and-tie portrait,
shows a handsome adult with no visible hint of effeminacy.

The newspaper account of the funeral remarked on the unusually
large crowd that filled the church: "Many beautiful flowers testified to
the esteem and affection felt for Mr. Say by all who had been in any
way associated with him."

Not everyone, not in 1920.

STANLEY GILKEY'S STORY provides sharp contrast with Edward
Say's in that it exemplifies the Court at its most lenient. It also shows
the advantage of being a skillful liar. When Dean Greenough wrote his
it-saddens-me letter to Gilkey's father, a Congregational minister, he
made it clear, as he had with Lumbard's father, that the Court had not
found his son guilty of improper sexual acts. He was nonetheless being sent from Harvard "for the moment" for three reasons:

> *First, he has, by reading and conversation found out too much
> about homosexual matters. Secondly, he has been most indiscreet
> in saying in a public restaurant that a certain student looked to
> him like a man guilty of homosexual practices. In the third
> place, he has been too closely acquainted with the ringleader in
> these practices, and has visited his room too often.*

The letter's hope-giving phrase "for the moment" indicates that
Greenough at least foresaw an eventual readmission. This violates the
pattern of clemency granted only to those for whom there was no direct
evidence of male-male sex. In Smerage's testimony he said that Roberts
claimed to have had sex with Gilkey and added that Gilkey had once
"gotten a little gay with me." Perhaps Roberts was so despised by the
Court that his bragging was discounted, and "getting a little gay" with a
fellow student did not cross the Court's line for eternal damnation.

Gilkey's father wrote back that his son had delivered his "malodorous message." The father then expressed hope that Stanley, "by manly conduct and other qualifications," would soon be readmitted to Harvard so that "the rest of his career may not be stamped or branded, and misrepresented by a penalty out of proportion to his delinquency." This was not the first time a parent suggested that the Court was overreacting.

To say that parents are biased in favor of their children would be a gross understatement. Yet parents are also more likely than nonrelatives to feel anger and indignation at their children for letting them down in such a shameful manner. This would be especially true for parents who sacrificed much to send their children to Harvard or who took pride in their presence there. No one would feel more strongly than a parent that their child had destroyed a rare opportunity with disgraceful behavior. Almost all of the parents, however, questioned whether the transgression warranted permanent banishment from Harvard and the lifelong stigma that expulsion carried. It seems that homosexuality was far more heinous in someone else's child.

Greenough's response to Gilkey's father was not encouraging, particularly about his son's chances for being readmitted in the fall. He said that the Court would not meet again until September and that its decision had been to suspend Stanley for at least a year. This had been the strong recommendation of the five Court members to President Lowell, "who felt absolutely certain about the inevitableness of his decision in your son's case and in certain of the others."

No further effort was made by Gilkey until the spring of 1921, when he wrote Greenough about the prospects for readmission. Greenough told him to reapply in September and to include testimonials from his employers. That fall, one year and three months after his expulsion, Gilkey was readmitted to Harvard and graduated with the class of 1923, a year behind schedule.

Later events would confirm that Gilkey was indeed gay and had been sexually active through his freshman and sophomore years at Harvard. By skillfully lying and steadfastly refusing to admit to any sexual impropriety, Gilkey was able to escape the grim fate suffered by others. His lies, however skillful, were often preposterous. If his frequent presence in Roberts's room was merely to borrow dinner clothes, he must have attended formal events three times a week.

The leniency shown to Gilkey was strong indication that the Court needed confessions in order to inflict its worst punishment: permanent expulsion. Without a clear admission of homosexual acts, the deans, even in their vengeful state of mind, realized their evidence was too thin for such drastic punishment. Had Smerage and Cummings known this and stonewalled the Court, as Gilkey had, their fates might have been very different. Neither boy was stupid, but they simply never imagined the Court would be so merciless or penalize honesty to such an extent.

Without doubt, readmission removed much of the curse from a student's suspension; it spelled the all-important difference between having a Harvard degree and not having one. By no means, however, did it provide a clean college record. A year's absence from Harvard had to be explained, and those seeking an explanation, which meant anyone considering hiring the student in question, was directed to the implacable Appointments Office. Like Gilkey, Lumbard had been readmitted and allowed to graduate, but for the next thirty-three years the Appointments Office informed anyone inquiring that he had been suspended from Harvard for moral misconduct, and if details were needed, they would be supplied.

Gilkey managed to sidestep this lifelong vendetta by embarking on a career that scoffed at such puritanical condemnation: the New York theater. He lived in Paris for two years, working for a bank, but in 1926 returned to Broadway to commit himself to the field he had always wanted. As a Harvard graduate who had acted and done other jobs in summer stock, Gilkey was a hirable commodity, if not necessarily as a performer, certainly as a manager. As it turned out, he did both but veered more toward managing and, eventually, producing. Over a twenty-year period, he produced ten Broadway shows, several of them hits.

Within two years of his return from Paris, Gilkey was hired as assistant to the talented and flamboyant director Guthrie McClintic. Although primarily homosexual, McClintic was married to the first lady of the American theater, Katharine Cornell, who later came to be known as gay herself. But this was insider gossip; to most of the world, McClintic and Cornell were revered theatrical royalty. Close associates assumed that McClintic and his young Harvard assistant had had an affair, at least in the early days of their working relationship.

Whether they had or not, Gilkey quickly proved himself a highly valuable asset to the McClintic-Cornell team. He organized their lives, acted as their manager, and even appeared in one of Katharine Cornell's plays, a 1928 adaptation of Edith Wharton's novel *The Age of Innocence,* directed by McClintic. Gilkey's primary duty, however, was tending the unpredictable and sometimes out-of-control McClintic. The madcap director in Moss Hart's 1948 comedy, *Light Up the Sky,* was based on McClintic, but a friend who knew him for years said he was nothing like that.

Whatever the nuances of personality, McClintic was clearly a handful. At one performance, a stage manager had to be restrained from inflicting physical harm on McClintic for having disappeared before the end of the play to take a young actor to a nearby steam bath for sex, barely making it back to the theater for the curtain calls. This was not an isolated incident. For all their eccentricities, the McClintics were at the epicenter of New York glamour and talent, blue-chip division. Their world was that of the fictional Margo Channing's town house in the film *All About Eve.* They knew everyone of importance of their day, especially everyone "amusing," and they were greatly admired.

Increasingly tired of paying large percentages to agents and producers, the McClintics assumed, and handed over to Gilkey, more and more of the tasks usually farmed out by producers. Eventually they formed their own production company, Cornell and McClintic Productions, and made Stanley its general manager. Katharine Cornell also had an assistant who became her lover, Gertrude Macy. While the dynamics of the byzantine four-way setup might have led to major friction between the two assistants, Gilkey and Macy became fast friends and eventually produced several Broadway shows together.

For many years Gilkey lived at 113 East 40th Street, in a beautiful apartment that opened onto a spacious garden. He entertained frequently and his annual Christmas parties were important events in the theater world. In 1939 Macy and Gilkey produced their first show, a review entitled *One for the Money,* which gave an unknown dancer named Gene Kelly his first speaking line. The show was a hit and was followed by *Two for the Show* in 1940 and *Three to Make Ready* in 1946, with Ray Bolger, a major Broadway star who had been immortalized playing the Scarecrow in the film *The Wizard of Oz.* Throughout the fifties Gilkey produced a number of shows, ten in all, and in 1962 he was named first general manager of the newly formed Repertory Theatre of Lincoln Center under Robert Whitehead and Elia Kazan.

Broadway press agent Sol Jacobson knew Gilkey well and worked with him on the three reviews and other shows. Reminiscing about Gilkey in 2003, Jacobson said, "Stanley was a charming guy and was practically my mentor. He got me started in the business with a job in Chicago. He was the general manager for the Cornell-McClintic Company, which was like working for family. The whole staff was very close, from Cornell down to the telephone operator. Like everyone else, I assumed Gilkey and McClintic were lovers, at least at first, but no one paid any attention to things like that. Certain things were assumed, but no one cared. I don't know if Gilkey had other lovers. He was very discreet, a real gent."

One of Gilkey's closest friends was the suave and beautiful actress Ina Claire, who had a distinguished theater career and is probably best remembered as the Russian countess in the Ernst Lubitsch/Billy Wilder film *Ninotchka.* After leaving the stage, Claire married a very rich man and moved to San Francisco. When Gilkey retired, he moved there as well. Jacobson recalls Gilkey telling him that every morning Claire would phone him and say, "Well, darling, what are we going to do today?"

In his Harvard fiftieth reunion report, Gilkey spoke about his theater career, then invited all his classmates to visit him in San Francisco where, he said, "I am hale and hearty—and swing, too." Five years later, in 1979, he died there at the age of seventy-nine.

Of all the students purged by Harvard in 1920, few had as enjoyable and stimulating a life as Stanley Gilkey. He had a long-term professional involvement with two of the most talented figures of the American stage. This placed him at the center of the New York theater world during what many would considered its greatest period. He was actively engaged in more than a few memorable productions, either plays of the McClintics or later his own. His circle of friends included many of the best-known theater and film personalities. His love life, one can only assume, was whatever he wanted it to be.

Would he have found his way to such a rarefied career if Harvard had expelled him permanently? Maybe and maybe not. It is difficult not to contrast Gilkey's forty-year joyride at the upper reaches of the New York theater with the inability of Keith Smerage to get beyond the chorus of *Blossom Time*. The Harvard degree surely helped Gilkey get past doors and, for Smerage, the lack of one surely kept doors closed. Both men, it appears, were actively gay, so their homosexuality cannot be cited as a reason for Smerage's failure. It is possible that an endorsement from Harvard in one case and a blackball in the other made all the difference.

NONE OF THE accused students of 1920 was dealt with as summarily and harshly as the two instructors, Harold Saxton and Donald Clark. Although Saxton was not officially connected with the university, he made his livelihood by tutoring Harvard students, so his banishment by the university had the effect of dismissal. (Since he lived with his parents in Cambridge, Harvard could not send him from the area.) Because he had graduated from Harvard, however, the university was still able to inflict its worst punishment on him: condemning letters to anyone considering him for a position.

Shortly after his encounter with the Secret Court, Saxton applied for a teaching job at Hallock School in Great Barrington, Massachusetts. The school naturally wrote to Harvard for a recommendation. This was before the dean's office turned such unpleasant matters over to the Appointments Office, so they were answered by Dean Edward Gay:

> *In the spring of 1920, Saxton became involved with certain*
> *undergraduates of such moral turpitude that the under-*
> *graduates were removed from the university immediately.*
> *Saxton, of course, was beyond our reach [had already*
> *graduated] but it is regarded as highly undesireable [sic] that he*
> *should be recommended for any position, especially that of*
> *teaching in a boys school.*

In that same year, 1922, Saxton, discouraged from seeking a teaching job, applied for a position at the Massachusetts Department of Education. But Dean Gay was not so easily sidestepped: "It is impossible for us to recommend Harold B. Saxton for any position whatever." Similar letters were sent out by the Appointments Office to other potential employers.

Determined to confront this rigid obstructionism, Saxton went directly to the Appointments Office to plead his case. Whoever interviewed him there was very favorably impressed with the personable young man. When the interviewer reported as much to his superior, he was told to look deeper into the files. He found a letter from Dean Greenough to the Appointments Office which said, "Make no statement implying Harvard had confidence in Harold W. Saxton '19."

The Appointments Office told Saxton it could make no further recommendations for him. Perhaps taking pity on Saxton, the person who interviewed him told him about Greenough's letter. Furious, Saxton demanded to see Greenough. During the meeting, the Court spelled out in more detail all the evidence it had on his homosexuality. The next day, Saxton wrote Greenough a note that not only admitted his guilt, if somewhat obliquely, but also carried a curious endorsement of the Court's antigay crusade. "I wish you to know," he wrote, "that you are justified."

This is all very difficult to understand, especially drawing solely on the meager bits and pieces that have survived. From his interrogation by the Secret Court, Saxton surely knew the charges against him. And the Court rarely minced words about its feelings toward the suspects, especially the older ones like Saxton. It is possible, however, that he did not know the extent of the evidence against him, and Greenough, challenged by Saxton, would have had no reason to withhold this.

On hearing the Court's evidence, Saxton undoubtedly resigned himself to the fact that his gayness had been proved. At the same time, he had learned enough about the machinations of the Appointments Office to know that this blemish on his record relegated him to a lifetime of job seeking with two choices: either omit any reference to his Harvard degree or restrict his job hunting to institutions not in a position to be picky.

In his fourth-year Harvard class report, Saxton is upbeat about a suspiciously large number of jobs in a short period: "After graduating, I first taught in South Carolina and Georgia. The following year I went to Kentucky then Martha's Vineyard. This last year I am head of the French Department at Hebron Academy in Hebron, Maine."

In the fifth-year report, the twenty-nine-year-old Saxton is listed as "lost."

DONALD CLARK WAS twenty-four when, after testifying before the Court, he was fired from the Harvard faculty and dropped from the Ph.D. program. Having earned a bachelor's degree and membership in the Phi Beta Kappa society at Wesleyan and a master's degree from Harvard, Clark was not quite as vulnerable to the Court's vendetta as those who had been denied degrees. But his entire life had been aimed at an academic career and, without a Ph.D., his ambitions along those lines had to be greatly reduced. Either by lying, falsifying records, or finding a gay-friendly dean, Clark taught for a while at Mills College in California; then in the fall of 1927, he helped the nine-year-old David Mannes School of Music create a department of cultural studies and taught there for a year.

Clark had literary aspirations and wrote one book of poetry, *The Single Glow,* which was published in 1933 by Villagra Press of Santa Fe. A recent Internet search turned up few copies, but one was in the private library of composer Arnold Schoenberg in Vienna and another was, ironically, in Harvard's Widener Library. It is also listed on a Voice West Web site under "cowboy poetry." Clark did a translation from the Italian of the letters of Christopher Columbus and another translation, this one from German, of Heinrich Mann's *In the Land of Cockaigne.* In addition to his writings, Clark also composed serious music. After contracting tuberculosis, he moved to Denver and got a job as the librarian of the National Jewish Hospital, one of the top tubercular hospitals of the day, since enlarged to include all respiratory ailments. He remained in that position until the disease killed him in 1943, at age forty-seven.

Given the esoteric and scholarly interests of Donald Clark, the only field for which he was suited was higher education. Even his books, by their arcane subject matter alone, prevented him from earning a living as a writer. He was a scholar and, from the evidence, a very good one. There is every reason to think he might have become a distinguished professor of Italian or German at Harvard, Princeton, or any university he chose.

He was clearly on track for such a career when he was stopped short by Harvard's Secret Court. Because of it, he never got his doctorate, a requirement for any teaching post at a top-level college, and he was blocked from positions in even secondary schools of the first rank by the damning letters from Harvard's Appointments Office. He was not trying to become a house proctor or gym coach or to occupy any other position in which his sexual orientation might have had some relevance. He was trying to become a teacher of Romance languages.

As it was, Clark's translations gave him certain standing in intellectual circles, but his jobs were minor compared with the career he would have had with a Harvard Ph.D. and the accompanying blessing of the Appointments Office. As it was, he spent his most productive middle years as a librarian in a tuberculosis hospital. His confessed crime was that he once made advances toward a student. Not only did the student refuse him, he reported Clark to the university authorities.

Clark appears to have been a kind and likable man, and his fine qualities as a human being, if not a scholar, did not go unnoticed. When he died, a columnist for *The Rocky Mountain Herald* who wrote under the erudite pen name of Childe Herald and was clearly a friend of Clark's, composed a touching tribute to this unknown, sad, and brilliant figure:

> Sometimes you stare at a typewriter wondering why you don't say what you ought to say. I feel that way about Don Clark. I went to his funeral Saturday and I'd like to write a book about good people and generous people and mean people and wicked people, calling them by name; a chapter about New Mexico, one about Denver, one about the magnificent applied Christianity of the National Jewish Hospital and one about music and wisdom and loneliness and courage. [Clark] wrote amusing essays and quips for patients he pretended were worse off than he. The last thing Don said was "It doesn't seem quite fair." And it wasn't.

The words "music and wisdom and loneliness and courage" lead into a summary of Clark's life and were evidently referring to him. The tribute ends with a glimpse of the kind of man that Clark was, then the columnist quotes his dying words. These wrenchingly sad five words probably refer to his incurable illness, but he might also have had in mind Harvard's crippling of what might have been an important academic career.

17

The Nathaniel Wollf Story

———◆———

THE CORRESPONDENCE INDICATES that none of the parents, on learning the reasons for their sons' expulsions, turned against their sons. All were supportive and sympathetic. It is worth considering the contrast between the acceptance of the grief-stricken parents with the harsh and prolonged vindictiveness of the Court. To be sure, Harvard had to worry about the good name of an august institution and the welfare of hundreds of students, while parents had to deal only with the tragedy in their own families. Still, Harvard's efforts to punish the unaffiliated Boston boys involved and to damage the career hopes of expelled students years, even decades, after they left Harvard indicate a deeper revulsion at homosexuality, a bedrock motive far stronger than the protection of the student body or the school's good name. Parents may have seen their sons as troubled and needing help. Harvard saw only the need to ensure that no other school or employer had to deal with such moral outlaws. For many of the former students, this translated into lifelong punishment. Lawrence Lowell's Secret Court was clearly on a crusade that went well beyond the institution's welfare.

Of the many parents who had to grapple with Harvard's harsh solution to its problem, none was more compassionate than the father of Nathaniel Stein Wollf. When Nathaniel arrived at his home in Buffalo, expelled just days ahead of winning his Harvard B.A. degree, he told the entire story to his father, a wealthy banker, outlining his history of homosexual acts that he had so candidly and trustingly told the Court.

After the father-son conversation, Nate Wollf sent Dean Greenough a telegram: INTERVIEW WITH FATHER MAKES ME PROUD TO BE HIS SON. Given the attitude of Greenough and his colleagues, it is doubtful if they shared Wollf's gratification at his father's tolerance.

Greenough's letter to Wollf's father had stressed the Court's admiration for the boy's honesty in telling them everything and held out hope for his reinstatement. At the same time, the letter left no doubt as to the revulsion with which the Court viewed his crimes. "We wish . . . to help him in his struggle to rid himself forever of any desire to indulge in the unnatural sexual passion which has for the moment beclouded his name." The cry for redemption has echoes of the Reverend Davidson kneeling in anguished prayer with Somerset Maugham's fallen heroine Sadie Thompson.

Wollf's father was not in good health, and his son's expulsion from Harvard for aberrant sex could not have helped his condition. Still, he wrote Dean Greenough an eloquent and measured letter that stressed his son's fundamental goodness, his honesty, and his fervent desire to reform and return to Harvard. The father appealed to the dean's compassion: "I am taking the liberty of appealing to you, not in your official capacity, but as a man, to do what you can to assist him. You know all are subject to mistakes, and the blessing is in those who can aid and advise in correcting and saving rather than otherwise."

Greenough suggested that Wollf go to Labrador for a year to work with Sir Wilfred Grenfell, a physician who had emigrated from England in 1882 to ease the destitution of the inhabitants by building hospitals and nursing stations. Dr. Grenfell did not need anyone at that time, so Wollf went to France to take premed courses in Grenoble. Throughout his time in France, Wollf wrote Greenough of his scholastic progress and his exemplary behavior. In December 1920, Henry Yeomans, who had resumed his duties as dean, wrote Wollf a letter telling him that he had consulted with the Court members and "the weight of opinion was decidedly against your being allowed to return." The absence of a mitigating phrase such as "at this time" indicates that the others did not share the clear tilt toward leniency in Greenough's earlier letters.

Before receiving this letter, Wollf had an even shaper blow: his father died in Buffalo. He returned immediately from France, so did not receive Yeomans's devastating news. In a letter to Greenough, Wollf, still unaware of the Court's negative verdict, said that his mother knew nothing of the reasons he left Harvard, his father having forbidden anyone to tell her. Now his mother insisted that he either finish college or go into business without delay. Could he please come to Cambridge to discuss the possibility of readmission? Crossing this letter was one from Dean Yeomans expressing sympathy for his father's death but also enclosing a copy of his letter sent to Grenoble saying that the decision was made: Nathaniel Wollf could not return to Harvard.

The earlier correspondence between Wollf and Dean Greenough leaves no doubt that Greenough believed Wollf should and would be readmitted. This favorable attitude only strengthened as Wollf acquitted himself so admirably in his time away from Harvard. Since most of the others on the Court relied heavily on Greenough's judgments, the unequivocal and blunt rejection of Wollf suggests the wrathful hand of Lawrence Lowell.

In the case of Kenneth Day, Greenough wrote to a colleague about his disagreement with Lowell's hard-to-explain obduracy against readmission. If the Harvard president also blocked Wollf, it is possible that he was angered by Wollf's greater age. Because he left Harvard in 1917 to serve in France for two years, he was twenty-five in 1920, when his other purged classmates were nineteen or twenty. It is also possible the decision was not made by Lowell but by Henry Yeomans, who may have overruled Greenough. This is less likely, since Yeomans repeatedly said how much better informed Greenough was than he on individual cases. Whoever reversed Greenough's drift toward clemency, the reasons are lost.

With Wollf's father gone, the role of family champion was taken over by a cousin by marriage, a urologist named Julius Waterman. He wrote a plaintive letter to Dean Yeomans pleading for answers to outstanding questions. Would Nathaniel ever be readmitted to Harvard? Could he go directly into Harvard Medical School after only three undergraduate years? Would Harvard block him from entering another college? With utmost courtesy, Dr. Waterman pleaded for answers as soon as possible "to clear up an almost unbearable situation at home."

Dean Yeomans's response is a monument of hardheadedness. He "thinks" Nathaniel will never be readmitted to Harvard. As to whether he might be accepted at the medical school of another university, he replied coldly, "That depends on the other university." Yeomans then proceeded to dash Wollf's hopes of entering another school. He wrote that any officer of Harvard who was asked about Mr. Wollf "will make a statement embracing all the facts which appear upon our record and will make the statement in such a way to preclude any misunderstanding."

Over a year later, Harvard received a letter from the registrar of McGill University in Montreal inquiring about Wollf, who he said claimed to have told "the whole story." The registrar asked how his case stood, whether "he told me everything or not," and "whether his case is really so bad that he should not be given another chance anywhere."

Yeomans wrote McGill's registrar and said that, from his report of their conversation, it is clear Wollf did not report the facts fully. But he could not give these facts without first notifying Wollf. He wrote Wollf the same day, saying he "[could] not send [McGill] any statement unless it is a complete one." Wollf telegraphed Yeomans to send McGill the full record. A short time later, Wollf received a letter from McGill saying his application had not been received favorably by the authorities.

A year later, Wollf had better luck in New York where, thanks to a contact on the faculty, he was accepted as a first-year medical student at Bellevue Hospital Medical College. From there he wrote Greenough a five-page typed letter, a last-stand effort for readmission to Harvard, which had now become an *idée fixe*. Wollf meticulously listed his activities over the past two years, the names of those who could vouch for his moral rectitude, tributes from various employers, his success at Bellevue.

His letter builds to an emotional crescendo:

When I left Harvard two years ago to begin my fight for
ᐧrehabilitation, you, Sir, said to me, "I fully expect you to get
your degree." These words have spoken in my mind whenever, as
in my defeat at McGill, the weight of my handicap seemed to
make further struggle futile.

Wollf insisted he had always been open about his Harvard problems when he "thought it would matter to those concerned. I have
even confessed to my mother, at what cost you can imagine, because I
could not let her continue to hold a false belief in me." With this letter
from Wollf to Harvard, his two-year campaign for reinstatement came
to an end. He was never readmitted.

WHEN WOLLF GOT his medical degree from Bellevue, he interned for
the year 1926 in Zurich, then studied psychiatry for three more years
in Berlin. By the time he had finished his studies, he had been associated with one college or another for twelve years. This is significant
because so much of his later life had little to do with medicine, but
everything to do with adventure and exotic experience. In fact, his life
unfolds like a cross between that of the adventurer Sir Richard Burton
and that of the nirvana-seeking Larry Darrell, the hero of Somerset
Maugham's novel *The Razor's Edge.*

Blessed with an income, Wollf pursued painting in Paris, where he
had one low-impact show. He became a spelunking enthusiast and
made annual visits to the caves at Ussat sur l'Arlege, in the French
Pyrenees. His interest in caves gave way to an interest in the Albi-
genses, members of a Catharistic sect who made a last stand against the
brutal Third Crusade in this area. Wollf subscribed to the belief that
the Holy Grail legend originated, at least in part, with the Cathari. He
became fascinated by the theory of a religious historian, Antonin
Gadal, who believed the Holy Grail might still lie hidden in that region.

For the next ten years, Wollf continued painting while he moved
from Marrakech to Barcelona, making frequent visits back to the Pyrenees. His two years in Morocco brought about a conversion to the

Muslim faith because, he later wrote, "of its philosophical content, its tolerance, its true democratic ideals [that are] a confirmation rather than a denial of my origin."

It was in Spain of the Republic that Wollf found his "true spiritual home." But he made a sudden shift from Muslim spirituality and his quest for the Holy Grail when, in 1935, he opened a nightclub in Barcelona called Gong. When his side lost the civil war to Franco and the nationalist forces, Wollf left Spain and resumed his painting career, living first in Greece, then in Holland.

From 1939 to 1942 Wollf lived in Mexico City and became, as he bragged in his Harvard twenty-fifth Anniversary Report, "the first regularly employed bullfight critic in history." He actually dabbled in the sport himself and took part in a few nonprofessional bullfights. After one of these, he informed his classmates, he landed in "the Bull-Fighters' Sanatorium with an embarrassing, but not too serious goring."

When World War II erupted, he returned to New York and contributed to the war effort by treating psychiatric problems in returning U.S. servicemen. He said, "The work was not as exciting as bullfighting, or even looking for the Grail, but it is a lot more satisfying." When the war ended, Wollf returned to Mexico City and continued practicing medicine.

Wollf never married and died in London in 1959. His lifelong bachelor status, combined with his choice of locales (Marrakech is famous for its boys, not its girls), his fanciful pursuits, and his foray into the nightclub business strongly suggest he was actively and probably merrily gay. Whether or not he had a long-term partner is not known since most of the information about him comes from his autobiographical sketch in his class's twenty-fifth Anniversary Report, printed in 1944 (although he never graduated, he was assigned to the class of 1919). This would have been early for an alumnus to proclaim his gayness to his classmates. (Although one alumnus of the 1918 class came out in a class report as early as 1963, gay Harvard graduates rarely acknowledged their homosexuality in the anniversary reports until the late 1970s.) Whether gay or straight, with or without a string of fulfilling love affairs, Wollf appears to have led a happy and exciting life.

It is possible that the ordeal of shame and unworthiness that Harvard, in its wisdom, put him through for two years, helped him to realize the shortness and preciousness of life. When his glamorous and exciting post-Harvard life is examined, one wonders why he cared so desperately about getting back into Harvard and struggling through medical school. Given his free spirit and his rovings through Europe, Africa, and Central America, it is hard to see what allure the starchy upper-middle class of Buffalo, New York, had for him, or why he so doggedly craved the Harvard emblem.

He probably saw this as the only way to prove his worth to his family, to expunge the disgrace of his expulsion. But once his two-year fight for redemption ended in failure—rude, abrupt, no-explanation, slap-in-the-face failure—he may have said the hell with it all and set out to be himself and have a good time. And like many before and after him, he found that there was much to enjoy beyond Cambridge, beyond the approbation of musty deans and away from the strictures and prohibitions of the hometown bourgeoisie. It is possible his persecution by Harvard's Secret Court taught Nathaniel Wollf to enjoy life to the fullest.

Whatever his motives, Wollf—with his brains, his good looks, his fluent French, German, and Spanish, his money—seized and savored the world's opportunities with a verve and imagination matched by few. If his entire drama can be seen as a contest between Nathaniel Wollf and A. Lawrence Lowell, it seems clear that Wollf won.

18

The Lester Wilcox Story

————◦◆◦————

WITH THE HOMOPHOBIC frenzy at Harvard in 1920, a number of factors combined to bring about the antigay hysteria and its strange tribunal. The exceptional homophobia of President Lowell was an important element, as was a similarly exaggerated horror of homosexuality shared by the five Court members. Some of this could be explained as adopting the attitudes of the resident alpha male, Lawrence Lowell, but it would be a mistake to assume such strong feelings were ubiquitous at that time, especially among educated men of the world. With Lowell and his deans, an unspoken awareness and dread of Harvard's queer reputation surely played a part, as did the damage homosexuality inflicted on the vision of the ideal Harvard man.

Another anomalous element was the remarkable flamboyance of Ernest Roberts and his giddy, in-your-face parties. Although homosexual activity abounded in America in 1920, it thrived in secret, away from the scrutiny of respectable society. Roberts's blatant celebrations of aberrant sexuality in the sacred groves of Harvard—as well as in dormitory rooms and corridors—would probably have drawn the wrath of many college administrations at any time down to the present.

But more than any of these factors, the primary impetus for Harvard's harsh reaction and the emergence of the Secret Court, at that time and that place, was the outrage of one man: Lester Wilcox. His grief and fury at his brother's suicide, his stormy visit to Dean Greenough to deliver evidence of undergraduate depravity, and his demand that Harvard take immediate action—all led directly to the Court's formation. Without Wilcox's supercharged response to the tragedy in his life, it is unlikely the Secret Court or anything like it would ever have come into existence. Sooner or later, the university would have become aware of Roberts's escapades and done something about them, but an entity as extreme as a gay-purging tribunal needed exceptional energy and passion to propel it into existence. That energy came from Lester Wilcox.

To some, Wilcox's demands for action from Harvard, as well as the thrashings he gave Dreyfus and Cummings, might seem excessive, even irrational, but less so when his state of mind at the time is considered. The suicide of a much loved younger brother might, by itself, have placed Lester in a highly emotional state. Beyond that was his conviction that his beloved brother's suicide had a culprit: the university that allowed a homosexual ring to flourish on its campus. Lester was not angry merely at the man he saw as his brother's seducer, but at the college that had been entrusted with his brother's welfare and had placed him in a dormitory swarming with predatory perverts. Even allowing for these aggravating circumstances, many in Lester's position would have stopped short of thrashing two gay men, forcibly extracting names of others, and demanding that Harvard expunge all the homosexuals in its midst.

Anyone evaluating past events must make every effort to view those events in the context of the period. When events are instigated by one person, historians must also try to view them in the context of that individual's personality and overall pattern of behavior. For this reason, Lester Wilcox's surprising background and even more surprising future life will be examined in some detail. His overall story throws light on the thought processes and psychological anomalies churning within him at the time of Cyril's suicide and may help explain his precipitate reaction to his brother's homosexuality, suicide, and the gay circle at Harvard.

Lester's homophobic rampage of 1920, when seen as one episode in a lifetime of countless unusual episodes, becomes more intelligible. His dramatic story might also help explain the sorry parade of militant homophobes, individuals who, throughout two millennia, have been able to fan the dormant fears and antipathies of an unconcerned crowd into savage action.

Lester was no Grand Inquisitor or Savonarola, but his psychological abnormalities—including his fierce sense of right and wrong, his powerful emotional responses, his skewed thinking on many issues, his obstinate infallibility, his intellectual brilliance—would have wide-ranging repercussions. These exceptional qualities would bring him considerable grief throughout his life, as they brought grief to many others besides the unfortunate Harvard students and teachers whose lives were destroyed by his crusade.

IN 2003 LESTER WILCOX'S only son, Richard, was tracked down in Eaton, New Hampshire, where he had retired from a notably varied career as a Congregational minister, a clinical psychologist, and a radio talk-show host. In a telephone discussion about his family, he was asked how it was that his father, in spite of a successful business career, had retired at the age of thirty-eight. There was a long silence on the phone, then Wilcox replied, "My father spent the last twenty-seven years of his life in a mental hospital."

ONE OF THE most important scenes in the entire drama of Harvard's Secret Court was the conversation between Lester and Cyril Wilcox in which Cyril confessed his homosexuality. Nothing is known about the brothers' conversation beyond the revelation itself, but from Lester's frenzied antigay behavior a short time later and from his hotheaded nature, it is safe to assume he did not take the news calmly. The sympathetic hand on the shoulder was not Lester's style. Even if he directed his wrath at Harvard and the circle of perverts it harbored, for the fragile Cyril, who was already dealing with the humiliation of expulsion, a barrage of censure from Lester would have been shattering.

However hard Lester was on his brother, Cyril's suicide a short time later must surely have instilled a degree of guilt into the incendiary mix of emotions roiling in Lester. His subsequent life would reveal how obsessed Lester was with his own infallibility, his own rightness in all his actions and judgments. Yet the slightest thought that he might have brought about, or even contributed to, his brother's suicide would have deposited an insupportable burden of guilt in even the healthiest psyche.

If Lester felt guilt over Cyril's death, he subsumed it in his feverish assault on Harvard's gay underworld. Even with this shift of focus, there had to have been some residue of belief, however deeply buried, that he had fatally failed his brother. Even if his self-recrimination was as mild as regretting not having offered supportive, lifesaving words, any degree of responsibility he might have felt at a brother's death was not the kind of guilt that would evaporate with time; rather, it would continue to eat at even the most robust ego scaffolding.

After Lester Wilcox's momentous May 22 meeting with Chester Greenough, he wrote the dean three letters with additional information over the next ten days. After that, there is no evidence Lester had any further interest in the homosexual pogrom he had launched. Even the anonymous letter writer, so disdainful of the Court's ineptitude, followed developments closely and, after the Court disbanded in July, wrote a critique of its failings. Lester, on the other hand, having provided Dean Greenough with "all the information you desire to put [Roberts] out of business," never made an effort to learn if Harvard had done so.

Lester was busy building his own life. He was doing well with his job at the Granite Mills in Fall River and in 1922 was named supervisor of the entire operation. In the same year he married Lucy French, also of Fall River. His mother was against the marriage on a number of flimsy pretexts, but Lester's son, Richard, is convinced the two women disliked each other from the start because they were so similar. Accustomed to wielding total control over her family, Mary was unhappy about a daughter-in-law who might threaten her sovereignty.

The couple found their own place in Fall River and, in short order, had two children—a daughter, Frances, born in 1923, and a son, the aforementioned Richard, in 1925. Even though Lester could be proud of running a prosperous textile mill while still in his early thirties, he was feeling underutilized and restless. He knew, as did his employers and many others with whom he did business, that he was a forceful administrator with an auspicious talent for the textile trade. He also knew that he would never get rich as an employee. He yearned to become the owner of a mill himself.

When he was offered a much higher salary with a New York textile firm, Heineman and Seidman, he took the job with the idea of making enough money to return to Fall River and buy the Granite Mills. The growing strain between his wife and his mother may have played a part in Lester's decision to move to another city. Things got so bad between the two women that, after moving from Fall River, Lucy refused to accompany Lester on visits to his parents.

In New York, Lester quickly established himself as an asset to his new employers. He and Lucy found an apartment in suburban Montclair and took on a housekeeper, a young black woman. Over this tableau of suburban tranquillity a dark cloud appeared and grew steadily darker. It was Lester's temper, which began to erupt for little reason at all around him: the maid, his children, but most frequently at his wife, whom he increasingly saw as his enemy. When angered by outsiders, Lester acted with even less restraint.

One day when his son, Richard, was about five, the boy punched the maid in the stomach, which disturbed the young woman quite a bit. That evening, her two brothers arrived at the Wilcox home and demanded money for the assault. Lester went into a rage at what he saw as an extortion attempt. Despite his small stature, he gave the two black teenagers thorough beatings. This readiness to take physical action, already seen with the beatings of Dreyfus and Cummings, had also emerged in his professional life. At the Granite Mills he had beaten two Portuguese workers merely for being late to work.

Lester's behavior in Montclair grew more erratic. He ordered an expensive tailor-made suit, accepted and paid for the finished garment, then refused to wear it. One day, having just arrived home, he announced that he was returning to Manhattan for the night. By his own account, he checked into a good hotel, then after an hour checked out and returned to Montclair. He felt no need to explain his strange action, merely stating that he had changed his mind.

After the stock market crashed in October 1929, Lester held his job for the first rocky months, but was then fired for what he cited as "personal differences." He would later say that his company's fortunes had not been affected by the Depression, eliminating economic conditions as a reason for his severance. It is more than likely that his increasingly odd behavior had much to do with his dismissal from a firm that had valued him highly. In fact, his wife would later voice this opinion. It was also a time when paying jobs were to be prized. He quickly got an even higher salaried job with a similar firm, Pope and Early. Here, too, he was fired after about a month. He offered no explanation.

During this grim period, his outbursts of anger at his family escalated to violence, and Lucy Wilcox began to fear for herself and her children. While it is easy to assume that Lester's job problems led to his troubled state of mind, the reverse seems to have been the case. The unworn suit and the one-hour hotel stay had nothing to do with the Depression or his professional life, which was fine at that time. Something inside Lester Wilcox's brain was clearly unraveling.

Like an out-of-the-blue *deus ex machina,* a group of North Carolina entrepreneurs invited Lester to come south to discuss his becoming chief executive of a textile operation they were establishing. Full of optimism, Lester and Lucy went to North Carolina, but this time it was Lucy who derailed their hopes. When they arrived, one of the backers invited the Wilcoxes to his home to discuss the proposition and become acquainted. Given the reputation southerners had for hospitality, it was surprising that the visitors from the North were entertained in the man's kitchen with pie and coffee. After their long journey, Lucy was so indignant at such offhand treatment, she strongly objected to Lester's taking the job. He acquiesced.

While many might agree about the inappropriateness of the North Carolina welcome, both Lester and his mother would later use this as an example of Lucy's willfulness and obstinacy. In future years, the other Wilcoxes saw the new mill as a last chance for Lester's salvation, a chance that had been vetoed by Lucy's ill-timed social sensitivities. They cited it as justification for Lester turning against his wife.

When the Depression entered its worst phase, with waves of bankruptcies, and ruined individuals jumping from windows (a neighbor up the street from the Wilcoxes committed suicide), Lester stopped looking for a job and took to his room, rarely coming out. He would sit alone all day, reading the newspapers and endlessly cutting out random articles which, over the years, the family has kept. Then his odd behavior ratcheted up a fateful notch. In one outburst, he threw a pot of boiling water at Lucy. This was the turning point. Mary Wilcox came down from Fall River and helped get Lester to a hospital, where he stayed a few days and was released. The medical advice was to take him back to Fall River, where he could be near his parents and other relatives.

Lucy's family owned a farm in Swansea, close to Fall River. It was called "the Lizzie Borden farm" because of a distant relationship. ("Everyone in Fall River is related to Lizzie Borden," Lester's son, Richard Wilcox, would later say.) No one was living in the place, and it was agreed that Lucy and the children should go there to live. Their departure may have been a flight from the increasingly deranged Lester who, for some reason, announced he would remain in Montclair for a few days. After he spent four days alone in the New Jersey apartment, the police were called—it is not clear why—and Lester was taken to Greystone Park, a state mental hospital. He remained confined there for a year.

When he was released, he joined his wife and children at the farm in Swansea, but the irrational behavior that had gotten him locked up quickly returned. There were terrible fights between Lucy and Lester. During one of these menacing outbursts, Lucy grabbed her two children and ran from the aptly named Lizzie Borden farm. Lester caught up with her and managed to grab his son by one arm. Lucy had the other arm, and the two adults stood yelling at each other while pulling the terrified child.

Speaking of the incident years later, Richard Wilcox said the tug-of-war had not hurt him badly, but he recalled thinking, This is so unnecessary. What is this all about?

In the struggle, Lester fell and Lucy managed to free herself and her children. Fearing for their lives, she frantically ran with them down the road toward the home of her sister. When she made it to the house, she hustled them all inside and locked the doors. Almost immediately Lester was pounding on the doors, screaming for his family to come out. Lucy's brother-in-law, Ezra, not a forceful man, demanded that Lester go away, and he did. On another occasion Lester tried to burn down the farmhouse that was the haven for him and his family. Lucy managed to extinguish the fire with a broom.

Lester may have had a previous encounter with arson. During the one and a half years he had been at Cornell twenty years earlier, a mysterious fire in one of the university buildings was thought by the authorities to have resulted from arson. Richard Wilcox, although unclear about his reasons, always felt his father had something to do with it. (Fall River experienced a horrendous fire in one of its largest mills when Lester lived there, but his son, Richard Wilcox, is quite sure his father was not involved.)

Another mystery about Lester's college years suggests he was something less than the straight-arrow he had appeared as a young man. He apparently got into difficulties at Cornell for drug use—morphine and cocaine. Lester, along with some other students, was disciplined by Cornell but not expelled. Although Lester's drug troubles provoked a small scandal, they were not the reason he transferred from Cornell. Rather, it was his desire for advanced math courses that the university did not offer. By the time Lester transferred to Harvard in 1911, he was a full-fledged cocaine addict.

Lester's student file in the Harvard archives, now sealed, contains a remarkable correspondence between the dean of students and Lester's father, George Wilcox. Harvard became aware of Lester's addiction when he was placed in the infirmary for a drug-related problem, perhaps an overdose. The dean's tone in the letters is one, not of condemnation, but of commiseration, and he seeks to arrive at the best way to help Lester with his habit. He tells the older Wilcox that Lester claimed to have first gotten hold of cocaine at his father's drugstore.

The dean wrote that he had consulted a medical specialist and asked, "If a boy had been taking drugs for a year or more, would he be able, on his own initiative, to stop, or whether if he were not carefully watched it would be possible to tell whether he had stopped entirely by merely having him looked over once every week or two to make sure that his weight was keeping up and his eyes looked as they should."

The dean eventually concluded that Lester's problem arose from having spent too much time alone. The solution was to assign Lester a carefully selected roommate, one who would be responsible for monitoring Lester at all times and making sure he did not slide back into his cocaine habit. The dean indicated that in order to induce someone to take on this task, Mr. Wilcox would probably have to pay the young man's room charges. The possibility of expulsion was raised only in the event that Lester did not stop his drug use. Even then, the expulsion would be to prevent Lester's habit from spreading to other students.

It appears from a shared address that the person they found to look after Lester was Earnest Hooton, who would accompany Lester, nine years later, to his momentous visit to Dean Greenough's office to denounce Harvard's gay circle. At the time Hooton shared quarters with Lester, he was a new instructor on the Harvard faculty and only four years older than his charge.

The Harvard administrator's letter to Lester Wilcox's father, with its warm solicitude and strained efforts to assuage Lester's addiction problem, stands in harsh contrast to the summary and remorseless expulsions of the gay students nine years later. In 1911, the dean knew that one of his undergraduates was a serious drug addict, but punishment or disciplinary action was not discussed. When the matter of expulsion was touched on, it was as a hypothetical in the event that Lester did not quit drugs. Even then, the expulsion would be to prevent other students from taking up Lester's habit, not to punish Lester.

* * *

WITH HIS WIFE and children at the Swansea farm, Lester's outbursts grew so frequent that he agreed to leave his family and return to live for a while with his mother and father. Back in his childhood home, Lester's behavior was no better. With his mother, he was the same coiled spring of resentments he had been with Lucy. On one occasion he treated Mary Wilcox to the same punishment he had given his wife: he threw boiling water at her. The whole family then agreed that Lester was mentally ill and had to be put away. Since he was lucid most of the time, the sad decision was discussed with him and he agreed—to the extent that he acknowledged he needed medical help. (He would later change this realistic self-view and insist there had been no valid reason for his incarceration.)

With his typical meticulousness, Lester went to see his insurance broker, an old friend, to make sure his insurance would pay out an income while he was hospitalized. The broker explained that payments would indeed be made, but because Lester had been designated as mentally ill, his wife would have to be appointed his guardian, and the money would go to her. On hearing this, Lester went berserk. He leapt up and grabbed his old friend by the throat and would have killed him if others in the office had not intervened.

Since both Lester and Lucy wanted the money for the same thing, the support of their family, there was no question of its disposition. His concern was control. Being forced to relinquish control to his wife made him feel more the incorrigible lunatic than being committed did. If he relinquished the purse strings to a woman he had come to hate, her victory in their struggle, whatever its cause, would be complete. If his wife and parents had any misgivings about institutionalizing Lester, they had none now. His mother and father signed the papers to commit him to the State Hospital for the Insane in Taunton, Massachusetts.

The Taunton State Hospital was a cluster of dark, gloomy, but well-built Victorian buildings on 137 acres of attractively landscaped parkland. The hospital grounds, which could have been those of a small New England college, once sat on the outskirts of town. They now seem remarkably close to the town's center for such a commodious piece of land. When Lester Wilcox was committed, Taunton had nearly two thousand inmates. Due to medications and a present-day reluctance to warehouse the mentally ill, Taunton's inmate population by 2004 had shrunk to two hundred.

Over the years, Lester's condition had a number of different diagnoses, but this was more a reflection of changes in psychiatric vocabulary than changes in Lester. When asked what his father's ailment was, Richard Wilcox responded, "Did you see the film *A Beautiful Mind*? Well, that was my father, a paranoid schizophrenic." His most frequent symptom—that is, his credentials as a madman—was to lash out violently when crossed about even minor matters. An occurrence that would not bother him ordinarily would, on a particular day, provoke a fierce outburst. For example, he fell into a routine of a weekly chess game with one of the doctors. One week the doctor did not show up as scheduled, and Lester went into a violent tantrum.

The most routine matters could provoke ferocious anger. Taunton required all inmates to shower at regular intervals. Lester hated showers and refused to take them. He would agree only to a gentlemanly bath at a time of his choosing. The nurses and attendants, feeling he was confusing asylum incarceration with a visit to a country estate, grew increasingly irritated by these inevitable battles. He was sternly told that Taunton did not offer baths, only showers, but Lester remained adamant. Eventually they had to forcibly throw him into the shower, which led to more than a few injuries for both Lester and the nurses.

For many years Lester gave only hints of his paranoia and delusions in his interviews or, more likely, in his offhand remarks to doctors or other patients. He believed his wife had had him put in the hospital only to get control of his money. He felt his mother was seeking to damage his life in any way she could. He was sure his wife was turning his children against him. In general, he was highly mistrustful of everyone. These glimpses of his skewed rationales were rare. Most of the time, Lester presented to the doctors the face of a completely rational, highly intelligent man. As long as the conversation stayed away from personal matters, he would appear totally sane, even brilliant, and talked knowledgeably on a wide range of subjects.

Always very canny, Lester learned quickly that his thoughts about his family and relationships with them were the areas that got him into trouble. His violent explosions were, he felt, normal reactions to intolerable outrages. It was only when he discussed such matters that others believed him to be crazy. While happy to talk to everyone about almost anything, he developed the simple ruse of refusing to talk about any subject even remotely personal.

During his periodic examinations, the Taunton psychiatrists worked assiduously to evoke some clue to his skewed thinking. Even a relatively innocent question such as "Do you feel your wife behaved badly toward you?" would inevitably get a response like "I do not wish to discuss that." Or "I prefer not to answer that question." These stonewall responses would be for all questions even touching on the personal, from the innocuous ("Do you think people treat you fairly?") to the highly charged ("Why did you throw scalding water at your mother?"). With no sign of emotion or displeasure, Lester would state with great civility that he chose not to respond.

Occasionally he would ridicule the questions. When asked why he had been fired from his first New York job, he replied, "Just put down that it was for political reasons. That's as good an answer as any." On one occasion he said to a fellow inmate, "I wouldn't give two cents for the doctors' opinions." Underneath the banter, however, was an acute alarm system for potentially dangerous questions; when this alarm went off, Lester was highly adept at avoiding an answer. Better to be thought an uncooperative witness than a lunatic.

On one of the rare occasions when Lester talked about himself, he spoke of an episode during his years in the navy in World War I. He was the executive officer on a small ship, and a line snapped loose, cutting off the leg of one of his sailors. This calamity, he said, disturbed him so much, it may have contributed to his illness.

This was a noteworthy observation from Lester for several reasons. First, he almost never admitted he had any illness at all. Second, it was an extremely rare attempt at self-analysis. Third, it sidestepped such highly personal traumas as his repeated castration by his overbearing mother, his hostility toward his wife, his brother's suicide and his possible contribution to it. He refused to discuss any of these evocative, therapeutically helpful, but far too personal topics, instead pointing to the loss of an unknown sailor's leg as a cause of his psychosis.

The hospital tried everything they could think of to break through the wall Lester had erected around his inner being and to induce him to talk about himself. This was a period when talk therapy was not just highly regarded but considered the only approach to curing mental illness. With his refusal to talk, the doctors felt helpless. They offered him privileges and concessions if he were more forthcoming. When he made requests—tobacco, an afternoon off the grounds, hard-to-find books—the doctors would seize on his desire and barter his request into a degree of cooperation. Lester would haughtily decline to take the bait. He denied them the merest crumb of his interior thinking—about himself, his family, or his situation. Most often, the staff would eventually break down and give in to his requests, getting nothing in return.

After a number of years of impasse, Lester developed an even more maddening evasion: "We have been over and over these questions," he would say wearily. "The answers are all in my medical records."

They were not, of course, and Lester's obstinacy ensured that he was denied the biggest concession, the one he most wanted: release from the hospital. While he may have gotten his books, his tobacco, even his private room, he was for years denied permission even to leave the grounds. To win the small battle over discussing personal matters, he paid the enormous price of his freedom.

At first, Lucy was afraid to visit her husband for fear he would harm her or her children. When, after a few years, she relented and drove to the hospital to see him, he came to the visiting room but sat in a chair with his back to her, refusing to look her way or speak to her. His mother, less wary than Lucy, never stopped her pleas to allow Lester to come home for Thanksgiving or Christmas. Finally the hospital agreed to one such furlough, but it ended as the doctors feared:

Lester attacked his mother. Although he did not injure her seriously, the violence was sufficient to end all such visits. Remarkably, it did not stop Mary Wilcox from requesting them. Lester also assaulted his mother when she came to see him at Taunton, but even this did not deter her from making visits.

The many eccentricities and oddities of Mary Wilcox sometimes suggested that she too may have had psychological problems. For instance, when interviewed by the doctors, she insisted there had never been any mental illness in either her family or her husband's. This is at best an exaggeration. Her husband's great-uncle had been hospitalized for severe alcoholism, her own father spent his last years in a crippling depression, and her son Cyril had killed himself. Then, too, there was the legendary Lizzie Borden only a chromosome or two away.

As the months at Taunton stretched into years, Lester threw himself into a number of intellectual enterprises. He worked on classic mathematical problems, including one that had gone unsolved for two hundred years. He taught himself German, French, Portuguese, and Esperanto. He became interested in the last language while at the Greystone Park hospital in New Jersey. For years he corresponded in Esperanto with a man he had befriended there who was probably a fellow inmate or one of the staff.

Lester enjoyed writing and wrote frequently—short articles for the hospital newspaper, tales for children, and short stories for no one in particular. He undertook a serious anthropological book on the distribution across the planet of species from the Eocene period. It is not clear when he began this work, but it remained a project for many years, up until 1949, when it was more or less finished. The book was never published but exists today in neatly typed manuscript form. In 2003 the eminent Rutgers anthropologist and author Robin Fox was asked to read Lester's book and give an evaluation. Fox describes Lester's theories in some detail, then writes:

> Put these things together and you have an account of the "distribution" of species through progressive marginalization of

weaker competitors. [Lester] applies this to various orders of nature, and to human races and languages. He also attempts in the final chapter to account for the evolutionary break between animal and plant life. . . .

This is very far from crazy. Lester is, on the contrary, quite smart, and well informed with the knowledge of his day. His ideas are original and an interesting way of looking at natural selection, which he understands very well.

Fox goes on to describe areas in which he feels Lester's ideas "verge on the nutty," but quickly adds, "Many people at the time held similar views, and his are no nuttier than theirs."

Lester had thoughts on a wide range of subjects, but his opinions were often difficult to categorize. For instance, he was politically conservative, but he had strong admiration for Franklin Delano Roosevelt. In general, he felt humanity was on a pronounced downward slide, and he was suspicious of everyone's motives—whether public figures, the people around him, or his family, especially his wife and mother. To Lester, everyone was rotten until proven otherwise, and the two women closest to him had focused the full weight of their rottenness on him. According to his son, Richard, who eventually got to know him well, Lester never even referred to homosexuals or people who were different in any way, let alone speak badly of them.

At times Lester was relatively content at Taunton, reading, writing, and receiving visits from other patients, staff, and occasionally from an outsider. Other times he was desperate to get away from the hospital. When he had been there three years, he pleaded with his mother: "Get me out of this place." Another time he obtained a key to the hospital gate and went off on brief excursions, always returning before he was missed (but never before he was "ready" to return). When the hospital staff discovered Lester had a key, they were frantic to know how he had come by it. When he told them that he had made a copy simply by careful observation of the real key, they were dumbfounded.

At a later date, Lester again got out the front gate—no one knew how. This time he was not content to stroll around Taunton and return to the hospital in time for dinner. He had a larger purpose. He wanted to see his hometown. Remarkably, he walked from Taunton to Fall River, a distance of fourteen and a half miles, and spent the afternoon visiting familiar sites: the family home on High Street, his grammar school, the Granite Mills. He would later pronounce the city much improved.

Stopping for a rest on the outskirts of town, Lester sat on a low wall overlooking the Taunton River. There, he was spotted by a cousin, who was alarmed to see her kinsman, who she knew was committed to the State Hospital for the Insane. Aside from this coincidence, it is surprising that the woman recognized Lester after so many years. She had no doubt it was he, however, and immediately phoned a warning to Lucy Wilcox, who had moved into a small house near the Swansea farm. Lucy immediately hid all the knives in the house and resigned herself to the terror felt by too many women when they learn an unbalanced person who wishes them harm is at large in the neighborhood.

Lester did not find his wife, but he got close. His aunt Ella, his father's sister, then an elderly widow, lived alone in a house not far from Lucy's. At home alone around midnight, she heard a rare and terrifying sound: loud knocking on her front door. With remarkable courage, she opened the door to see an unfamiliar man, old and disheveled, standing before her.

"Why, Aunt Ella," Lester said pleasantly, "don't you recognize me? It's your nephew, Lester."

"Well, Lester," she said evenly, "what a surprise to see you. Wait right there, there's something I must do. I'll be right back."

She closed the door and went directly to the telephone and called the police. She returned to the front door and told Lester to come inside, then kept him in conversation until the police arrived. Since no one recalls how Lester reacted to this betrayal, he probably took it calmly, but Aunt Ella always felt guilty about having turned in her nephew, who had done nothing untoward. According to family members, Lester seemed much more pleased with himself for having pulled off his illicit outing than angry at being caught.

When his son, Richard, was in his late teens, he returned to Swansea from military school. When his bus made a stop at Taunton, the boy got off on an impulse and went to visit his father. Because of Lucy Wilcox's fears, he had not seen Lester since he was a child. At first the hospital staff was uncooperative, insisting that visits had to be arranged in advance. Richard said he was Lester's son, that he had been away at school and had not seen his father in years. They relented and took him to Lester.

Before Richard said anything, his father looked up from his chair and said, "What took you so long?"

Father and son developed a close relationship, and for Lester's remaining years, Richard visited him often. Increasingly he got permission to take his father off the grounds for a few hours. Richard grew intent on bringing about a reconciliation between his parents. This was no easy task. Lucy, again fearing her husband, refused to visit him. For his part, Lester persisted in his belief that Lucy was the cause of all his woes. From the moment he was institutionalized, Lester continued to believe that Lucy kept him locked up for no other reason than to receive the $250 a month in insurance money, which she lived on.

Young Richard played on his mother's contrary nature and told her the doctors did not want her to visit Lester. The stratagem worked, and an indignant Lucy immediately set out for Taunton. Lester was not pleased to see her, but little by little he warmed to her visits. Eventually, Lucy began a campaign to have Lester moved to a nursing home near her. As he entered his sixties, Lester's health began to deteriorate.

On August 3, 1957, Richard went to see his mother. She looked at his face and said, "He's dead, isn't he?" When he nodded yes, she cried.

WHILE THERE IS a possibility that Lester Wilcox's incipient madness in 1920 contributed to his over-the-top campaign against Harvard gays, there is also the possibility that the trauma of discovering his younger brother was actively homosexual—followed almost immediately by his suicide—may have fed the psychosis that emerged ten years later. Then, too, it could have worked both ways: Lester's shock and horror at Cyril's homosexuality and death may have started him on the downward spiral into madness. At the same time, his inchoate madness may have energized his antigay campaign to avenge his brother's death.

This theory becomes even more plausible if one factors in the likelihood of Lester's guilt at having excoriated his brother for his fall into homosexual depravity. Even though one can trace a thin chain of rationality in Lester's odd and precipitate actions, it does not mean they were untouched by the insanity that ran in the Wilcox family.

Mental health professionals say that, of all human afflictions, the one that causes the most pain and suffering is schizophrenia. Not only does the sick person suffer, but everyone around him or her suffers as well. And the suffering is not merely the anguish at a loved one's misfortune, it is also the agony, humiliation, and fear that goes with closeness to the insane. Further compounding the suffering is the duration of the illness: it lasts a lifetime.

With his tendencies toward physical and verbal abuse and his attempts at arson, Lester Wilcox made life an unpredictable hell for his parents, his wife, and his children. In his twenty-seven years in an institution, he gave considerable grief to doctors, nurses, and other staff. Harry Dreyfus probably did not quickly forget the beating Lester had given him, nor, for that matter, did Eugene Cummings or the two brothers of Lester's black cleaning woman or the two Portuguese men who arrived late for work. Who knows what traumas he inflicted on his coworkers in the textile business? And of course, there were the Harvard students and town boys whose lives were damaged, if not destroyed, by Lester's antihomosexual rampage.

To say his attack on Harvard gays was the direct result of his derangement would be to overburden the logic of cause and effect. A perfectly sane person might have done the same thing. Still, lynch parties and witch-hunts most often come about when one consumed individual exhorts others to his or her level of passionate outrage. That level may have a degree of insanity in it, but if it connects with a receptor in the crowd's network of responses, the insanity can appear to the crowd as a clearer vision, a deeper perception. At least two of the obsessed girls in Salem in 1692, Ann Putnam and Betty Parris, had insanity in their families, but their crazed behavior contributed strongly to an entire community's being possessed for many months by witch-hunting insanity that resulted in twenty executions.

Humans are tinderboxes of potential hatred, fears, and violence. Sadly, igniting them is not difficult. Throughout history, one of the most effective sparks is the obsessed madman, or at least an individual whose mental unbalance is linked to one of our species' dormant furies. Whether the focus is morality, patriotism, misanthropy, or racial antagonisms, an artful, eloquent madman, an individual consumed with the urgent necessity for action against a perceived wrong, can induce sane people to do insane things.

Lester Wilcox fulfilled that function when he set into motion Harvard's crusade to eradicate homosexuals from its midst. That his exhortations fell on ears particularly susceptible to these fears and hatred must be seen as unfortunate happenstance. But then, many such crusades and vendettas may owe as much to chance exigencies.

The splendid writer John Knowles, some years after the enormous success of his first novel, *A Separate Peace,* wrote a novel called *Spreading Fires* that had as its theme the contagion of insanity. The setting is the French Riviera, where a young American has rented a fully staffed villa and is entertaining friends. The host realizes that the resident cook is behaving in an increasingly deranged manner. Since a lunatic servant is inconsistent with his view of a posh Riviera holiday, he ignores the signs in the hope that the bizarre behavior will pass.

The tension in the house grows as the host can no longer hide the alarming situation from his guests. When the cook's derangement rises to a menacing level, the host and the now-terrified guests also start behaving irrationally until they are all nearly as insane as the cook. Knowles builds his theme of spreading madness to a horrific dénouement.

Something similar may have occurred when the soon-to-be-insane

Lester Wilcox stormed into Dean Greenough's office and demanded Harvard take action against the homosexual clique that brought about his brother's death. Greenough and his cohorts, their brains teeming with horrendous images—dormitory orgies, seduced freshmen, Harvard's queer reputation—may have gone a little crazy, too.

THREE YEARS BEFORE Lester Wilcox's death, Richard Wilcox received permission from the Taunton hospital to take his father to his fortieth reunion at Harvard. At the various social events, Lester did not run into anyone he had known. For the main ceremonies they sat in the balcony to listen to the speeches. The picture is haunting: a small, toothless, inconspicuous man, sitting with his son in the Harvard hall, unknown and unrecognized. One can only wonder if Lester, in spite of his legendary intellect and brilliance considered even for a moment, or was even aware of, the powerful influence he had had on the august institution around him, how he had provoked the proud university into actions it would, eighty years later, profoundly regret.

It is not known if Lester ever gave a thought to the conflagration he launched on the Harvard campus—or ever showed any curiosity about the way in which the inquisition unfolded. If he had, given Lester's stubborn nature and his self-awarded infallibility, it is doubtful he would have felt any remorse. If asked his feelings about the wrecked lives of the students, the shattered parental dreams, the shame and embarrassment that Harvard would come to feel, he would probably have given the same answer he gave the psychiatrists at Taunton when they veered too close to the core of his insanity: "I do not care to discuss that."

19

Homophobia's Long March

———◆———

THERE ARE FEW topics as difficult to analyze and discuss as homophobia. It is a mind-set about which humans have a welter of conflicting attitudes, violent manifestations, tortured justifications, self-deluding denials, and much hypocrisy. This has been true throughout history and in all parts of the globe. In spite of recent tectonic shifts in public perceptions and a greater awareness that homophobia is unjust and irrational, the confusion and contradictions are still very much present. The tangled attitudes toward what is already a complex human trait and the muddled rationales make it very difficult to arrive at a clear picture of what homophobia is and where it comes from.*

Most historians and social scientists agree that homosexuality itself has existed to roughly the same degree in all times and places. While the numbers may have remained relatively constant, gay visibility has fluctuated widely, depending on the prevailing climate. The levels of homophobia have fluctuated as well, and a pattern emerges: the greater the visibility, the greater were the antihomosexual feelings. For homosexual men and women, history has been a grotesque seesaw: guarded toleration followed by angry backlash.

---

*Even the terminology reflects the confusion. "Homophobia," from its Greek roots, means "fear of the same" but has come to mean "aversion to homosexuality," which is fear of the unsame, quite a leap. "Sodomy" means any unnatural sexual act but has evolved to mean male penetration of another male. Even the word "homosexuality," from its roots, means "sex with the same." But the "homo" prefix, meaning "same," is mistakenly thought by many to refer to "male." The illogicalities abound.

Religious doctrines and strong individual aversions have guaranteed that a degree of homophobia is present at all times. While official positions in modern Western nations have invariably been antihomosexual, and this attitude is written into the laws, rulers and governments often ignore the problem but at times lunge forth in deadly purges. The same is true of most of the world's nations. While the inquisitions and punishments may have been sporadic, an underlying attitude that homosexuality is evil and wrong has been present more often than not.

America, with its odd mix of religiosity and open-minded liberality, has been as conflicted about homosexuality as any nation. In 1976 the highly respected U.S. newsman Mike Wallace said on the air, "Most Americans are repelled by the mere notion of homosexuality." Yet a scant thirty-five years later, two of the most popular television shows are about (lovable) gay men, and a highly rated talk show is hosted by an openly (lovable) gay woman. In 1998 twenty-two-year-old Matthew Shepard was beaten and killed for being gay; in 2005 state-sanctioned gay marriage is poised to become an inevitability throughout the United States.

After thousands of years of grappling with the omnipresent phenomenon of humans attracted to their own gender, humanity is still unsure how to deal with homosexuality, or even how to feel about it. More often than not, however, the feelings have been negative, and despite a considerable reduction of the fire-and-brimstone abhorrence, the world still abounds in hostility toward homosexuality.

Given the historic pervasiveness of homophobia and its tenacious survival in a more enlightened, less goblin-fearing world, it is tempting to think of it as a fundamental aspect of human nature, a genetically inscribed disposition that can be evoked by circumstances and which manifests itself in various strengths, from mild condemnation to murderous hate. Anthropological historians, however, challenge facile genetic explanations by pointing to societies in which homosexuality has been accepted, even admired.

Most famously, the ancient Greeks saw nothing wrong with physical love between older and younger men, and even saw advantages to their culture in male love affairs. The Chinese have a long tradition of homosexuality, especially in the educated and ruling classes, even though the practice was disdained by Confucius and the Taoists. Although the Koran comes down against homosexuality, Muslim societies have often been accepting of it, with periods when physical love between males was extolled in poems and novels. In modern Afghanistan, religious law is far harder on illicit sex between a man and a woman than on sex between two men. Perhaps because of this, sex between young males is tacitly condoned, but only until they marry.

Among the natives of New Guinea and various American Indian tribes, sex between men, at certain times—initiations, rites of passage—was sanctioned by tribal leaders. In the United States of 2004, an underground sexual phenomenon has broken into the public consciousness. "On the Down Low" is the expression African-American males use to designate the widespread practice of men having sex with other men while considering themselves heterosexual and leading predominantly heterosexual lives. Within the black community, the practice is criticized because of the unfairness (and danger of disease) to wives and girlfriends, not because it is sinful or abnormal.

Still, many of these gay-tolerant societies and subcultures, if examined closely, have their homophobic aspects. The ancient Greeks, so often portrayed as having created a homosexual utopia, found endless ways to carp at homosexuals but always stopped short of condemning the practice itself. Irritated social critics of the day constantly excoriated one type of male homosexual or another: men who were too boy-obsessed, men who neglected their families for boys, men who were effeminate, men who dressed outlandishly, boys who prostituted themselves for advancement. To the Greeks, homosexuality was okay, but a line was drawn at the excesses it led to. The list of line-crossers, however, was suspiciously long.

Even Plato, who had extolled man-boy erotic love in *The Symposium,* appeared to have changed his mind late in life. In *The Laws,* he calls homosexual love "unnatural." Speaking through "the Athenian" (who, most scholars believe, voices Plato's own views), Plato sees men who love boys as inferior beings who lack the moral fiber to resist their urges. Among the reasons put forward by Plato (or by "the Athenian") for this disapproval is that homosexuals have abdicated their roles as procreators; their sexual practices (along with masturbation) "murder" the human race. Plato also made the ludicrously false claim that homosexuality does not exist among other animals. (It is disheartening to think that one of the primary architects of Western thought should have such faulty powers of observation.)

"The Athenian" waxes even tougher on homosexuals: the few who give into homoerotic urges are a danger to the State and should be suppressed. While it is not certain that Plato himself held these views, the evidence is strong that most Greeks of the day did not hold them. None of the other Greek writers, so critical of every aspect of their societies, spoke out against homosexuality per se, then so rampant in Greece, or condemned it with the sweeping brush of the elderly Plato.

For all these pockets of acceptance, however, such societies were isolated interruptions in the historic tide of hostility toward homosexuals. Against the centuries of opprobrium and censure, gay-friendly cultures are rare enough to appear curious anomalies rather than proof that there is nothing in human nature that recoils at the notion of sex between people of the same gender.

SOCIETIES IN WHICH homophobia is the prevailing attitude invariably base their hostility on religious dogma. In case anyone might feel that God's condemnation was insufficient reason to hate homosexuals, more earthbound rationales are plentiful. One of the most frequent is Plato's gripe that homosexuality is not procreative. Because many religions hold that the one and only purpose of sex is procreation, same-gender sex is seen as contrary to the divine plan. Because homosexual acts produce no progeny, they are undeniably for pleasure only, lust for lust's sake. Since Christianity and other religions tend to consider *any* pleasure as cosmic thin ice, homosexuality was highly suspect to begin with, but the absence of offspring was proof

that God disapproved. That homosexuality does not lead to repro-
duction evokes a related charge: it undermines the family.

Of the many justifications for denouncing homosexuality, the most
powerful has always been religious doctrine. Homosexuality is wrong
because God says it is. This has been true of many, if not most, religions to varying degrees—from the mild disapproval of Confucianism
to the virulent abhorrence of the Judeo-Christian tradition. Inevitably
the religious positions on homosexuality have influenced the laws and
traditions of the societies that they guide. Religious injunctions became useful weapons for secular leaders to wield when they felt homosexuality was getting out of hand.

Of all the cultures that have condemned homosexuality, none have
experienced such prolonged hostility or such deadly purges as Europe after the advent of Christianity. But this didn't happen right
away. In fact, in his masterly study of attitudes toward homosexuality
throughout European history, *Christianity, Social Tolerance, and Homosexuality,* John Boswell painstakingly makes the point that attitudes
toward homosexuality, as reflected in church doctrine and secular law,
were for the most part quite tolerant until the thirteenth century, when
the first death sentence for homosexuality was imposed. Until then,
homosexuality was generally accepted; where prohibitions existed
they were rarely acted upon. This changed abruptly in the thirteenth
century—Boswell is far better at documenting the change than at explaining its causes—when a virulent homophobia erupted and has
dominated Europe until modern times. Two primary explanations he
offers are the lessening importance of urban centers as rural areas
emerged in importance and the concentration of political power in au-
tocratic rulers, but they raise as many questions as they answer.

Whatever the causes of the homophobia that consumed Europe during the past eight centuries and that spread to the European-dominated
parts of the globe, it was strengthened by the Jewish teachings in the
Old Testament and a few admonitions in the New Testament, most
forcefully in the Gospels of St. Paul. It is worth noting that, while
early Christian theologians, the creators of the modern church, had no
trouble soft-pedaling other aspects of Jewish law, they embraced Old

Testament admonitions against homosexuality with a fervor and zeal that might have alarmed pre-Christian Jewish scribes. This is even more remarkable considering that, in the entire Bible, only eight passages clearly address homosexuality, whereas the scriptures repeatedly dwell on countless other sins. As Suzanne Pharr points out in her book *Homophobia: A Weapon of Sexism,* while there are only a few warnings against homosexuality, the Bible has literally hundreds of injunctions against unfair distribution of wealth. Yet no Christian tribunals have ever been set up to ferret out and burn exploitive landowners and financiers as they repeatedly did with homosexuals.

One of the harshest biblical injunctions, the one most often cited by those legislating against homosexuality, is the Holiness Code in Leviticus, which says that homosexuals should be put to death. Christian leaders and secular rulers seized on this one sentence, but blithely ignored the Holiness Code's insistence that many others sins— adultery, incest, bestiality—mandated a death sentence: even children who cursed their parents should, according to Leviticus, be executed. All these transgressions have been dismissed and forgotten *except* the injunction against homosexuality.

The Bible story that was the primary justification for eight hundred years of homophobia was the destruction of Sodom and Gomorrah by a vengeful God incensed at the cities' relish for sodomy. While some scholars in recent years have held that this story is not about homosexuality at all, that this reading is a misinterpretation of the Hebrew text—and there is much persuasive evidence behind this theory—it nevertheless became the basis of eight centuries of homophobia and must be dealt with, in any examination, as medieval Christians interpreted it.

As an admonition, this Christian redaction of the tale implies a far more frightening possibility than mere damnation for sins. The Sodom story served to warn Jews, and later Christians, that if they countenanced sodomy in their midst, the innocent would perish along with the sinners. This posits an exceptionally high level of godly wrath, far more frightening than the usual list of "thou-shalt-nots," with an emphasis on keeping oneself sin-free in order to avoid an eternity in hell. The Sodom story says something quite different. You could be a paradigm of virtue yet still be dragged to hell because of the sins of others. What your neighbor does *is* your business. Not only is your survival at stake, so is your admission into heaven.

Leaders responsible for the fate of their country or principality— assuming they were believers, and most were—would have been monstrously derelict if they closed their eyes to rampant behavior among their citizenry that could bring about the destruction of their realms. God punishes all those who sin, but for homosexuality, God punishes entire cities. This uniquely powerful story was invoked each time church or secular leaders felt that homosexuality was becoming a threat to their communities, and it was the scriptural foundation for countless purges and inquisitions.

While the founding councils of the Christian church for the most part condemned homosexuality and advocated severe punishments, it took twelve centuries before repressions became deadly. Since homosexuality was so prevalent and so clearly abhorrent to God, it became a convenient scapegoat for every disaster. Famines, floods, even commercial declines—all sent shudders of Sodom-and-Gomorrah fear through the rulers and their people. This blame-the-gays response exploded with the Black Death that broke out in the 1340s and, for almost a century, devastated Europe. Homophobes of the day could not have asked for a more ghastly demonstration of God's wrath. (Over six hundred years later, the Reverends Jerry Falwell and Pat Robertson—with the advent of AIDS and, later, with the World Trade Center tragedy—tried to make the same wages-of-sin connection, but both times were shouted down by a more enlightened public.)

In his excellent book *Homophobia: A History*, Professor Byrne Fone documents centuries of homophobic mayhem through the Middle Ages and the Renaissance. Even before the plague, European nations were beginning to panic about the spread of sodomy. The Spanish referred to it as the *"pecado nefando,"* the unmentionable sin, and, in 1265, made it punishable by death. Stoning and castration remained the punishments of choice until Ferdinand and Isabella's Grand Inquisitor, Tomás de Torquemada, changed that to burning alive. Records are incomplete, but it is known that in three Spanish cities between the middle of the sixteenth and the end of the seventeenth centuries, sixteen hundred people, mostly males, were prosecuted for sodomy, and roughly three hundred of them were executed.

Italy, widely considered a pesthole of sodomy in that period, was no more lenient. In Florence, a 1325 law decreed castration for homosexuals, but this was later upgraded to torture and death. Several cities publicly castrated offenders and left them hanging on display for three days before drowning them. In Italy from 1432 to 1500 some fifteen thousand people were tried and two thousand convicted. Such brutalities were common throughout Europe at the time, with the actions of outraged rulers encouraged by the Church. A few countries, however, had exceptionally virulent homophobic outbreaks. One of the worst was Holland—now among the world's most gay-friendly nations—where a brutal eighty-year purge was launched in 1730.

Several curiosities emerge from the grizzly statistics. The number of actual executions, while appalling to most present-day thinking about homosexuality, was still relatively small. Three hundred executions in Spain over 150 years is not a large number—two a year—when compared to the thousands upon thousands who were accused, and the hundreds of thousands who undoubtedly were sexually active with their own gender. The inhuman punishments, always highly public, were obviously intended to discourage homosexuality, not to rid the area of homosexuals.

In spite of the sadistic and terrifying sentences, it is remarkable how little they deterred homosexual activity. Around 1500 the Florentine governing council, after inflicting some of the cruelest and most energetic purges, finally admitted failure and changed their eradication policy to one of containment.

Those who still consider homosexuality a choice would do well to consider the young men of Spain, Italy, or Holland who indulged in this despised behavior, knowing that it could lead not to a flower-bedecked wedding and a happy conjugal life, but to public castration and death by fire. Fone's history is a tragic tribute to the power of the sex drive and the impossibility for vast numbers of people to channel their drive where others would like.

HOMOPHOBIA IN THE past thousand years was by no means confined to Europe or Christianity-dominated countries. China has had crackdowns from time to time, as have most of the Muslim countries, which were generally tolerant. Ancient Indian Sanskrit art depicts homosexuality in an approving way, but when the Muslim Moghul empire conquered northern India in 1526, its rulers inflicted some of the most barbaric punishments on homosexuals, including hot pokers up the rectum and always death. Eventually, attitudes toward same-gender sex returned to toleration but in modern times have been reverting to hostility. Most blame this on the British, who arrived as conquerors bristling with Victorian moral certainties.

In China in the 1950s, a government crackdown on homosexuals in Shanghai resulted in the execution of thousands of gay men. The Communist government deplored the proliferation of homosexuality, which it claimed resulted from the westernization of China's major cities. It is ironic that officials chose to view homosexuality as a western import when a stronger case could be made that *homophobia* was a western import. Wherever the aversion came from, it suggests much about the homophobic potential in all people that China's millions could be so quickly converted from seeing homosexuality as a harmless anomaly to seeing it as a capital offense.

In England, the degree of punishment fluctuated over the centuries, but homosexuality was always a serious crime and deplored by authorities. One of the ugliest outbreaks of homophobia occurred in 1810, when a tavern on London's Vere Street was raided and some thirty men were arrested for homosexual conduct. What made this episode so memorable was not the harshness of the punishments—only six were convicted and given prison sentences of one to three years—but the virulence of the public hatred toward the accused.

Before going to jail, the guilty were sentenced to stand for varying times in a pillory. As the hour for this public humiliation approached, large crowds formed and wagons appeared loaded with dung, offal, rotting fish, and parts of dead dogs and cats. These items were sold at high prices for the crowd to throw at the pilloried men. When the prisoners were brought forth in an open cart, the barrage began and increased in repulsiveness and ferocity as the cart reached the pillory. In a frenzy of hatred, the crowd screamed insults as they showered the men with their cartloads of filth. One observer was quoted in the newspapers as saying, "It was the most enraged populace we ever saw."

It is hard to explain such loathing. Even murderers and child molesters did not inspire such savage rage (although heretics did, which suggests an interesting parallel). It is doubtful the crowd's fury stemmed from terror at suffering Sodom and Gomorrah's fate. Even the most homophobic God would not destroy a city the size of 1810 London for harboring a mere thirty homosexuals. Nor does moral outrage appear to be the cause. Among the homosexual prisoners' most vociferous tormenters was a group of prostitutes who had paid well for seats close to the pillory. The overall spectacle seemed to ignite buried reserves of homophobia that may have stretched far deeper into human history than the Old Testament.

England's most famous episode of homophobia followed the Oscar Wilde trials of 1895. While this tragedy made many thinking people reconsider the religion-backed vindictiveness toward homosexuals, it convinced many more that Wilde's crimes were so horrendous as to make all those guilty, regardless of their place in society, deserving of the harshest punishments. Instead of proving the destructive potential of mindless homophobia, Wilde's sorry fate, with his trials' revelations of the pervasiveness of male-male sexuality, made most people of the day feel a need for tougher laws and more aggressive enforcement.

It is not surprising that the Puritans were vehement in their opposition to homosexuality. In the mid-seventeenth century, the Massachusetts Bay Colony's governor John Winthrop was not alone in feeling that the settlers had to be *more* righteous and pure than their countrymen in England. Sodomy was a major concern. Clergymen railed constantly against it and, in most of New England's colonies, it was one of the few crimes punishable by death. The South was equally fanatical on the subject. In a 1776 revision of Virginia law, no less a liberal spirit than Thomas Jefferson wrote the section on punishment for homosexuals:

> Whosoever shall be guilty of Rape, Polygamy or Sodomy with man or woman shall be punished, if a man, by castration, if a woman, by cutting thro' the cartilage of her nose a hole of one half inch diameter at least.

IN SPITE OF the many pockets of tolerance, even acceptance of homosexuality throughout history and around the globe, there has almost always been at least an undercurrent of censure and a reflexive aversion to same-gender sex. More remarkable than the global and historic pervasiveness of this human mind-set is the level of rage and hatred that is present during the epidemics of homophobic hysteria. What is behind such hostility and revulsion?

The biblical basis of homophobia does not work as an explanation in that the Bible is extremely hard on many behaviors that have never evoked the kind of pogroms, mob rage, and vigilante executions that homosexuality has provoked. Many sins considered major in the Old Testament have long since been ignored except for rare observances in the most fundamentalist sects. If one believes the Old Testament to be no more and no less than the word of God, then the Sodom and Gomorrah story, as it has come to be interpreted, leaves no room for argument.

But if one believes the ancients who wrote those texts were too quick to assume the cities' destruction resulted from one cause only, or too quick to assume the cause was homosexuality rather than rampant lewdness, as many believe, then other possible explanations come to mind. Like the Jerry Falwells and Pat Robertsons of today, homophobic priests in biblical times may have used the day's disasters to dramatize their condemnation of behaviors they deplored. In other words, innate homophobia may have inspired the otherwise baseless interpretation that the disasters proved God's wrath at homosexuality.

A further weakness of the biblical explanation is that it ignores the flourishing of homophobia in other parts of the world and in other cultures, cultures that do not base their morality on the Old Testament. It is unlikely that the gay-slaughtering Moghul rulers in sixteenth century India had ever head of Sodom and Gomorrah. Or that the Communist leaders of 1950 Shanghai were haunted by this Old Testament tale.

The fear that homosexuality is destructive to the family and undermines communities undoubtedly had validity at one time, but does not in the modern world. In an earlier, underpopulated world, colonial villages, small farming communities, isolated tribes were held together by families—a husband, wife, and children. Sexual free agents in their midst were thought to have—and probably did have—a pernicious effect on the entire community. But on today's overpopulated planet, even the poorest people have a mobility unknown in earlier times. Men and women who do not fit the family mold are free to move to more congenial areas. In the present time, ever increasing numbers of people, gay and straight, have made it clear that they do not want a world in which the traditional family is the only option, a world in which all others are outcasts.

A frequent justification for homophobia is that homosexuality is non-procreative and therefore unnatural and sinful. The Bible, especially St. Paul, comes down hard on sex that does not lead to children. The contemporary writer, Andrew Sullivan, points out, however, that the Catholic Church has no problem with an infertile couple marrying and having sex. The idea that sex between men and women, even married couples, is all right *only* for producing offspring seems to have vanished long ago, if indeed it ever had much of a following.

One of the most basic arguments against homosexuality is that it is wrong and unnatural because most people do not do it. Writer Gore Vidal came up with an ingenious demolition of this statistical approach to pinpointing sin. If the only acceptable sexual act is the one done by the most people, then the most "normal" form of sex would not be man-woman intercourse, but masturbation, which would clearly win, well, hands down, if numbers were the criterion.

Another common reason for antipathy toward homosexuality is that the action most ascribed to gay men, anal sex, was for nonenthusiasts quite disgusting. Because of the unfortunate double duty of the anus, the practice was seen as filthy and depraved. But in this regard, heterosexuals are only slightly better off, which is perhaps the reason the argument rarely gets spoken. Then, too, most sexual acts are repugnant to anyone not excited by them. (If the titillation-disgust pattern holds throughout the species, evolutionary theorists could have a merry time trying to figure out the adaptive advantage.)

UNDERLYING ALL OF the rationales for despising homosexuals is an assumption that homosexuality is a matter of choice, that men and women fall into this behavior because of an absence of moral strength or a leaning toward depravity. Science has now shown that homosexuality is not a matter of choice but of genetics and prenatal biological anomalies. However convincing the science, an even stronger refutation of the choice concept can be found in the thousand-year history of the legal persecution of homosexuals. What sane person would risk castration or being burned alive if he or she had other, "acceptable" outlets for sexual desires?

Throughout his book, Byrne Fone, who probably knows more on the subject than anyone, sees the virulent homophobia he chronicles as a result of fear, or, to use his expression, "the horror of difference." In his final paragraphs, however, Fone raises the possibility that homophobia may be innate, that it "is more than learned (if unexamined) bigotry and intolerance. For some, it seems to have the force of a command of nature." Professor Fone stops just short of saying homophobia may be an evolved characteristic that exists, to one degree or another, in all humans. But there is considerable evidence this is the case.

Whenever a genetic basis for a behavior is suggested, those unaware of the advances of behavioral genetics are quick to fear that by claiming a trait is inborn, it is therefore "natural" and inevitable, so must be accepted. Nothing could be further from the truth, and no geneticist has ever suggested such a thing. Humans are riddled with nasty impulses and innate dispositions that are ignored, rejected, or overruled. These may be the detritus of early human development, traits that at one time may have had an evolutionary purpose, a survival advantage, but that are detrimental to modern life or conflict with other biological impulses. As the geneticist Richard Dawkins has written, every time humans use contraception, they are overruling their genes, which agitate persistently for more babies. Genetic impulses can be weak or strong, but if unrecognized as the mindless part of our makeup, they become stronger.

Before examining a number of clues to a biological basis to homophobia, it should first be pointed out there is an obvious survival value for any hardwired attitude that discourages a practice that threatens man-woman sex. Two male australopithecines were no better at making babies than two male commodities traders. It is not unreasonable to suppose that an antipathy toward homosexuality became hardwired into the species in order to keep randy males focused on women and randy women focused on men. If evolution has fine-tuned the human for an attraction to the opposite sex, it may have thrown in a species-wide aversion to homosexuality as a device to strengthen the opposite-sex focus of those individuals insufficiently fine-tuned.

It is in fact far easier to build an adaptive rationale for homophobia than it is for homosexuality itself, which has flourished throughout the millennia—in spite of a clear disadvantage for the species' long march to overpopulation. Gayness has always presented staunch Darwinists with one of the knottiest problems and reduced them to such tortured rationales as the evolutionary advantage of the sissy uncle who stays home by the campfire protecting the women and children while the real men are off slaying mastodons. Homophobia needs no such logical contortions. By seeing to it that most people despise, ridicule, and harass men-loving men or women-loving women, the highly sexed "normal" males were more likely to stick to the warm bodies that would result in offspring.

Simply having an evolutionary advantage doesn't make a trait genetic. College spring breaks probably benefit the species' future, but few geneticists would argue we are hardwired to strip naked on bars and throw up. There are many more specific reasons to suspect a genetic component to homophobia. All of the evidence is circumstantial, but then it is not possible to find an eyewitness to a million-year-old alteration in our DNA.

An excellent clue to the possibility of a genetic basis to any trait is its emergence throughout history and across cultures. This is certainly true of homophobia. Another is the irrational virulence of the hatred same-gender sex can inspire: the dung-throwing prostitutes of Vere Street, the judiciary that can sentence one of England's greatest writers to hard labor in prison, and the countless Europeans who, for centuries, cheered the public castrations and burnings of hundreds convicted of homosexual activity. The rage and hostility, if not the punishments themselves, go far beyond that shown almost all other crimes. Moreover, the speed with which a populace can be whipped up into a homophobic frenzy suggests the presence of internal receptors that connect and respond to the external inveighing.

Yet another clue to a genetic basis is the dearth of logic in an emotion that has produced such dire and forceful actions. If practiced among adults, homosexuality produces no victims or physical damage, unlike many crimes that do not evoke similar levels of outrage. An equally puzzling manifestation of the special loathing reserved for homosexuals has been the long-standing use of homosexual epithets to excoriate adversaries. Throughout Europe in the Middle Ages and the Renaissance, the most scathing insult one man could make to another was to call him a sodomite. Substituting the slur "faggot," the same is true today among schoolchildren. The crime itself is awarded a special vocabulary—or even worse, denied *any* vocabulary. From the Middle Ages down to Harvard's Secret Court, righteous men referred to homosexuality as "unspeakable," "disgusting," or, in the Spanish phrase, a "crime that cannot be mentioned." No one hesitates to mention adultery, murder, or child abuse.

Another possible clue to a genetic basis is the homophobia and self-hatred that exist among gay people themselves. Until recently—

until Stonewall, really—homosexuals in the advanced nations docilely accepted the opprobrium of the rest of the world and were content just to be able to pursue their desires without being harassed or locked up. In Third World nations, that is still the case. Many gays feel the same revulsion as do straights at the extreme effeminacy and outlandish behavior of some gays. The use by some gays of antigay slurs in verbal battles, the attaching of gay labels to disliked people, and the way some gay men address each other with feminine names or pronouns (you are not a man but a woman), all are signs of an ingrained homophobia that may go beyond social conditioning.

For direct, personal evidence of a possible inborn homophobia, a useful exercise would be to compare one's reactions on encountering two different scenes. The first would be seeing two men or two women kissing passionately in a public place. The other would be to spot a thief in the act of stealing. Both scenes would trigger a degree of disgust in many people, but the disgust at the display of homoerotic feelings is of a different order. It draws on a different template of affront and is more viscerally felt. It is a feeling that is less amenable to the persuasions of reason. The viewer might consider both actions wrong, yet the kiss harms no one, is not illegal, and is consensual, while the theft harms someone and is against the law. When one's attitudes and responses defy logic, it is a good time to suspect the presence of a genetic nudge.

For many people, including even some gays, tableaux of same-sex eroticism evoke responses that seem to reach beyond cultural and religious laws, beyond the individual's upbringing and socialization, beyond his or her standards of appropriate behavior. Call it a gut feeling, a reflex, or a spontaneous reaction, but it is there and, in the absence of countermanding impulses, can be powerful.

As with any genetic impulses, one's awareness of possible biological manipulation can greatly raise one chances of overriding it. If homophobic feelings are recognized as an atavistic response, a weak strand of evolutionary detritus in our makeup, it might spare us from the usual self-deluding reaction: a quick scouring of our catalogues of rationales and pretexts in the hope of coming up with intellectual justifications for attitudes that discredit us, are hurtful to blameless people, and have no basis in reason.

Many of the historic, cultural, and religious explanations of homophobia become nonsensical when we consider the brutal murder of Matthew Shepard in 1998. Does anyone believe his two killers brooded about the non-procreative side of Shepard's homosexuality? Were they obsessed by the Old Testament injunctions again sodomy? Were they products of a puritanical society that was against all sex? Were they fighting the deterioration of the American family? Were they victims of a power elite that used homophobia to keep minority groups in line? Were they terrorized by anyone who was different? Terrorized enough to kill? All of these constructs become absurd when considering these two ignorant, unsocialized, hate-filled hooligans.

Of course, the capacity of such sorry clods to hate and inflict violence can be tapped by different manipulators, but did anyone care enough about these losers to manipulate them? In their street-world of dropouts and druggies, hatred of gays may have been a boost to acceptance, but could that alone have fired them up enough to risk life in prison? To be sure, their hate was legitimatized, even inflamed, by institutional condemnation of homosexuality, mainly by the church, but institutions also condemn violence and murder and Shepard's killers had no trouble sloughing off those injunctions. Surely many elements contributed to the tragedy—the killers' drunkenness, their subculture's homophobia, maybe even a dislike of Shepard—but none of these things would have moved them to murder had there not been something inside *them* that empowered them to commit such a vicious and extreme act.

It is difficult for contemporary men and women to be too surprised at such antigay violence, or indeed the violence toward gays throughout history, when they consider some graffiti spotted on the wall of a notorious public toilet in a Harvard building in the 1990s. Someone had written, "Kill all the faggots."

Underneath, someone else had written, "Why?"

Then below that, in yet a third handwriting, was written, "Because they must die."

So even at Harvard, the dialogue continues.

*   *   *

POPULAR PSYCHOLOGY HAS it that homophobia springs from individuals who are most threatened by male homosexuality, men who share these erotic feelings but, fearing and detesting such inclinations, hate those who give in to them. This was probably true of Shepard's two killers, who frequented gay bars. Such sexually conflicted individuals, the theory goes, are the most militant opponents of the practice and the ones most likely to move aggressively against gays.

While this explanation of homophobia strikes many as too facile, if not too self-serving for homosexuals, a scientific study at the University of Georgia in 1996 gave considerable credence to the theory. Two groups of straight male students were assembled; one group was unabashedly homophobic, the second was indifferent to homosexuality. Both groups were "wired" in an ingenious if uncomfortable way to monitor degrees of arousal, then shown gay pornography. The homophobic group registered a significantly higher level of arousal than those men with a live-and-let-live attitude.

This finding does not necessarily replace the gene-basis theory. A mild homophobia hardwired into most humans can be activated by many things—fear of God's wrath, anxiety over the disintegrating family, an aversion to anything abnormal. Repressed homosexuality may be just one of many triggers.

If it is found that homophobia has roots in the human genome, what difference would it make? For one thing, establishing a biological component would undermine the claims of various religions that homosexuality is an affront to God's laws. One can argue with DNA or human nature; one can't argue with God. An awareness of an evolved leaning toward homophobia might also reduce the respect paid to this particular "gut feeling" by the many people who have that reaction.

If there is a genetic disposition against homosexuals and it goes unrecognized, it has the destructive potential of a dormant killer mold that, under certain conditions, could be reactivated. History has proven all too often that the human is a tinderbox of potential hatreds, aggressions, and violence. If within each human sleeps the same homophobic response mechanism that inflamed the Renaissance Italians, the Spaniards of the Inquisition, the colonial Americans, and the U.S. government during the Eisenhower Administration, it would only take a Savonarola, Torquemada, another Senator Joe McCarthy, or a more charismatic Jerry Falwell to ignite those dormant, discarded, nucleotide acids that made evolutionary sense in humanity's precarious early days, but now are irrelevant and contradict what it has come to mean to be human.

20

Loose Ends

———◆———

ALTHOUGH THE SECRET COURT was only in session for three weeks, the effects of its actions lasted half a century. It had lifelong repercussions for the expelled students, one of whom, Joseph Lumbard, died in 1999, an astonishing seventy-nine years after he was ordered to leave Harvard. The repercussions were great as well for the students' families, mainly parents, who were left with unshakable burdens of grief and shame. It destroyed the careers of two professional academics. And it brought about, directly and indirectly, the deplorable suicides. And finally, the Court created an indelible stain on Harvard's history, in spite of the administration's assiduous efforts to conceal its existence.

Did the men of the Court realize they were ruining lives? How could they not after Cummings's suicide? Did they care? Did they truly believed the moral stakes were so high that one student's life was inconsequential? Cummings took his life on the very day he learned the Secret Court was expelling him. When that unambiguous disaster failed to mitigate or allay the punitive zeal of Lawrence Lowell and his judges, it left no doubt about the momentous gravity with which they saw their mission. In the meticulous records of the Secret Court and the well-recorded prominence of its members' subsequent careers, there is no evidence that any of them had the slightest misgivings about their actions against homosexuals in 1920.

The record makes clear their primary motivation was a conviction that homosexuality was a terrible wrong and a sin beyond redemption.

Anyone who could engage in sex with his own gender, even once, was a permanent threat to decent people and had to be banished. The abhorrent vice made a mockery of the vision of the ideal Harvard man that guided the judgment, if not the lives, of these academics. Beyond their personal repugnance, they felt that eradicating the blight from the campus was their duty; healthy students had to be protected from infection. This idea that normal but morally weak students were being put at high risk permeates the Court's thinking.

In fact, it may have been the reason Lowell was so obdurate about readmitting Kenneth Day. Lowell may have recognized in Day one of the normal boys who should have withstood the temptations pushed on him by the hopelessly depraved, but lacked the moral fiber. By seeing some of the guilty as irredeemably homosexual—an idea that comes close to a belief in the congenital nature of that sexual preference—Lowell may have felt a higher abhorrence for the casual switch-hitter.

A final motivation for the Court was undoubtedly the reputation Harvard had for attracting and harboring "fairies." If the cloistered men of the Court were not aware of this before, the information was forced upon them by Keith Smerage's angry letter ("Harvard has a reputation for this sort of thing that is nation wide"). At Yale University in the 1950s there was a song dear to all, or most, undergraduates. Perhaps it was the same song Smerage heard at Princeton in 1920:

> You can tell a Harvard man about a mile away
> Cause he looks *(clap, clap)* just like he'll blow away . . .

Surely aware of this reputation, the men of the Court also knew the potential for public scandal in the antics of Roberts's giddy circle. But it is doubtful if they were aware of this prior to Lester Wilcox's visit. They needed to be informed about the happenings in Perkins Hall. Indeed, they needed considerably more information in general before they could act. Wilcox provided all of this. He also provided the furious energy to set them into motion. It may not be too much to say the Secret Court came into existence in May 1920 because of the outrage of a psychotic cocaine addict.

IF PRESIDENT LOWELL saw Kenneth Day as the breakdown of his ideal-male defenses against perversion, a moral Maginot Line the enemy had overrun with appalling ease, Day's future life throws considerable light on one of the Court's prime contentions: the contagion of homosexuality. That an innocent heterosexual like Kenneth Day could be drawn into the erotic diversions of the gay group would seem to be telling corroboration of the Court's belief that normal boys could readily be infected with the gay disease.

When Day's life is viewed in its entirety, however, his case proves the opposite. Assuming that Day was, as his daughter said, an enthusiastic heterosexual, that he was not just playacting for fifty years and through three marriages, his brushes with gay sex must be seen as sexual opportunism of a lusty and frustrated young straight man. The important point is that, however extensive his sexual activity with other young males, it did not affect his future sex life in the slightest.

All evidence is that Ken Day was biologically programmed to be a heterosexual. The minute he was in a position to have a broad choice of amatory partners, he unfailingly chose women. Of all the students involved with the Court's judgments, the ones who were fundamentally gay—Gilkey, Wolff, Smerage, Say, Saxton, and Clark—put the pain and humiliation of their Harvard disgrace behind them and lived out their lives as active, if extremely wary, homosexuals. The ones who were basically straight, such as Lumbard and Day, went on to solid, fulfilling marriages with women.

There was no contagion. If anything, the straight students' dabbling in gay sex, and the devastation the punishments they suffered, or came close to suffering, made them more aware of the recklessness in 1920 of toying with a form of sex that was not their first choice. For them, sex with other males was not their only option, as it probably was for the others. Their erotic experiments on the Harvard campus also made them men with broader experience of the realities of the world around them and, inevitably, more tolerant of fellow humans with different erotic response mechanisms. Even more, their tangle with the Court's brutal justice inevitably made them more sensitive to the misuses of power. Such qualities are not misplaced in a federal judge; for Joe Lumbard, at least, Harvard had inadvertently provided him with an important component of his judicial education.

What did the Court accomplish with its lethal inquisition? From its point of view, there were definite positives. It had rid the campus of the most notorious perpetrators. It had protected other students from lubricious predators living among them. It had also instilled terror in the hearts of others engaged in—or even contemplating—these activities.

On the negative side were the destroyed lives and the suicides. There was the judicial ineptitude of expelling heterosexuals like Kenneth Day and permitting homosexuals like Gilkey to graduate. More lastingly, Lowell and his Court had left their beloved Harvard forever vulnerable to charges of the worst sort of ignorance, bigotry, and absence of compassion. They had shown a harsh vindictiveness toward homosexuality at a time when the most thoughtful opinion saw the condition as, at worst, an anomalous pathology, and some experts saw it as today's enlightened opinion sees it, as an innate disposition. The ignorance and bigotry can be explained and, to a degree, forgiven. The lack of compassion cannot. What they saw as "the problem" could have been resolved with far less cruelty and devastation.

IT IS INTERESTING to speculate on the reaction the men of the Secret Court would have if they were to visit today's Harvard. If, in 1920, Harvard acted with more homophobia than other universities, it now leads the pack in gay acceptance. The comasters of Lowell House, Diana Eck and Dorothy Austin, are an openly gay couple. The minister of the historic Memorial Church, which shares domination of Harvard Yard with the Widener Library, is the Reverend Peter J.

Gomes, who is also openly homosexual. Dorothy Austin is an associate minister of that church as well as chaplain to the university.

In 1983 the Harvard Gay and Lesbian Caucus was formed with official sanction from the university. After a meeting in 1985 with the president and Fellows of Harvard College, an antidiscrimination policy was declared for the entire university, including discrimination on the basis of sexual orientation. In 1994 the Caucus began publishing a bimonthly magazine, *The Harvard Gay and Lesbian Review,* which attracted such a broad audience, it has recently been renamed *The Gay and Lesbian Review Worldwide.*

While eighty years seems a short time for such a total change, it did not come about quickly. In 1930 Harvard's legendary professor of English literature, F. O. Matthiessen, wrote to his male partner, "Have I any right to live in a community that would so utterly disapprove of me if it knew the facts?" In 1950, five years after his lover died, Matthiessen jumped from a twelfth-floor window of a Boston hotel. For such an open and honest spirit, the "disapproval" that surrounded him—and the hypocrisy it demanded—must have played a part in his unbearable despair.

In 1960 Harvard made little effort to save one of its graduates, Smith College professor Newton Arvin, one of the country's foremost literary critics, when he was arrested after the discovery of gay pornography in his Northampton apartment. Although ten years earlier Harvard had invited Arvin to replace F. O. Matthiessen on its faculty, it stood by and watched the destruction of his career as a result of some photos of naked boys.

As recently as 1998, when noted financial writer Andrew Tobias wrote a coming-out article for *Harvard Magazine,* it produced a flood of angry mail from alumni, not just old grads, denouncing the journal for printing such filth. If anything sets Tobias's self-revelation apart from those of countless other gay men, it is the disgust he felt about his own gayness and the terror of discovery he suffered as an undergraduate in the late 1960s. He acknowledges awareness of an active gay subculture during his Harvard years, but wanted no part of it.

Still, Tobias's candid reminiscences caused outrage in certain Harvard precincts.

So homophobia is still alive at Harvard and perhaps, in spite of enormous strides toward tolerance, always will be alive in some form or other. There is nothing to say that a backlash from current tolerant attitudes is impossible, even in the United States, even at Harvard. All it would take would be some Taliban-like zealots to take control, any group from the many now flourishing throughout the United States who believe they are hearing the voice of God when they are really hearing the darker corners of their Pliocene genomes.

GIVEN THE MANY homosexual purges and persecutions since the Secret Court went on its crusade, and the possibility of more in the future, it is important to stress the two aspects of this particular outbreak of homophobia that set it apart. First, it happened at Harvard, not only one of the world's great citadels of civilization's finest strivings, but an institution that for its nearly four centuries has successfully fought off intolerance, dogmatism, and bigotry. Second was the vindictive tenacity of the university in ensuring that the stigmatization of the expelled students would persist throughout their productive lives. Some had fallen through the career cracks, so had sunk below Harvard's reach, but others, like Joe Lumbard, had the audacity to continue moving up in the world, so their names were periodically presented for Harvard's blessing and received the damning report.

A third distinguishing aspect of Harvard's gay vendetta was its pitiless implacability. Not only was it undeterred by Cummings's suicide, it was also undeterred by the clear possibility that many active homosexuals had eluded the makeshift net and continued their Harvard careers unscathed. Repeatedly the Court was told by students under interrogation—and even more vociferously by the anonymous letter writer—that it was overlooking countless active homosexuals. It is hard to understand how this awareness wouldn't have caused the

Court to ease up on the unfortunate few who had been caught, if only after four or five years.

Another oddity of the Court sets it apart, mainly because of Harvard's reputation as a preeminent seat of learning: its ignorance of, or obliviousness to, the day's most advanced thinking about sexual inversion. With all the many attempts at "cures" for homosexuality in the nineteenth century and well into the twentieth century, and with the respected theories on the subject by serious researchers like Havelock Ellis, it is the more remarkable that Harvard saw the matter not as a medical one, but purely a moral one. This thinking enabled the members of the Court to believe that the solution lay solely in discipline, not in counseling or treatment.

They seem to have been less interested in the condition than in the behavior—which is what they were enjoined to deal with, to be sure. Still, any awareness that gayness might be an illness or an innate condition would surely have mitigated their brutal treatment of the students they found guilty. Some of the Court's questions suggest a mild interest in how these students became as they were—especially its inquiries into masturbatory habits, which was then a popular causative theory. But for the most part, causes be damned, the Court wanted to rid Harvard of the infestation and to punish severely the perverts who threatened Harvard's good name. And if a town boy was drawn under its scrutiny, the Court would see to it that he lost his job. Moral frenzy clearly took precedence over administrative pragmatism.

Regardless of the Court's attitudes toward homosexuality and the ranking of its crusade among other gay persecutions, Harvard's 1920 antigay tribunal will always be a landmark of magisterial unfairness and a cautionary parable of a powerful institution run amok. It presents a spectacle of wise, learned men, who, because of their leadership qualities, had been pulled from Harvard's faculty and given responsibility over thousands of the nation's best and brightest, reacting to a discipline problem with panic, intemperance, and unconsidered righteousness.

Taking into consideration their concern for other students, their dread of scandal, even a conviction they were dealing with sin of a high order, the evidence points to one conclusion: the underlying motivation that raised their inquisition and their punishments to such an excessive level was the same homophobia that motivates skinheads, barroom brutes, and the man who wrote on the wall of a public toilet, "Kill all the faggots."

MANY MEN AND women walk the planet with consciences weighted down with past decisions: generals who sent legions to unnecessary deaths, judges and juries forced to acknowledge they had sentenced innocent people to execution, surgeons whose mistakes caused patients' deaths. No evidence exists, however, that Lowell and the members of his Court ever felt the slightest remorse about pillorying eight Harvard students and two instructors.

When Kenneth Murdock presided over his baronial table at I Tatti, his guests invariably were artists, art historians, collectors, and all-purpose aesthetes like Harold Acton and Lincoln Kirstein. At a safe estimate, a good 50 percent of his esteemed visitors were homosexuals, most of them openly so. One wonders if Murdock, as he basked in his guests' brilliance and renown, ever thought back to the days when he worked assiduously to destroy the lives of young men guilty of no other crime but having the identical sexual nature as the men and women he was now so proud to be entertaining.

Could there have been a rationalization? An exonerating distinction? Whatever Murdock might have come up with to justify his actions in 1920, he would have trouble escaping the fact that any one of the homosexual guests could have been a Harvard student who might have felt the ruinous force of his righteous wrath. And the same fate might have befallen other illustrious Harvard students such as Leonard Bernstein, Virgil Thomson, Philip Johnson, John Ashbery, William Burroughs, and Frank O'Hara. Instead of becoming internationally renowned figures in the arts, social trophies at great houses in Europe and America, they could have ended up with the Appointments Office's automatic blackball, disgraced embarrassments to Harvard and in fifth-rate jobs like Day and Clark or suicides like Cummings and Smerage.

It is doubtful if Murdock or the other Court members ever learned the devastation their harsh punishments had on many of the lives they disrupted. There is no reason for them to have known of smart and attractive Kenneth Day's failure to obtain a position worthy of his abilities, or the brilliant Donald Clark's desultory pilgrimage from one ignominious position to another, or Harold Saxton's pathetically saying the Court was "justified" in forever blocking him from a decent teaching job, the odd car crash of Edward Say, or the sad career and suicide of the ebullient Keith Smerage.

The Court apparently never considered that it was pummeling men who were already, in a sense, "down." The young person new to gayness must first work through the arduous process of admitting to himself he is gay. Then he must struggle with the terrible risks involved with being himself, acting in accordance with the dictates of his fundamental nature. Finally, he is faced with making the giant leap into total openness, to present himself to the world as an unashamed, undepraved, unrepentant homosexual.

What makes this so difficult and so perilous is the institutionalized homophobia of institutions like Harvard in 1920. The young homosexual inevitably feels bad about himself. It doesn't take long for him to learn what much of the world thinks of gays, but when an august institution hates gays even more than did the little boys on the playground, he knows he has been dealt a very bad hand.

History has repeatedly shown that society's most virulent condemnations and most brutal punishments are no match for the juggernaut drives of lusty young people who happen to be attracted to their own sex. Harvard's 1920 inquisition seems pale when compared with the public castrations and burnings at the stake of the fifteenth and sixteenth centuries. But the results were the same in that lives were destroyed.

Those expelled by the Secret Court were not merely martyred for having committed acts the Old Testament designated sins. Keith Smerage with his gardens and scrapbooks; Ken Day with his brains, good looks, and charm; Nathaniel Wolff and his adventurous, altruistic nature; Donald Clark with his literary prowess in four languages—all had much to offer the world but ran afoul of a vision of the ideal Harvard man, a prototype that had been hammered together by a three-century procession of great educators and paragons of manhood. Ralph Waldo Emerson, William James, Theodore Roosevelt, and the university's eminent presidents—all earthly giants consumed with a vision of *the Harvard man*, the pristine, glowing product of their life's work. The Secret Court's victims did more than damage this fantasy; they sullied and poisoned it for all the others. They were the deadly fungus that could annihilate the majestic forest, the virus that could kill off a noble race.

The benefit of a superior education is that it makes students realize the infinite variety of the universe and the destructive potential of rigid visions of the way things should be. The speed with which sexual mores change and the wild fluctuations in attitude toward homosexuality should have indicated—at least to educated men, if not to the Salem witch judges—the dangers of setting up harsh tribunals and meting out severe punishments based on ancient taboos, arguable premises, and shifting attitudes.

Despite all the damage done by the Court to the students it found "guilty"—to their psyches, self-esteem, and future prospects—none of the Court members left behind any sign they gave it a thought. One likes to think, however, that when the retired Lawrence Lowell, shooting game in Africa or speeding in one of his collection of roadsters, thought of his fat, talented, gay sister who died at age fifty-one; or when Henry Yeomans stood alone on his family farm outside Spokane congratulating himself for his unwavering and lifelong veneration of his mentor, Lowell; or when Chester Greenough rummaged through the human diversity in his beloved Melville, Whitman, and Hawthorne; or when Dr. Roger Lee attended self-congratulatory psychiatric meetings on the most enlightened views about sexual deviance; or when Edward Gay edited *The Times Picayune* in wide-open and famously tolerant New Orleans; or when Kenneth Murdock preened among his gay luminaries; or when any one of them confronted a gay son or daughter—they might have reconsidered their fire-and-brimstone rigidity in 1920 and might have come to view the purged students' crimes as less horrific, less deserving of life-wrecking punishment.

One can only hope that they might have arrived at a more compassionate perception of human differences, even sexual ones. Or hope that at some point in the administrators' lives a wisdom would have settled on them to make them realize that, whatever shame these boys brought on themselves, whatever dangers they presented to the Harvard man, real or idealized, whatever punishment the rules mandated, or however much they exacerbated atavistic loathing deep in the deans' natures, these men, too, had a right to lives.

Epilogue
Discovering Secrets

———◆———

WHEN THE COURT concluded its business, its files were locked in storage boxes and kept in the administration offices in University Hall. The five hundred pages of documents—interrogation notes and letters from students, parents, and other schools the expelled boys tried to enter—sat unnoticed for decades. For many years, however, people in the office must have known the subject matter in the boxes; a memo regarding Joe Lumbard's suspension dated 1953 is correctly filed with the other material. This was thirty-three years after the Court adjourned.

But thirty years is not eighty years, and eventually the boxes were overlooked totally. In a periodic housecleaning they were sent to the Harvard Archives in the Nathan Pusey Library to be catalogued and stored. They sat there unnoticed for some years, then were designated for recataloguing in the 1990s. Andrea Goldstein was one of the archivists assigned the task of going through the material. Right away she realized its sensational nature. When asked if she or perhaps a colleague had alerted a journalist to the files' contents, Goldstein stiffened. "In this business, we have professional ethics."

As Goldstein and the others set to work recataloguing the files, they began referring to the collection as the Secret Court of 1920. Eventually this became the name that designated the files in the updated online catalogue.

One of the most remarkable aspects of the entire story is that someone in the dean's office, aware of the files' embarrassing nature and the very different image of Harvard that they projected, did not quietly destroy them. In fact, it is extraordinary that the five men of the Court, so obsessed with secrecy, had not themselves destroyed their records in 1920, as soon as they adjourned. As for their transfer to the archives, Andrea Goldstein commented that whoever sent them probably did not realize what was in them.

While this is a possibility, something else may have caused the files' preservation, both when the court adjourned and years later when they were sent to the archives: Harvard's enormous pride in its rich history. This position was well articulated by Sydney Verba, the director of all of Harvard's twenty-nine libraries and a key player in the subsequent drama of the files' release to *The Crimson,* Harvard's student newspaper.

"We are one and a half times as old as the United States," he said in 2003. "The Harvard Archives are one of the great historical repositories of the nation. It is a huge record of American higher education and too important to doctor or edit."

Early in 2002 a writer for *The Crimson* was in the archives researching an altogether different subject when he came across a reference to "the Secret Court of 1920." Intrigued by the title, he made a request to see the material and was told the files were sealed on the grounds that the papers concerned disciplinary matters. A formal request was made to the dean of the college, Harry R. Lewis, and was turned down.

Now the entire *Crimson* staff was intrigued and worked for two months for the release of the files. Harvard has a rule about disciplinary records of individual students. They can only be released if the records are over eighty years old, or if the individuals mentioned are dead. Since eighty years had passed and the students involved would have been over one hundred years old, *The Crimson* felt on safe ground. An appeal was made to the university archivist, Harley P. Holden. An advisory committee was formed, and they made a decision to release the files, but with the names blacked out.

Quite remarkably, *The Crimson* was still not satisfied. Its feeling was that redacting names implied there was something "embarrassing or criminal" about the students' sexual orientation. This might have been true in 1920, the newspaper staff argued, but was not in 2002. (Amazingly, centuries-old antisodomy laws had been struck down by the Massachusetts Supreme Court only a few months earlier.) *The Crimson* appealed the decision to withhold students' names, but this time was turned down.

Over the next months, eight staff members of *The Crimson* went to work and, through remarkable detective work—poring over year-books, archive records, alumni albums, newspaper stories, and student folders—they were able to learn the names of all the principal students. They contacted surviving family members, who, even in the more enlightened age, may not have been thrilled to learn that their venerated grandfather or great-uncle had been thrown out of Harvard for being gay. Two of the families contacted later said they had looked into suing *The Crimson*.

Verba had said the university's only reason for withholding names was to avoid embarrassing the families. So while *The Crimson's* position was undoubtedly politically correct, at least some of the families were undoubtedly embarrassed.* Verba had steadfastly insisted on the preservation of the Court's files and had been instrumental in their eventual release. He nonetheless sounded a note of wistful regret when he said, "If the cataloguers hadn't affixed the word 'secret' to the files, it is unlikely anyone would ever have notice them."

In November 2002, *The Crimson* published its account in three parts in *FM (Fifteen Minutes),* the paper's weekly magazine. Two parts summarized the Secret Court story; the third was a deservedly self-congratulatory account of *The Crimson's* discovery of the material and struggle with Harvard's administration for its release. The articles attracted some national press attention—*The New York Times* ran a story in its Saturday paper (November 30, 2002)—but daily newspa-

---

*When the daughter of one of the students expressed her dismay at a belated airing in this book of her father's sex-based difficulties at Harvard eighty years earlier, the offer was made to change her father's name. After thinking it over, the daughter declined.

pers are not geared for eighty-year-old stories, and the scandal was quickly forgotten.

The president of Harvard, Lawrence Summers, issued a judicious statement: "These reports of events long ago are extremely disturbing. They are part of a past that we have rightly left behind. I want to express our deep regret for the way this situation was handled. As well as for the anguish the students and their families must have experienced eight decades ago."

President Summers was later quoted as saying the affair was "abhorrent and an affront to the values of our university. We are a better and more just community today because those attitudes have changed as much as they have."

In a private conversation two years later, Summers said, "It is hard to comment intelligently on the university's reaction in 1920 as I am not thoroughly familiar with all of the details of that situation. However, I do ask myself repeatedly, Are we administrators doing anything now that will look as bad in eighty years?"

When discussing the subject of the lengths to which a university should go in stigmatizing students for their undergraduate misdeeds, President Summers, who clearly felt that homosexuality did not fall under the heading of "misdeed," posed a hypothetical question: "If a student is caught plagiarizing someone else's work, how many years should this remain on his record?"

While this is a shrewd analogy (especially to put before a writer), and it squarely addresses a university's problem in dispensing or withholding information about former students, the answer is not difficult and has been found by the U.S. criminal-justice system. Extremely grave crimes, such as child molestation, that present serious threats to the community should remain indelibly on an individual's record. Lesser crimes, those that deserve punishment but not throughout an entire lifetime, should not. In 1920 this principle was in effect in U.S. laws, but Harvard clearly believed that homosexuality fell into the former, grave-threat category.

*   *   *

WHILE PRESIDENT SUMMERS'S abhorrence of the 1920 Secret Court was shared by most of the university when the story came to light in 2002, it was not held by everyone on campus. A letter to the editor appeared in *The Crimson* on December 7 arguing that the articles were wrong to call the Secret Court's action "cruel persecution" when it was instead "a very appropriate disciplinary move by the College." After denouncing the university's permissiveness to all sexuality, but especially homosexuality, the letter writer went on to say, "The college should reestablish standards of morality and strongly consider disciplinary measures for those who violate them." The writer's name was Gladden J. Pappin, of the class of 2004.

The letter was so counter to Harvard's prevailing zeitgeist of tolerance and acceptance, some thought it was a joke. But it was not. Pappin was the editor of a campus publication for conservative Catholics called *The Salient.* Although it represented "a tiny minority," in the words of one student, it sent shock waves of outrage throughout Cambridge. This dismay was not limited to the university's liberal majority; because of Pappin's letter, two editors resigned from *The Salient.*

Of course, there was a barrage of mail denouncing Pappin's letter. One of the most eloquent, by David A. Smith, concludes: "Who will be left out of Pappin's university? Who amongst our friends, colleagues, mentors and teachers will be cast out beyond the locked gates of the Yard? Mr. Pappin, Harvard is not the Puritan college of 1636 or the New England finishing school of 1920; Harvard is the great research university of 2002. We changed and ceased to fear the diversity and freedom that tolerance permits. So should you."

Members of Harvard's gay community had reservations of a different sort about the *Crimson* articles. They feared that in today's soundbite culture, word of a purge of Harvard gays would dissuade worthy candidates from applying. This position was well stated by Robert Mack, a founder of the gay and lesbian group at Harvard: "I'd hate to think some terrific young person would focus on this one episode in the university's history. They might rule it out as a choice saying, 'Oh, Harvard, they persecute gays.'"

A top university administrator and a longtime member of the Harvard faculty was asked about such fears and about other negative fall-out when word of the Secret Court's antihomosexual purge surfaced. "Harvard has been around a long time. We have survived the 1967 students riots and supplying the brains behind the Vietnam war. We have survived Cotton Mather and the Salem witch trials. We do not see ourselves in the business of protecting Harvard." He thought for a minute and added, "We are not like the Catholic Church." He quickly asked not to be quoted.

Perhaps. But in 2005, after the research for this book was completed, all reference to the Secret Court files was mysteriously erased from the online catalogues of the Harvard University Archives.

Acknowledgments

I WOULD LIKE to offer sincere thanks to the many people who helped me with this project, offering a special gratitude to the family members of the victimized students for whom this story could not have been a pleasant recollection. Deep thanks are also due to my inspired editor, Charles Spicer, who brought me this idea and was extremely helpful with ideas for optimally organizing the at-times unwieldy material. In alphabetical order, my thanks to Elena Castedo, John Copland, Linda Cunha, Sandy Epstein, Robin Fox, Nancy Day Henderson, Jane Hilvey, Harry Kraut, Joseph E. B. Lumbard, Robert Mack, Michael Murphy, The New York Society Library, Robert Percy, Robert Richardson, Douglass Shand-Tucci, Lawrence Summers, Sydney Verba, Richard Wilcox, Perry Deane Young, and Jean Ziegler. I also want to express my gratitude to Harvard University, which was generously cooperative in my investigations; in particular, to Andrea Goldstein and the staff of the Harvard Archives, who were unfailingly helpful throughout my frequent stakeouts in their domain.

Select Bibliography

Amory, Cleveland. *The Proper Bostonians.* New York: E. P. Dutton, 1947.

Chauncey, George. *Gay New York: Gender, Urban Culture, and the Making of the Gay Male World, 1890–1940.* New York: Basic Books, 1994.

Duberman, Martin. *James Russell Lowell.* Boston: Houghton Mifflin, 1966.

Fone, Byrne. *Homophobia: A History.* New York: Picador, 2001. First published in 2000 by Henry Holt, Metropolitan Books.

Gould, Jean. *Amy: The World of Amy Lowell and the Imagist Movement.* New York: Dodd, Mead, 1975.

Heymann, C. David. *American Aristocracy: The Lives and Times of James Russell, Amy, and Robert Lowell.* New York: Dodd, Mead, 1980.

Kahn, E. J., Jr. *Harvard Through Change and Through Storm.* New York: W. W. Norton, 1969.

Katz, Jonathan Ned. *Gay American History: Lesbians and Gay Men in the U.S.A.: A Documentary.* New York: Meridian, 1992. First published in 1976 by Thomas Y. Crowell.

Loughery, John. *The Other Side of Silence: Men's Lives and Gay Identities; A Twentieth-Century History.* New York: Henry Holt, 1998.

Meade, Marion. *Bobbed Hair and Bathtub Gin: Writers Running Wild in the Twenties.* New York: Doubleday, Nan A. Talese, 2004.

Morison, Samuel Eliot. *The Founding of Harvard College.* Cambridge: Harvard University Press, 1935.

———. *Three Centuries of Harvard, 1636–1936.* Cambridge: Harvard University Press, Belknap Press, 1936.

Robb, Graham. *Strangers: Homosexual Love in the Nineteenth Century.* New York: W. W. Norton, 2003.

Russell, Ina, ed. *Jeb and Dash: A Diary of Gay Life, 1918–1945.* Boston: Faber and Faber, 1993.

Shand-Tucci, Douglass. *The Crimson Letter: Harvard, Homosexuality, and the Shaping of American Culture.* New York: St. Martin's Press, 2003.

Starkey, Marion L. *The Devil in Massachusetts: A Modern Inquiry into the Salem Witch Trials.* With an introduction by Aldous Huxley. New York: Time Books, 1963. First published in 1949 by Alfred A. Knopf.

Townsend, Kim. *Manhood at Harvard: William James and Others.* Cambridge: Harvard University Press, 1998. First published in 1996 by W. W. Norton.

Wilcox, Richard French. *The Shadow of the Wind.* New York: Vantage Press, 1979.

Wolfe, Thomas. *Of Time and the River: A Legend of Man's Hunger in His Youth.* New York: Charles Scribner's Sons, 1935.

Yeomans, Henry. *Abbott Lawrence Lowell, 1856–1943.* Cambridge: Harvard University Press, 1948.

Index